Motherself

Motherself

A
MYTHIC ANALYSIS
OF
MOTHERHOOD

KATHRYN ALLEN RABUZZI

INDIANA UNIVERSITY PRESS
Bloomington and Indianapolis

Portions of this book appeared in "Family" by Kathryn Allen Rabuzzi.
Reprinted with permission of Macmillan Publishing Company, a Division
of Macmillan, Inc., from *The Encyclopedia of Religion,* Mircea Eliade,
Editor in Chief. Copyright © 1986 by Macmillan Publishing Company.

Library of Congress Cataloging-in-Publication Data

Rabuzzi, Kathryn Allen.
Motherself : a mythic analysis of motherhood.

Includes index.
1. Motherhood.   2. Self.   3. Mother-goddesses.
I. Title.
HQ759.R23   1988   306.8'743   87-45247
ISBN 0-253-33844-1
ISBN 0-253-20471-2 (pbk.)

1 2 3 4 5 92 91 90 89 88

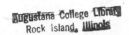

Contents

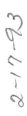

2-17-93

ACKNOWLEDGMENTS

Many friends and colleagues have supported my efforts in writing this book. I especially want to thank my children, Daniel, Matthew, and Douglas, and Professors Lee Bailey, Robert Orsi, Joseph Ramisch, Ellen Umansky, and Mary Jo Weaver for their helpful suggestions at various stages of my writing. My husband, Dan, deserves special recognition for his patience throughout.

I dedicate this book with love to two very special mothers, Dorothy Sawyer Francis Allen and Frances Sullivan.

Introduction

As I was walking down a sleazy section of Second Avenue in New York City a few years ago, a voice suddenly intruded on my consciousness: "Hey, Mama, spare change?" The words outraged me. Not because the man was begging. All New Yorkers are used to that. Nor even because, although begging, he addressed me in an annoyingly patronizing, all-too-familiar male chauvinist way. All women are used to that. No, what so particularly angered me was hearing the word "Mama" from his lips. Although I had by then been a mother for many years, never till that moment had I seen myself as "Mama" in such an impersonal, external context. In the man's speaking I beheld myself anew. "I" disappeared, as though turned inside out, and "Mama" took my place.

Besides precipitating this shocking dislocation of self, the beggar's words enraged me for another reason. He was taking Her name in vain. His "Hey, Mama," despite its personally devastating effect on me, was as meaninglessly devoid of content as "Hey, Bud." That I should think this strange thought even as I walked impassively by the importuning man made me wonder. Who was this "Mama" that I was thinking of as "Her," with a capital "H"? What power lay hidden behind that once familiar, now strange word?

It wasn't until a recent trip to Vienna that I began to understand. While there, I visited St. Stephen's Cathedral. Like most cathedrals, this one contains numerous effigies of the Madonna and Child. On this particular occasion I lingered to gaze first at one, then another image. Gone was my accustomed Protestant unease with Mary. These pervasive images of mother and child tugged at me with a strange power I could almost see. What I was feeling existed at a level far more fundamental than the one named by the words "Mary and Jesus." Here was the raw power of a special kind of unity composed of mother and child.

Should I Have a Baby?

This moment in St. Stephen's revealed a force far deeper underlying the ubiquitous Mary-Jesus image than I had ever previously experienced. The wonder of that moment has remained with me. It is especially strong whenever, as increasingly happens, a young woman tells me of her indecision about whether or not to have children.

"Should I have a baby?" she will ask. This is a question that was seldom raised before the pill became widely available in the 1960s. Before that time it was more customary to hear: "I'm going to have a baby." Each utterance, in its own way, may betoken intense anguish. Having a baby without choice may feel like being consigned to hell. All those plans for graduate school, a career, college, or even high school—gone, poof! Yet as increasing numbers of women are discovering, the agony of choice can be just as great. Consciously having to think what it means to become and be a mother means a woman must assume responsibility for one of the most important decisions in her life.

Part of the agony of her choice is necessarily practical: How can I manage both a career and a child? How can my partner and I maintain this lifestyle if I don't continue my career? If I take a leave of absence can I ever fulfill my potential as a trial lawyer, a research scientist, a software engineer? Despite these valid professional and economic concerns, having children is still generally acceptable to most women.

What is not always acceptable, however, is being a mother. An underlying argument of this book is that a woman trying to decide whether or not to have children should reconceptualize this important question. Instead of asking herself, Should I have children? she should ask, Do I want to become a mother? Seemingly the two situations are synonymous. Yet asking, Should I have a baby? is not at all the same as asking, Should I be a mother? The first question readily connotes adding something extra to your life. Particularly in the context of our highly acquisitive society, it is easy to think of a baby as one more "thing" to enhance your life, in much the way that a house in the suburbs or a Mercedes might. But asking, Should I become a mother? realistically shifts the focus to where it belongs—onto the selfhood of the mother. By no means is this shift of questions meant to preclude the father. It is simply the case, however, given the nature of biological difference coupled with the androcentric world in which we live, that most men do not experience the same kind of radical change in selfhood when they become fathers that women do when we become mothers.

By making this shift in her thinking, a woman can readily see that the central issue of her agonizing decision really is not economic. Instead it is symbolic. Ultimately, the meaning motherhood will have for a woman is far more significant than the dollar cost of raising children. But just what being a mother means is often not clear to her. What is very clear, however, is that generally speaking in contemporary Western cultures being a lawyer, a doctor, or a broker is "important." Being a mother is not. Therefore, instead of deciding whether or not to have *children*, a woman must refocus her question. She must grapple with the very serious issue of whether or not to become a *mother*.

Some Necessary Questions

To decide whether she should become a mother a woman needs to ponder such questions as: What does being a mother mean to me? If I never become a mother, how do I imagine I will feel later on in life when it is too late to change my mind? To what extent will becoming a mother affect my sense of who I am? What are the relative valuations as I experience them, of being an engineer, a cancer researcher, a respected novelist, for example, and being a mother? How does my culture define these different roles? Whose valuation matters most to me? My own? Or that of someone who is influenced directly by androcentric attitudes? Or, conversely, that of someone reacting against such attitudes? Where do my concepts of valuation come from? Are fatherhood and motherhood equivalently valued?

These are just a few of the many complex and vexing questions a woman must probe thoroughly, rather than sweep aside, if she is to find any answers to this perplexing question: Should I choose or reject motherhood?

Issues

Within the context of the framing question of this book, Should I become a mother? there are two important related questions. As a woman, who do I want to be? How can I become that person? These questions, which are really about self-actualization, are simultaneously religious and psychological. From a religious perspective the question of who to be often emerges out of consideration for a life yet to come in some future world. By contrast, the present world is of paramount concern to psychology. Nonetheless, practically speaking, the effect on the individual is the same whether the context is religious or psychological. The psychological question, What self do I wish to be? equals the religious one, Who must I be as I live out my time on earth?

Almost universally throughout history, regardless of whether the context has been religious or psychological, a single answer to this question has prevailed for women: You must be a mother. Not only has this maternal role been chosen by women, but androcentric cultures worldwide have enforced it as the norm for women as well. Except for those who chose a life religiously dedicated to virginity, few alternatives have been possible for most women until recently. That is not to say that women have not often been something else as well—agriculturalists, merchants, traders. But cross-culturally throughout history to actively repudiate motherhood has been essentially unheard of. Only in the Western world during the past quarter century have more than token numbers of women done so. It is just now that women are able to choose not to be mothers without experiencing ridicule or censure from their culture.

At the same time that many women now choose not to become mothers themselves, some also vociferously oppose motherhood in general. Undeniably not all women can or should become mothers. Many are miserable in that role. But it is also true that not all women want to reject motherhood, either. To be forced into the role against your will because androcentric thought declares motherhood to be "woman's destiny" is deplorable. Equally deplorable, however, is the reverse notion that only women who engage in careers and relinquish motherhood are leading worthwhile, liberated lives. Furthermore, this supposedly feminist viewpoint is anything but the message of liberation it claims to be. Instead, it is an equally imprisoning viewpoint which, by inverting the original patriarchal dictum, is itself just as patriarchal. Instead of valuing the natural biology of women, this repudiation of motherhood thoroughly denigrates it. It rejects woman's birthright in favor of the right to do what men do. But why is what men do automatically declared "better"? Implicit in this valuation is the assumption that woman's natural function is inferior to participation in the public sphere in which "work" takes place (as if mothers do no work!). No patriarch could be more scathing in his denunciation of women.

Instead of saying that one role is better than another it is far more appropriate to see both as necessary, exciting, and equally valid ways of being in the world, as conversely both may be dull and inappropriate, depending on the individual woman and her particular circumstances. The only inequality involved in the two roles is the fact that women, unlike men, are biologically constructed in such a way as to be able to carry, bear, and nurse children. Thus we have the luxury, so far denied to men, of choosing both roles if we so desire, although apart from these biological constraints, as chapter 5 suggests, a man can also follow the way of the mother. It is to celebrate this natural luxury of women that I have written this book.

The Meaning of Motherhood

Understanding how deeply significant the role of motherhood can be to a woman is not always easy in contemporary culture: Nowadays we lack ready access to the necessary vehicles for doing so. That is partly because, despite the growing phenomenon of worldwide fundamentalism, the generalized belief system of Western culture as a whole is secular. To find language, concepts, and images appropriate to the deepest meanings of life has traditionally necessitated some sort of religious context. Our current, predominantly secular culture, with its heavy emphasis on material gratifications, therefore presents some problems. For instance, traditional icons of motherhood such as the images of the Madonna and Child that so transfixed me in St. Stephen's Cathedral in Vienna no longer automatically reach an entire community of believers as they once did. While some individuals—usually, believing churchgoers—still experience their power, many people have little or no exposure to such images. Still others, exposed to them, can feel in them nothing but dead relics of a religious past that does not personally touch them.

Nonetheless, despite the predominantly secular system of thought in the desacralized postmodern cultures of the twentieth century, even the least traditionally religious among us occasionally encounters the continued, if fleeting, existence of forces that once were called goddesses, gods, and savior heroes. All these forces continue to possess meaning for human life, although that meaning is now more commonly interpreted as psychological rather than religious, when it is recognized at all.

Salvation and Selfhood

As givers of meaning these presences once known as goddesses, gods, and savior heroes can be said to provide salvation. But salvation is not a concept generally thought to exist in a predominantly secular context. Salvation as it has been popularly understood in a traditional Christian context has typically referred to another time and another place. Although centuries of argument and reflection have yielded various opinions on this issue, lay understandings of Christian salvation have focused almost exclusively on Heaven, a place where life, transfigured, continues *after* death. Since the Enlightenment, such belief in an afterlife has become increasingly difficult to sustain, however, so that within the Church as well as without, many people no longer think of Heaven, if they even use the word, in traditional terms at all. Instead, they necessarily emphasize the only other possibility—*this* life here and now. In keeping with this shift in emphasis from life *after* death to life here and now, the traditional theological concept of the soul has now largely been replaced, particularly in secular theology, by the concept "self."

This replacement of soul by self especially concerns women seeking to understand the potentially deep meaning of motherhood. This is so because a woman's decision about whether to become a mother is basically a decision about what kind of self she will be. In an earlier age, if she were Christian, she would have worried about saving her soul. Nowadays, if she believes she has only this one life on earth to live with nothing further to come, her concern necessarily shifts. Now each moment counts, not because of its effect on an anticipated afterlife but for its own sake. Therefore a woman must constantly ask herself, Am I being and becoming the self I most want to be? If not, I must do something right now to ensure that I do because I have no second chance to make up for any mistakes I make in this life.

This contemporary emphasis on life lived here and now illustrates perfectly what it means to say we live in a secular age. The kind of theology which reflects this move away from a future-orientation to a here-and-now perspective is variously referred to as postmodern, post-death-of-God, and post-Christian. Such contemporary theology is open to the charge that it is becoming psychology. But that charge reflects a false dichotomy in the thinking of those who level it. At issue is the capability of the psyche to be a location of sacredness. Few would say that nature cannot function as such a location. But when it comes to the psyche, many dissent, because they confuse the psyche with an individual's personal ego. But such a reduction of the psyche is totally inappropriate to what this "place" really is. This issue is important for women deciding whether to become mothers because basically theirs is a decision involving both psychological and religious dimensions. To emphasize one at the expense of the other is to fail to do full justice to the drama of motherhood. This is a drama to be played out in the arena of the psyche itself.

The psyche, which functions so importantly in the deep meaning of motherhood, can be described as a "place" in which both divine and demonic elements of a collective nature manifest themselves. Understood this way, the psyche is simply a different way of naming what many religions traditionally call "Heaven" and "Hell." Instead of locating those sacred spaces up in the sky and down below the earth, individuals who employ the metaphor of the psyche relocate both spheres within the depths of the human individual. In no sense, however, does this relocation identify the divine with the human ego. Rather it asserts that the forces once conceptualized as goddesses and gods may as easily reveal themselves through dream and image as through nature, history, or divine revelation from "on high." It is to these forces, by whatever name, that a woman trying to decide whether to become a mother must pay careful heed, for these erstwhile deities are the dramatis personae of her story. This is true whether the story she chooses at any given time is androcentric or gyno-centric. The difference between the two stories, as she will discover, lies not in the characters but in the perspective from which they are perceived and perceive themselves.

The psyche within which these goddesses and gods unfold their drama is the ground on which the theologian and the psychologist now increasingly meet. In meeting on this common ground of the psyche, they are healing a split more apparent than real. Before the Enlightenment, cure of souls was the province of the priest. But because of the split between body and soul which has governed Western thinking ever since the time of Descartes, science came to be viewed as material (that is, bodily), religion as spiritual (that is, as connected with the soul). Because the psyche came to be associated more closely with the body than with the soul, psychology developed predominantly as a medical rather than a religious specialty. But just because the "theos" (or feminine "thea," as the case may be) in theology has become increasingly problematic for those theologians who consider themselves post-death-of-God or post-Christian, that does not mean that theological ways of understanding have also died. Conse-quently, a woman, even in our own postmodern secular culture, may still experience motherhood as a way of being that would once have been called sacred.

What the problematic nature of the "thea" and "theos" of contempo-rary theology means is that previously taken-for-granted ways of con-ceptualizing, hence of articulating, no longer work. Talk of heaven no longer rivets all Christians as it once did. Yet talk of incarnating an authentic self very often does. Consequently, the important theological concept of incarnation, which is another way of speaking of selfhood, has altered considerably for many people. Because choosing to become a mother is choosing to become or incarnate a particular kind of self, some understanding of incarnation can help a woman trying to make this very difficult decision.

Incarnation

Earlier in history, incarnation referred exclusively to the physical embodiment of God as the Christ (or as various other divine savior figures in other traditions). Although the religious drama of the birth of the savior hero Jesus—his life, crucifixion, death, and rebirth—still figures prominently in the experiences of many believers, for many the time and place of that drama have shifted. Once the Christ story was generally construed as a historical, once-only event that took place long ago in the Holy Land. For fundamentalist believers this is still the case. But for many individuals a psychological interpretation has replaced the historical one. This shift makes the Christ story primarily a timeless, mythic event repeatedly re-enacted in the human psyche. The life lived in Christ now becomes the life any individual leads, Christ being the image par excellence of self. Within this framework the incarnation of self is thus the incarnation of Christ in any individual. Or turned around, the incarnation of Christ is now the incarnation of authentic selfhood. For those who consider themselves non- or post-Christian, the term "Christ" simply drops away; "self" entirely suffices.

From a feminist perspective, however, this way of construing Christian theology is often problematic, not because of its post-Christian shift in emphasis, but because of what it retains from the original tradition. Whether you retain the word "Christ" or not, the underlying conception of "self" implicit in that view of incarnation is ambiguous. As contemporary Roman Catholic requirements for the priesthood indicate, for many people, maleness is a prerequisite for following the example of Christ. In the West, the concept of self, like that of the ensouled individual which predates it, has long been masculine. As the work of Carol Gilligan demonstrates so effectively,[1] Western models of the relatively recent concept of self have necessarily been male because creation of models and testing of hypotheses by such influential psychologists as Freud, Piaget, and Erikson have all been based on male experience and male norms. That means that for women, questing for selfhood as that quest is traditionally presented often dooms us to failure. Not only do we usually not measure up to the male norms, we *cannot* possibly do so by definition. Even if we can squeeze ourselves to fit into their male form, we may contravene some of our own inner needs, desires, and experiences in the process. Consequently, in questing for selfhood as it is traditionally defined, some women find themselves engaged in a fruitless enterprise.

When this happens, what used to be a search for salvation through finding Christ turns into the familiar contemporary psychological quest for the self. In either its traditional religious or its contemporary secular form, this quest for something larger than mere ego is typically presented through the vehicle of the quest of the hero. Where that quest was once told through mythic tales, now it is more often presented in psychological jargon. Essentially the one telling of the tale is a modernization of the other. Whether understood as myth or psychology, this story of the quest of the hero is the quest that all humans, women as well as men, enact in some fashion if they are questing for selfhood.

Whether this ancient quest tale works for a particular woman largely depends on how she understands it. If she hears the language of the tale as referring to males, then questing for selfhood may involve playing a woman's version of a male self rather than enacting what feels like her own genuinely gynocentric mode of being. Some women adapt deftly to this male pattern. Others find it ill-fitting and awkward at best; typically they find it impossible to adapt to this male pattern without becoming male-identifiers.

Other women hear the story differently. For them the male language and imagery are not bothersome because they hear beneath both an androgynous model of spiritual questing that construes sex and gender as incidental, not essential, to selfhood. In this view the almost universal maleness of the savior hero is no more fundamental than the "Fatherhood" of God. Whether the spiritual quest is for self, Jesus, or God, physical embodiment is beside the point. What counts instead is spirit, which has no body. While the language and symbols of the spiritual quest may sound male, what they point to is beyond sexuality, hence the male imagery is unimportant. In this view, sexual difference does not essentially define a person's selfhood. Mystical techniques of spiritual questing traditional to religious traditions throughout the world largely reflect this view. After all, your bodily attributes scarcely matter if you spend your time mainly in prayer, whirling, davening, fasting, silence, chanting mantras, ingesting hallucinogenic drugs, or performing yogic exercises. Living in solitude or darkness can readily take place without reference to sexuality. The aim of the spiritual quester in such cases is traditionally loss of what more worldly individuals think of as embodiment and even selfhood. Within such a framework, to think of the hero as specifically male is believed irrelevant. The hero is simply the one who quests for spiritual enlightenment without regard for bodily attributes or impediments.

Altered to its secular counterpart in which "salvation" means fulfilling oneself, this androgynous model sees women and men as essentially the same, sexual difference being no more essential than such differences as eye or hair color, fatness or thinness, and the like. Selfhood, in this view, is basically the same for women and men. If a woman hears the familiar quest tale this way, then she can activate her quest by playing out the part of the hero without feeling uncomfortably male-identifying in the process. For her the hero and the self are both beyond sexuality.

But not all women experience either themselves or the quest tale in quite this way. This does not necessarily mean that these women construe sex as essential to determining selfhood. Rather, they may consider that reconceptualizing an androcentrically biased world as an androgynous one is begging the issue. For them, bodily experience does matter: A woman's body is *not* the same as a man's. To celebrate this body rather than to deny or ignore it is critically important. Fortunately, for such women, it is not necessary to choose between either an androcentric or an androgynous understanding of the story of the quest of the hero. Another possibility exists, to which I have given the name of "the way of the mother." In this story of the way of the mother it is no longer the hero alone who stands as a model of selfhood. Now it is the mythic Mother Goddess from whom he issues who takes center stage. In contrast to the heroself (whether construed androcentrically or androgynously) that the hero models, the Goddess is the underlying model for "motherself."

In no sense should this way of the mother be reduced to a literal reading which says *every* woman should be a mother. To so reduce it would be to misunderstand my intention completely. Instead, it should be read as one possible way of being in the world which, given the capability for motherhood natural to most women, recognizes positive value in an experience otherwise often ignored, glossed over, or denigrated. In fact, motherhood accords more closely with the lived experiences of many women in the world than does the complementary myth of the hero. As the quest of the hero is but one way of seeking spiritual fulfillment, so too is the way of the mother that leads to motherselfhood.

Motherself

It is the thesis of this book that the selfhood of a mother differs significantly from that of a nonmother. In Western cultures the central image for selfhood is that of the hero. Although theoretically the hero was meant generically to stand for individuals of both sexes, actually, like so-called "generic man," the hero is a thoroughly androcentric construction. Just how thoroughly androcentric this concept is becomes readily apparent to anyone who reads a representative sampling of the thousands of hero tales in myths, fairy tales, and novels from cultures around the world. For every Wonder Woman a reader encounters, ten Supermen appear.

According to mythologist Joseph Campbell, in his exhaustive study, *The Hero with a Thousand Faces,* the following series of stages characterizes this monomyth of the hero's quest. These stages are the call, refusal of the call, supernatural aid, crossing the first threshold, the belly of the whale, the road of trials, the meeting with the goddess, woman as the temptress, atonement with the father, apotheosis, the ultimate boon, refusal of the return, the magic flight, rescue from without, and crossing the return threshold.[2]

Told in endless variations, this mythic quest is always, Campbell assserts, "the one, shape-shifting yet marvelously constant story that we find."[3] Its hero may, although typically with great difficulty, be female as well as male. However, in its basic version the quest of the hero is the story of the male child breaking away from the world of his mother. This world of the mother is the mundane world he must transcend to reach the "higher" world of the father. When a female "hero" is substituted, the tale as traditionally told becomes full of awkward permutations designed to make it "fit" the altered mother-child relationship. Consider, for example, the motif of "woman as temptress."

For a heterosexual woman the motif of "woman as temptress," as it is traditionally presented, is entirely alien. To make it work, the story must be altered to such an extent that the woman's variant comes to seem deviant from the original. It is precisely this kind of "deviant" variation from male norms that Carol Gilligan discusses when she analyzes concepts of selfhood and behavior for women. To counter this sense that women's selfhood and experiences depart negatively from what androcentric teachings construe as the *human* norm, this other pattern, the way of the mother, which appropriately fits women's own gynocentric experience, must be explored.

In contrast to the singleness that forms selfhood as it is ordinarily conceived according to the pattern of the hero, selfhood in the mother consists of a binary-unity. It is therefore simultaneously two and one at the same time, its parts consisting of mother and child in varying degrees of relationship to each other. A further distinguishing feature of this selfhood of a mother that significantly differentiates it from that of a hero is its form. Motherselfhood is physically gynocentric (in contrast to hero-selfhood, which is not), based as it is on a biological condition of woman in one of her possible life stages. That does not mean, however, that motherselfhood is therefore necessarily ideologically gynocentric as well. That depends on the particular woman and her predilections. After all, a woman may range in her attitudes from extremely patriarchal to radically feminist. Neither womanhood nor motherselfhood automatically dictates ideology. In and of themselves, both are ideologically neutral. What is true, however, is that both womanhood and motherselfhood lead women to experience ourselves, and life in general, differently from what the single "norms" of maleness and selfhood imply is true. Consequently, if a woman who is a mother realizes that the selfhood she experiences differs significantly from that promulgated in androcentric cultures as "normal," she will be able to accept and understand her experiences more easily than if she believes she is somehow "deviant."

A word of reassurance may be in order: Just because the pattern needed to acquire motherselfhood is called the way of the mother does not mean, however, that it applies only to women who are literally mothers. Rather, it is a pattern which takes its name from the single capacity capable of distinguishing most women from *all* men. Though based on an actual, physical capacity, the way of the mother is meant to be construed metaphorically as well as literally. In its metaphoric sense, it should be as readily applicable to nonmothers (including the rare man who opts for this way) as to mothers. Furthermore, because the term "mother" is so highly loaded with all sorts of connotations ranging from the sickly sweet sentimental to the darkly negative destructive, "motherself" may automatically alienate some readers. Such automatic alienation would be unfortunate. The connotations, after all, reflect reaction against patriarchy as often as they do acceptance of it. Either way, they conceal the underlying power inherent in the word "mother" when it is not patriarchally contaminated.

The Way of the Mother

To find and give voice to a pattern appropriate to this gynocentric process of creating selfhood was not easy. Like it or not, we all live in cultures still largely dominated by androcentric assumptions. As many feminists have pointed out over the years, finding voices authentic to women's experience is appallingly difficult. Not only are the languages and concepts we have all inherited male-oriented, but historically women's experiences have been interpreted for us by men and male norms. Consequently, to assert absolutely that any woman can speak from an entirely gynocentric perspective is suspect. The words in this book must therefore be considered merely an *attempt* to do so.

Just finding a framework appropriate for such a gynocentric pattern reflects the difficulty of this enterprise. I firmly believe that the gynocentric pattern I call "the way of the mother" predates that of the quest of the hero. Nonetheless, because the heroic quest is universally known and the mother's way largely unvoiced in a formal sense, I have been forced to use the androcentric male myth as my point of departure. I do this, despite the fact that it violates my gynocentric sense of "reality," in order to make as clear as possible within the androcentric world we live in, concepts that are inherently too gynocentrically complicated to work with any other way. Therefore, to provide the necessary framework to develop the gynocentric myth, I have relied heavily on the work previously mentioned of mythologist Joseph Campbell, *The Hero with a Thousand Faces*.

As his title suggests, in this book Campbell thoroughly analyzes the concept of the hero. He draws from an enormous range of sources to support his thesis that the hero's quest, found in all cultures in all times, functions as an archetype for the human quest for selfhood. Yet despite this otherwise convincing claim to universal application, the hero's quest has not universally applied to *women*. Only in the past quarter century can it be said that large numbers of women have been free to try following this pattern in a physical sense, and these are mostly women from highly complex postindustrialized cultures like our own.

To argue, as many would do, that the hero's quest is only a metaphor for an inward, spiritual journey is not satisfactory: from a gynocentric perspective, which does not dichotomize between the two, it is necessarily both inward and actual; both bodily and spiritual. In contrast to the reductive, dualistic tendencies characteristic of androcentric theoretical structures, those inherent in gynocentric thought are relational and holistic. Consequently, from a gynocentric perspective, this traditional quest of the hero cannot adequately fit the needs of a woman attempting to develop the selfhood appropriate to her sense of herself as a woman.

Indeed, traditional wisdom would appear to support this view. Instead of following the hero's path in traditional societies and in the literatures that reflect those societies, females have traditionally been expected to follow quite a different route. But unlike the myth of the heroic quest, which women must also try to follow whenever we hope to survive in the "transcendent" spheres of male power, this route has not been specifically named. It is this generally unnamed pattern, stripped of the androcentric baggage which has slowly accreted to it since the inception of patriarchy some 12,000 or so years ago, to which I have given the name of the way of the mother. Although many contemporary feminists would argue that this is precisely the pattern from which feminism strives to "free" women, I disagree. What feminism seeks to disavow are the distorting androcentric versions of this pattern, which alternately denigrate and demonize it, thereby destroying its inherent meaning. My purpose in this book is to restore to women the ancient deep meaning of this truly gynocentric mode of being in the world. By no means does this imply that the way of the mother is the only way a woman can enact her spiritual quest. It is, however, a way that allows a woman to fully accommodate herself as a woman, with woman's experience the norm instead of a deviation.

In one sense the way of the mother is the "same" story as that of the quest of the hero. But what makes this familiar story of the hero seem so different when it becomes the way of the mother is its shift in perspective. In the familiar hero's quest, the hero is by definition just what the word "hero" implies: "He" is the center of interest, the protagonist who is typically a force for good. Repeatedly he engages in a series of life-and-death struggles with various forces of evil that wish to prevent him from acquiring or retaining the special gifts for which he is questing. Typically one of the forces of evil he encounters is a monster whose qualities are either implicitly or explicitly those of the archetypal "bad" mother. Thus, as in the case of Jonah, the hero may experience the horror of engulfment within a monster's belly. Or he may battle the temptation to incest presented by a seductive mother goddess.

By contrast, in the story of the way of the mother, the figure who is a monster from the perspective of the hero is no monster at all. Instead, she is the mother, protagonist rather than antagonist, in this telling of the archetypal story which is simultaneously romance and battle between mother goddess (the mother) and hero (her child). It is out of this changed perspective that this whole "new" story, the way of the mother, emerges. Furthermore, it is within this "new" story that a woman trying to decide whether or not to become a mother discovers the kind of selfhood engendered by motherhood and fully appropriate to a naturally gyno-centric understanding of the world: motherselfhood.

The overall similarity between this way of the mother, which produces motherselfhood, and the quest of the hero, which produces hero-selfhood, does not mean, however, that what appears to be the "same" step is experienced identically by both mother and hero. From the mother's perspective many events that the male hero views negatively seem positive. Conversely, many events he values highly seem negative to her. Such reversals frequently dwarf the similarities between these two patterns in ways of enormous consequence to women who try to incorporate both patterns into their lives.

This is not to say that a woman cannot, does not, or should not live out both patterns in her life. It is almost impossible for a woman not to live out the androcentrically imposed norm of the quest of the hero at times, despite its frequently incongruous application to her own selfhood. A woman who tries, within the bounds of possibility, to live out this pattern of the hero in those situations where it seems essential, such as in the world of the public sphere, can also live out that of the mother and vice versa. Countless women do so every day. What it means, however, is that in any given moment a woman cannot simultaneously live out both patterns. When she is enacting the woman's variant of the heroic quest, as she is apt to do at work, a woman cannot at the same time follow the way of the mother. She needs to bear in mind always that the underlying pattern for that role differs significantly.

Basically the hero of the quest tale is the child. A mother unaware of this identity of the hero, who tries to play the hero herself, will end up as a child among her own children. Sometimes this is both fun and appropriate. But she cannot always relate to her children as both hero and mother, without greatly confusing them. Unless a woman recognizes these distinctions, she cannot appropriately live out the role necessary to any given moment. Nor can she satisfactorily evaluate the issue of whether or not to become a mother in the first place if she does not understand that two very different, conflicting life patterns are involved here. As long as she knows which one is which, she will be able to function appropriately. Stepping into the "wrong story" at the wrong time, however, is a bit like walking inadvertently into a time warp with no understanding of how to get back into the right one.

This distinction means that a woman must understand how the emphases of the two stories respectively alter them. These emphases will differ according to whether the principal player is the mother or the hero. And with these shifts in perspective and emphasis comes a corresponding shift in sequence. The order of events necessarily differs for the two main characters. The mother brings the hero into being in the first place. But this event, so central to the mother's experience, does not even form part of the hero's consciously recollected experience. That difference alone guarantees that their respective points of departure will differ significantly.

Because this difference in perspective is so critical, Part I focuses exclusively on the dramatis personae of the way of the mother. Chapter 1 looks closely at the Palaeolithic and Neolithic Great Goddess, who, as both forerunner and progenetrix of the ubiquitous hero, is the archetypal image of the mother. Chapter 2 traces out the evolution of father gods as the logical outcome of the discovery of paternity, while chapter 3 shows how, with this development, the previously subordinate role of hero sons tends to coalesce with that of the elevated father god. Chapter 4 explores the concept of selfhood as it is represented by the figure of the hero. A contrasting model of selfhood, based not on a unitary but a multiple vision of self, is the archetypal Jungian vision of self, the subject of chapter 5.

Chapter 6 presents a still different vision of self, motherself, which is neither completely single like that of the hero nor multiple like that envisioned in polytheistic images of self. This concept of selfhood, which is based on the mother-child relationship, is the one engendered by the way of the mother.

Part II moves from description of the dramatis personae who characterize quests for selfhood to analysis of the particular quest that is the focus of this book: the way of the mother. Chapter 7 presents an archetypal mother's story told in the manner of a fairy tale. It then analyzes the motifs essential to motherselfhood. Chapter 8 concentrates on the body mystery connected with actually being a mother, approaching motherhood from within the experience itself instead of externally through accepted androcentric perspectives. Starting with the next chapter, the remaining chapters more closely parallel various stages of the quest of the hero as Campbell details them. Chapter 9 focuses on the sexual nature of the call to the way of the mother, contrasting it with the very different qualities inherent in the call of the hero to his adventure. Chapter 10 considers the motif of the threshold. For a woman this motif is highly ambiguous, tending either to force her into a traditional "doormat" role or to lead her out of her own story and into that of the hero instead. Chapter 11 then explores the space on the other side of the threshold, giving the "inside" story of the folkloristic motif Campbell refers to as "the belly of the whale." Chapter 12 shows how difficult it is to navigate this interior space beyond the threshold without the traditional folkloristic supernatural helper. In this case the helper is the goddess Persephone, an extremely useful guide for a woman embarking on the way of the mother.

Part III focuses on the motif of ordeals, beginning with pregnancy, the theme of chapter 13. Whether or not a woman experiences pregnancy as an ordeal depends largely on how she conceptualizes it. Chapter 14, for which I have coined the term "womansins," analyzes the kind of soul searching that is natural and essential to a woman experiencing her first pregnancy. Chapter 15 concludes the section on ordeals by focusing on the familiar motif of temptation which, in the case of a woman, is the temptation so readily offered by androcentric constructs and values.

Part IV leads into the realm of the Fathers, the counterpart of the better-known realm of the Mothers. In contrast to the hero, who must struggle against the temptation to remain a dependent infant attached to his mother, a woman must struggle against the temptation to become a pseudo-man. This is an important issue every woman must cope with if she is to make her way successfully along the way of the mother. Chapter 16 argues that atonement with the androcentric value system of the Fathers is absolutely the wrong approach for a woman struggling to create her genuinely gynocentric self by following the way of the mother. Chapter 17 expands this argument by stressing the need for precisely the opposite behavior on the part of a woman: estrangement from the Fathers in order to find her own way. Finally, what often turns out to be the most difficult task in a woman's struggle with the Fathers is facing her own attitude toward helping to decreate patriarchy. This is the theme of chapter 18.

Part V centers on the concept of atonement with the Goddess. As chapter 19 suggests, even knowing how to meet the Goddess is difficult in a patriarchal culture. Nonetheless, meeting Her can be managed if a woman learns how to recognize Her. Chapter 20 explores the meaning of mystical marriage with the Goddess, showing how this important concept applies equally, but in different ways, to lesbians and to heterosexual women. Chapter 21 centers on the mysteries of the Goddess, both in ancient myth and in a woman's experience of childbirth.

The concluding section of the book develops the critical motif of the return from childbirth. Chapter 22 discusses such threats as stillbirth, infanticide, and postpartum depression. Chapter 23 speaks of a different kind of peril to a woman trying to return, that of repudiating the very meaning of her experience. The final chapter, "Theft of Women's Mysteries and Boons," cautions against various dangers to women, chief of which is womb envy. While this concept of womb envy is by no means new, what is startling are some behaviors exhibited in contemporary Western culture which suggest that this envy did not die even when men discovered their own role in reproduction. What makes these attempts so threatening to women now, however, in a way they never were before, is the distinct possibility that men may now be able to satisfy their envy of women's powers literally as well as symbolically. Hitherto, threats to steal the mysteries and boons associated with the way of the mother have been just threats. But now men have nearly developed the capacity to steal the most precious boon of all: the ability to bear and give birth to human life. The book closes with a warning about the great danger these threats of men to steal the boons of women pose, not just to those who would follow the way of the mother, but to all humankind.

One final distinction is useful in considering this gynocentric quest for selfhood, the way of the mother. It is helpful to recall Adrienne Rich's distinction between the two senses of the word "motherhood." On the one hand, "motherhood" refers to the condition of a woman as she relates to her children, whether natural or adopted. To the extent that this condition enriches and fulfills her, this personal experience of motherhood is positive. On the other hand, "motherhood" is also an institution which, until very recently in the West, has confined the majority of adult women to a single role in life. For a woman to rebel against this negative *institution* of motherhood is comparable to a concerned Roman Catholic rebelling against the Church as institution with all its strictures against women. This latter kind of rebellion in either case is often an essential political act. But to rebel against the underlying symbol is very different: It is to commit a sacrilege within the context of the symbol. It is very important to bear this distinction in mind, for all too often the two meanings of motherhood are confused. When that happens the meaning of the Mother image with all its deep mystery is altogether lost.

To reject the image of the mother, as many modern women do, is to favor patriarchal values that focus instead on the image of the individual hero. Women's current situation, in which we do not always recognize the richness of our own inherent nature, is not unlike that of Adapa, the ancient Mesopotamian Adam who lost humanity the boon of eternal life. It happened this way: Adapa was fishing one day when the south wind capsized him. In fury, Adapa cursed the wind and all was calm for seven days. The god of heaven inquired why the wind was down and sent for Adapa. Meanwhile, the god Ea advised Adapa how to behave to receive mercy; above all, he must refuse the bread and water of death he would surely be offered. All took place as Ea had foretold until the servants of the god of heaven offered food and drink. Instead of the food and drink of death, they offered Adapa the bread and water of life. Not knowing the difference between them, Adapa refused the gift of immortality.

Do we as women not behave with equal blindness? Not understanding the value of the special quality of selfhood motherhood bestows, often all we can hear is the high praise patriarchy accords the achievements of the hero. Longing to be heroselves, we ignore the possibility offered by our own way of the mother.

PART I

Dramatis Personae

CHAPTER I.

Mother Goddesses

The *Bhagavad Gita* asserts that "the disciplined man [sic], having abandoned the fruit of action, obtains enduring peace; the undisciplined man, impelled by desire, is attached to the fruit and is bound" (v:12). Similarly, the way of the mother may be judged either solely in terms of its fruit—children—or more broadly as a particular way of being in the world. But understood narrowly, as a means to the single end of producing children, the way of the mother ceases to be the model for a certain way of being in the world. When that happens, in effect, it ceases to be. A woman may have children yet refuse to become a mother in any but the most superficial manner. But if a woman embarks on the way of the mother, then elements other than its very important fruit—children—become deeply significant to her as well.

The way of the mother is the counterpart of the familiar quest of the hero. Logically both these patterns of human existence should be equally celebrated. Yet this is not the case. The quest of the hero is so well known as to be a recognizable mythological motif found in cultures throughout the world. By contrast, the way of the mother is a configuration ordinarily not even named.

Consider the statement of psychologist Norman O. Brown that "coitus successfully performed is . . . a return to the maternal womb."[1] These words, which are so clearly both androcentric and heterosexual, completely ignore the basic sexual experience of women (and gay men), although possibly lesbian women, like heterosexual men, experience what Brown describes. But that very ignoring says something crucial about woman: Woman, who, as in this instance, is frequently made interchangeable with mother, must necessarily predate the hero. As mother, she has already lived out a substantial portion of her life before the hero is even born. Yet from the hero's perspective, the world necessarily begins only with his own birth. Anything that happened before did not, in an experiential sense, exist for him. That means that the experience of the mother before his birth cannot be told from the perspective of the hero. What he speaks of instead, as do those speaking about him, is necessarily his own, androcentric experience. In the rare instances when the woman's story has been told, therefore, it has seldom been presented except through the distorting lenses of the hero's perspective. In such instances, two processes inevitably reshape, hence distort, the story of the mother. First, when it is presented androcentrically, as the words of Brown suggest, her experience is ignored, while that of the hero is assumed to be universal. Second, in many other instances, instead of being ignored, the experience of the mother is imagined from the perspective of the hero. If her experience and experience of her are pleasing from an androcentric perspective, they are typically idealized. Conversely, if they are offensive, they are demonized.

But this story of woman as mother did once exist in highly potent, nonandrocentric form. Like the dramatis personae of the more familiar, complementary quest of the hero, the characters of this story are three: mother, child, and father. Mythically they are Mother Goddess, Hero Son, and Father God. In its most original manifestations, however, in the earliest period of human development, the story has but a single player: the Palaeolithic Mother Goddess.[2]

During the Palaeolithic period, which bequeathed to all subsequent cultures the earliest themes of concern to humanity, religion focused mainly on fertility. Consequently, birth and generation, problems of subsistence and continuing food supplies, death, and afterlife were of major concern. The focal symbol for these interconnected themes was the life-giving mother; her attributes readily became secondary symbols.

Material evidence in the form of large numbers of "Venuses" firmly embeds this female focal symbol in the Upper Palaeolithic period in Eurasia (c. 22,000 B.C.E.). Overexaggerated secondary sex characteristics and pregnant bellies characterize these figures, as in the case of the well-known Venus of Willendorf. By the time of the Neolithic and Chalcolithic periods (c. 7000-3500 B.C.E.) in Old Europe (roughly southeast Europe from Czechoslovakia to the Aegean) and the Near East, a full-blown Great Mother Goddess is well established. The forms in which She appears there universally characterize Her in agricultural societies. Her worship is strongest in these cultures because of Her discerned likeness to the all-important earth whose cycles of fertility and decay so dominate crop-planting cultures. In the two other major kinds of archaic societies, She never attains such prominence. These are patrilineal totemic cultures such as occur variously among some Native American and Australian tribes (others being structured along matrilineal totemic lines), the Baganda of Uganda, Africa, and the Santals of Bengal; and patriarchal nomadic cultures, most notable in the desert societies of the Near East that eventually spawned the Judeo-Christian-Islamic complex. Almost everywhere the Goddess is worshipped, She is associated with the earth from which all vegetal life springs. Simultaneously, She is often also connected with the vegetation itself, usually in the form of grain, generically referred to as corn. Hence, She is commonly both earth and corn mother.

Earth and related vegetal phenomena such as grains are not the only natural elements associated with Her, however. Water, the medium from which humans originally emerged onto land, also functions as her habitat, as with the ancient Mexican goddess of the waters, Chalchihuitlicue, and the water mother common to the ancient Karelians and other Finno-Ugric peoples. Sometimes, as with the Japanese sun goddess Amaterasu or the pre-Islamic Mother of the Heavens, Al-Lat, or the Egyptian sky goddess Nut, the traditional associations of earth with motherhood, and sky with fatherhood reverse; accordingly, the abstractions normally attached to motherhood alter. Ordinarily, however, one of Her primary attributes is chthonicity, that is, earth-rootedness. This attribute not only links her to the fertility of earth, primarily associated, at least visually, with earth's surface, but also with its opposite—death. In this connection She ties to the dark, hidden interior of earth in which the dead are "planted." At the same time, She connects to ideas of rebirth, based on analogies with planting: just as seemingly "dead" seeds are placed in the ground only to "rise" in due time, it is believed that dead humans restored to the maternal womb of earth will subsequently regenerate as well.

About 12,000 years ago, patriarchal revisions of the original story of this Goddess who constellates the pattern of meaning known as the way of the mother began distorting it. They did so (and have continued to do so) through various interconnected processes common to patriarchal thought, generally with devastating effect on the ways motherhood came to be represented by this Great Goddess figure. Specialization is one such process. When specialization occurs, qualities originally mixed together as attributes of the single Goddess are separated out to form distinctly separate goddesses. This happens in the Homeric pantheon when Artemis and Aphrodite, for example, both lose their original fullness of personality and become mainly associated respectively with hunting and erotic love. In similar fashion, motherhood, especially in monotheistic cultures, has typically been severed from all other potential and actual attributes of womanhood. Hunting, wisdom, sex, war—all such qualities of the holistic, undifferentiated goddess—appear totally unconnected with motherhood as it is construed in patriarchal thinking. What is left of the original powerful Mother Goddess in contemporary patriarchal cultures is little more than the sentimentalized image for which Mother's Day was invented.

Related to patriarchal disintegration of the holistic Goddess through specialization is a different process that polarizes "good" and "bad" qualities into beneficent and terrible goddesses. Such Terrible Mothers of death and destruction as the Hindu Kali, the Aztec Coatlicue, and the Greek Medusa typify this trend. Splitting of this sort dichotomizes the originally unified birth-death cycle of nature in which Mother Earth gives birth. After She does so, as in the Greek story of Erichtonious, or the Pueblo myths which portray humanity emerging from Shipapu [Pueblo], the womb of Natya Ha 'atse, the Earth Mother, She eventually takes back her dead for burial. Then Her cycle is complete. But the patriarchal process of polarization forever alters this original completeness of life and death by creating separate goddesses who preside over death in the under-earth realm. Such are the Greek goddess Persephone and the dread Sumero-Akkadian Ereshkigal, figures once coalesced with, but now distinctly separate from, such beneficent counterparts as Demeter and Ishtar. Without question, such polarization drains the original Great Goddess of Her power fully as much as the process of specialization does.

In a variant process whereby patriarchal thinking alters the powers of the Goddess, the specialized single goddess is multiplied, usually into a triad, as in the case of the Viking Norns, the Greek Horae, or the strange *matres* and *matrones* figures from the Celtic and Germanic provinces of the Roman Empire. The *matres*, usually portrayed as draped figures holding children and baskets of fruit, are triple attributes of fertility, as the Norns and Horae are dreaded images of death. Sometimes such triplification results in trinitarian representations involving different stages of motherhood as in various ubiquitous Virgin-Mother-Crone triads (the Hindu Parvati-Durga-Uma, the Celtic Macha, the Morrigan, and the Badb, for example). Just what purpose such triplification serves is not certain. It is not, however, a reunification of the original Goddess, for each of the three units retains her separate identity. Rather, it seems to be a means of amplifying, hence emphasizing, each selected power separately. As with the related processes of specialization and polarization, multiplication thus serves to further depotentiate the once all-powerful Mother Goddess. By separating out, even emphasizing, Her formidable powers in these ways, patriarchal thought was eventually able to render Her ineffectual.

Whether this once powerful Great Goddess so prominent in Neolithic agrarian societies is actually a single goddess bearing many names or many goddesses embodying the same or similar characteristics is a topic of continuing scholarly debate. Certainly the proliferation of Her names is staggering. In Babylon and Assyria She is Ishtar; in Canaan, Astarte; in Egypt, Isis; in Phrygia, Cybele; in pre-Hellenic Greece, variously Rhea, Ge, and Gaia; in Vedic India, Prithivi; in ancient China, Ti; in Inca Peru, Pachamama; and so on through hundreds of names in as many different cultures. Yet despite these many names, the debate about Her presumed singularity or multiplicity does not differ significantly from philosophical arguments over the biblical God: Is He actually "the same" God for all His many worshippers?

In prepatriarchal cultures in which the Goddess especially flourished such as those of Old Europe, pre-Hellenic Greece, and pre-Vedic India (Harappa, Mohenjo-Daro), not dominated by nomadic pastoral peoples, the Goddess is associated with both motherhood and virginity. Patriarchy subsequently separates the two and opposes them to each other. In a gynocentric thought pattern, which does not constantly split wholes asunder, this connection is not strange at all. Moreover, until the discovery of stockbreeding and planting, humans presumably did not understand the reproductive role of men. That means that out of the half million to million years of hominid existence, it has only been during the last 12,000 years or so that humans have understood the concept of paternity. Before this understanding evolved in human thought, it was largely assumed that birth took place by parthenogenesis, that is, without fertilization, solely through the mother's reproductive capability. A mother was therefore originally understood as sole creator of life, hence as a powerful figure in her own right. The emergence of a child out of her body would have been one of the two greatest of all possible mysteries, the other being death. A woman's ability not only to reproduce her own likeness, a girl, but also to create her opposite, a boy, must have seemed miraculous.

As the procreative contribution of males became apparent, however, the role of the Mother Goddess as central symbol of life and death slowly began to shift. Two ways this shift occurred are particularly significant. First, she was eventually replaced, thousands of years later, notably in the monotheistic religious complex of the West, by the Father God. Second, Her consort son, who was originally subordinate, before becoming equal, eventually surpassed Her. The relative positions of Mary and Jesus well exemplify the result of this metamorphosis.

Through various processes of androcentrization such as these, the once powerful Great Mother Goddess who constellates within Herself the deep meaning of motherhood lost Her original position as central deity of humanity. In the wake of Her gradual demise, the related high esteem in which the powers of female procreation were held suffered an equivalent decline. Instead of women's powers for motherhood, it was now men's for fatherhood that came to be worshipped. With this shift into a patriarchal way of understanding the world, the original shared reverence for the ancient way of the mother slowly disappeared.

CHAPTER 2.

Father Gods

Startling as it may seem from the vantage point of our own androcentric culture, paternity is not really self-evident. After all, the logic of cause-and-effect relationships is usually only apparent when the two are closely connected in time. When an effect takes as long as nine months to occur, even the most observant individual is unlikely to think: Aha! pregnancy and childbirth result from coitus. Furthermore, the most obvious sign of pregnancy, the swelling body, only becomes visible long after the time of insemination. Consequently, that connection, too, is not readily apparent. Thus universally prevalent beliefs in virgin birth, or parthenogenesis, are not that strange.

Given such beliefs, it is scarcely surprising then that motherhood should be so highly venerated by prepatriarchal humans. For some unfathomable reason women, and women alone, could reproduce themselves. Even more astonishing, women could reproduce those unlike themselves, males, as well. Men, on the other hand, could reproduce neither, no matter how hard they might try. Childbirth was unique to women.

Was women's great power related to the fact that their bodies mysteriously produced blood once a month? Somehow out of this blood new life sometimes emerged. Blood must therefore hold the secret. But why only women's blood? Not only that: How and why could women also produce magic fluid from their breasts to feed their babies? In these two secretions must lie the secrets of reproduction and maintenance of life. As sole possessors of these interconnected secrets, women in Palaeolithic and Neolithic cultures wielded a power above and beyond that of men. That power placed women in a class apart. In face of such awe-inspiring capability, these different beings, or the powers they represented, were necessarily worthy of worship. It was in women's form, therefore, that deity was initially understood.

But eventually the male's role in procreation became evident. Once it did, the original cast of characters in the story of the way of the mother expanded to include her mate. From that time on, the power of the Great Mother Goddess has slowly eroded. Exactly how or when this significant awareness occurred is unknown. As long as humans subsisted primarily on food obtained opportunistically through frequent gathering and occasional hunting, this recognition of paternity was unlikely to occur. Not until humans, in one of their great cultural transformations, abandoned hunting and gathering in favor of agriculture and stock breeding could the necessary connection between coitus and insemination be made. Placing a tiny seed in the ground, only to have it duplicate the plant from which it originally grew, sufficiently resembles human coupling for awareness to dawn. Instead of planting a seed in the earth, the man "planted" his hot liquid in the woman's dark interior. Furthermore, once humans became stockbreeders, they could even more readily correlate their own sexual acts with those of animals. That made the male role in procreation indisputable. Once the importance of the male in this hitherto woman-only mystery was understood, ritual and mythic celebration of fatherhood inevitably followed.

The exact sequence of this development is not as certain as it sounds, however.[1] The most archaic manifestations of divine paternity almost everywhere reveal a concept known as the "High God." Found even in some twentieth-century cultures, He is exemplified by figures such as Kupon among the African Tschwi, Baiame among some of the aboriginal Australians, and Puluga among the Andamanese. As might be expected, the abode of this High God is the sky. Myths from almost every tradition tell of the mating of this Father Sky with Mother Earth, although in a few cultures, such as that of the ancient Egyptians, the imagery reverses, making the sky female, the earth male. Typically this union creates the other goddesses and gods. Sometimes it also results in all earthly creation, often belatedly through a second generation of creative deities. Just how early in the development of humanity this concept of mother earth and father sky arose is not known, but it is definitely present from Neolithic times on, when inscriptions and myths testify to its existence.

What makes this concept of the High God especially difficult to place in the development of human thought is the fact that the fatherhood He implies is not always specifically biological. Consequently, it seems likely either that this idea of biological fatherhood took hold slowly or that this god actually predates understandings of paternity. Given the necessary absence of myths from this preliterate era, combined with the lack of any archaeological evidence to suggest His existence in the Palaeolithic period, there is no way to know for sure just how He fits into early religious thought. From contemporary archaic cultures, however, it is possible to draw some inferences. Often fatherhood in these cultures is more strictly creative, a distinction made apparent, for example, in the terms *Bawai* and *Apap* which the African Tschwi and Teso peoples respectively apply to convey the fatherhood of God relative to creation. In this way of conceptualizing the term, fatherhood is more akin to artistic creation than biology. This makes the High God a "father" even if He does not participate in the well-known marriage of Mother Earth and Father Sky. Similarly the early gods known in myths are often primarily makers or creators as well, rather than biological fecundators. The particular god known as the High God is also typically so far removed from his creation—the world of human affairs—that he becomes a *deus absconditus*, an absent god too remote from and unconcerned with human affairs to receive much worship. Such a concept of "fatherhood" does not seem at all odd if we think back to our understanding of the term in childhood. Typically, the last aspect of fatherhood a child learns about is insemination.

In a less archaic pattern of thought, however, biology definitely influences ideas of divine fatherhood. Instead of being a fairly abstract depiction of creation, the mating of Father Sky with Mother Earth is often made concretely sexual. In this pattern the son begotten of their union supersedes his father to become in his stead the mate of his mother. This happens, for instance, when the Greek Zeus replaces Ouranos or the Babylonian Marduk supplants the fathers Anu, Enlil, and Ea. Concomitantly, the earlier sky associations give way, and the son-god comes to be worshipped either as a weather deity like Zeus or an agricultural god like Marduk. Typically the agricultural son-gods "die" with each harvest, only to be "reborn" each spring. It is they who figure so importantly in myths and rituals connected with the Neolithic Great Goddess, functioning both as Her son and Her lover.

In marked contrast to this biological, often chthonic, fatherhood is the refinement of sky-oriented fatherhood apparent in the monotheistic religions. These include Judaism, Christianity, Islam, and the dualistic Zoroastrianism. All four developed out of patriarchal nomadic breeding societies which retained more of the archaic religion than did their matrilineal agricultural counterparts. The biblical Yahweh, for example, is thought to have emerged from the celestial Western Semitic deity, Ya, Yami, or Yahu. The ancient Palaeolithic Mother Goddess who flourished so fully in the Neolithic period among the Mediterranean peoples who looked to the earth for sustenance did not develop fully in these traditions. In the wide-open, parched lands of rock and desert out of which monotheistic patriarchal religions emerged, the primary symbol was not earth but sky. And few cultures other than that of the ancient Egyptians have associated the mother figure with the sky.

Seemingly these sky-oriented traditions would denigrate birth as well as mothers. Oddly, however, this is not the case. One of the most striking attributes frequently credited to father gods in almost all patriarchal cultures is that they give birth in some fashion. As with the high gods mentioned above, these gods are "fathers" whose model appears to be the mother who gives birth, rather than the father who inseminates. One of the most ancient examples occurs in the Babylonian epic which tells of the god Marduk creating humanity after first destroying the older goddess-centered order in which the goddess Tiamat, representative of chaos, had been the principal figure. Marduk does so by taking the blood of Kingu, Tiamat's second husband, saying: "Blood I will mass and cause bones to be. I will establish a savage, 'man' shall be his name."[2] In this way, the male god "begets" all humanity out of the blood of another male. In so doing he bypasses the female entirely, being completely sufficient unto himself, as originally the Mother Goddess was believed to be.

Similarly, from ancient Egypt comes a tale in which it is the male god who is solely responsible for engendering humanity. In Egypt no one myth dominated, since separate gods were revered in different religious centers. But in Heliopolis, it was the sun god, variously known as Atum, Ra or Re, Khepri, Horus, and Re-Harakhti, who created humanity out of his own tears: "O ancestor gods, behold mankind, which came into being from my Eye."[3] This idea of a male creator giving birth to humanity out of his tears is found also in ancient Greece where, according to one tradition the Titan Prometheus creates humanity, either out of earth and water or out of his own tears.

And in Teutonic mythology according to the *Vafprudnismal* it is again a male who "gives birth" to all humanity. This time it is the Frost giant Ymir, who one day falls asleep and becomes totally covered with sweat. Out of this bodily exudate a man and a woman are born from under his left arm.

And of course the creation of humanity in the Judeo-Christian tradition gives to the human male as well as to the Father God this power of birth which is naturally woman's. First it is God the Father who "gives birth" to man: "Then the Lord God formed man of dust from the ground, and breathed into his nostrils the breath of life; and man became a living being" (Gen.2:7). Subsequently, it is indirectly Adam: "So the Lord God caused a deep sleep to fall upon the man, and while he slept took one of his ribs and closed up its place with flesh; and the rib which the Lord God had taken from the man he made into a woman and brought her to the man" (Gen.2:21-22).

As if such mythic usurpation of women's natural powers were not enough, in ritual too, fathers often mimic the maternal role. Initiation rites for boys, particularly among various Australian aboriginal groups, frequently reveal the fathers of a tribe functioning as male mothers. This happens when they ritually imitate menstruation and "give birth" to the young male initiates. Such sexual crossing over introduces into the concept of fatherhood several conflicting themes. Sometimes fatherhood is as self-contained as motherhood in its parthenogenetic form. In that case no partner is needed. At other times, however, fatherhood projects a "maternal," nurturing quality far different from the remoteness associated with the archaic Sky God. Then again fatherhood sometimes de-emphasizes sexual differentiation completely. This de-emphasis occurs in fertility figures like the Babylonian god Marduk, who is sometimes described as a female, and the Egyptian goddess Isis, who is occasionally portrayed as a male.

This brief look at the development of the concept of the Father God who so greatly altered the role of the Great Mother Goddess indicates how complex and uncertain His history is. Although the precise time of His arrival in human thought cannot be ascertained, once the concept He represents became integrated into human thinking, He soon became supreme in the nonagrarian cultures of the Middle East. By contrast, in the fertile lands where agriculture was practiced, both in that region and in such fertile areas of Europe as the lands around the Mediterranean, the Palaeolithic Mother Goddess, of whom little is known, developed into the so-called Great Mother whose myths and rituals we still know today. It is She who functions for women as the model of selfhood expressed by the way of the mother, much as Her hero son models a complementary form of selfhood in the quest of the hero.

CHAPTER 3.

Hero Sons

In the story known as the way of the mother, it is not only the Father God who both opposes and usurps qualities possessed by the Neolithic Great Mother Goddess. Her son/consort, the prototype of the hero, also does so. Even in his seemingly weakest form, as infant, he is generically deified as the Divine Child.[1] Archaeological finds, including various vase paintings and figurines depicting infancy themes and rituals, place the concept of this archetypal Divine Child at least as far back as the Neolithic and Chalcolithic periods (c. 7000-3500 B.C.E.) in Old Europe. Various mythic motifs connected with him tell of his birth and subsequent maturation into the beautiful youth worshipped as a young god of vegetation. As such, he is born only to die and be reborn again.

In the story of the son-god's passion is reflected the course of the yearly harvest. Told and ritualized in countless variations, a representative example comes from the Cult of the Infant Dionysus, originally celebrated in Boeotia and Crete. Subsequently, worship of this particular form of the Divine Child became almost universal in Greece. In this cult, the infant Dionysus-Zagreus is ritually dismembered. According to the mythic tradition, it is the Titans, the generation of Greek gods generated by the mythic marriage of heaven and earth, who first enact this passion story. They do so by luring the child with various toys such as rattles, knucklebones, a top, a ball, and a mirror. They then proceed to cut him to pieces, cook him, and eat him. In some versions the child is subsequently resurrected by the Earth Mother Rhea. It was she who participated in the original mating of heaven and earth which produced these very same Titans who then destroyed the infant Dionysus. This death and resurrection theme, common to the complex of images central to agrarian religion, finds in the child, or alternatively the seed, an appropriate image of renewal.

The worship accorded this divine child was originally that directed to the Mother Goddess. The cases of Ishtar, Astarte, and Cybele, all of whose son-consorts were originally of secondary importance, are illustrative. With time, however, in each pairing, the child (originally of either sex as suggested by numerous Sumerian female Marduks) ceases to be merely the child or sacrificial consort. Instead he becomes more and more venerated in his own right. Christianity epitomizes this process whereby the Divine Child eventually eclipses his own mother.

Images of a Divine Child as hero-god are by no means confined to Eurasia. They are particularly common in Native American mythology of North, Central, and South America. In this mythology a common motif focuses on the "Wonder Child" who grows almost instantly from baby to strong youth or adult, as, for example, do the Siouan Young Rabbit and the Algonquian Blood Clot Boy. This pattern is typified by the Haida story of Shining Heavens: One day a Haida woman was digging on the beach. Hearing a cry from a cockleshell, she uncovered it, only to discover the baby, Shining Heavens. She took him home, and he almost immediately grew up, thus showing his supernatural power. In this story, the "mother" no longer even bears him; instead, she merely "uncovers" him from a shell. At other times, the power of the child hero is such that he can make plans in utero, as do the Iroquoian twins Good Mind and Evil Mind. Here again, the role of the mother is eclipsed by that of her own children, even before they exist as physically separate individuals. What is especially noteworthy about all these divine children is the way they so often usurp powers that belong by nature to their mothers.

Despite many obvious differences between them, these early mythic images indicate that the functions of mothers and their hero sons are often much alike. Even the conception known as "hero" may be, in its original sense, a gynocentric rather than a patriarchal idea, although scholars are by no means universally agreed about the matter.[2] In this view, heroes were originally men who were sacrificed to the pre-Hellenic Hera, long before she became the shrewish wife of Zeus, a role into which she was cast by patriarchal invaders of Greece. But before these many waves of patriarchal invaders entered Greece starting about 25,000 B.C.E., Hera was a mother goddess to whom "Hera-sacred-men," or heroes, were sacrificed as her martyr bridegrooms. So widespread throughout Europe was her cult that as late as the eighth century C.E., her Saxon temple at Heresburg (Hera's Mount) was destroyed by Charlemagne's forces. This connection of heroes to Hera allows for an important recognition of an underlying connection between heroes and mothers. It is important for two reasons. First, it allows contemporary women and men who have grown up thousands of years after these connections were all but obliterated to re-see motherhood. Second, the often close connection between the mother and the hero suggests that the mother role provides an overlooked potential for human salvation.

In traditional Western symbol systems it is either heroes or divinities who bring salvation. Furthermore, heroes are almost invariably male. For every heroic female character nine Sir Galahads exist. The Princess in the Grimm's tale of "The Twelve Brothers," who remains mute for seven years to save her siblings, is representative of the exceptions.

In fact, all the dramatis personae of traditional tales, not just heroes, are characteristically defined along rigid sex lines. The importance of this sex segregation to women trying to decide whether to follow the quest of the hero or the way of the mother cannot be overstressed. Consider the female characters in myths and fairy tales who are young and beautiful; they are either good or evil with no gradations in between. The good ones are heroines, exemplars of "the eternal feminine," who, like Cinderella, must be rescued by the hero rather than saving themselves. If they are evil, they are portrayed, like the Sirens, as destroyers of men. The hero must fight to preserve himself from such "evil" women.

This kind of reversal is precisely what happens whenever the quest of the hero becomes instead the way of the mother. Even in old age, such women characters remain just as rigidly dichotomized. Good women are presented as maternal helping figures, Wise Women, whose advice heroes must seek in order to succeed. Evil ones are witches and ogresses. Such splitting is yet another manifestation of the specialization directed by androcentric thinking at the originally holistic Neolithic Mother Goddess.

Such specialization is not directed only at women. Androcentric thinking is ecumenical in its application of processes which split apart original wholes. Consequently, male figures are just as rigidly portrayed as females. An older prototype of the hero is the mature male who wields great power and authority. As with his archetypal female counterparts, he may be either good or evil. In his good form he is typically a wise old man, a benevolent king (often the father of the heroine), or a powerful god. In his evil form he is usually an ogre or dwarf, a despotic king, or a devil figure. The important point to note is that despite apparent similarities, the two sexual groupings differ importantly: *Active* figures in most tradi-tional tales are both heroic and male. Passive figures are typically, albeit not exclusively, female. Consequently, the long-held Western association of women with inaction and men with action is given added emphasis through mythic characterizations of this sort. That mothers should be seen as nonparticipants in the "real" world is therefore scarcely surprising.

Fortunately, nontraditional tales have long abandoned such rigid configurations of character. Nonetheless, fixed sex roles have governed most cultures until relatively recently. When such rigid sex roles prevail, salvation is rarely mediated through a woman or by means of imagery connected with women. Woman-connected imagery simply is not "seen" because it fails to match the expectations and assumptions of any andro-centrically patterned community in which it appears. If such imagery is recognized, it is usually considered "deviant." Typically, such "deviant" salvation is renamed. Then, because it is coming through the "wrong" channels, it is called either "witchcraft" or "damnation."

For example, in Christianity, salvation can only come through the divine savior-hero, Christ. Without His intervention an individual will be damned. While Roman Catholicism acknowledges the power of Mary to intercede with her son, ultimately only He can grant salvation. Protes-tantism, largely eschewing Mary, disallows even that much feminine influ-ence.

Commonly fairy-tale counterparts of the Christian savior myth are construed purely as entertainment. Often they are relegated to the nursery. But these stories can be read on many levels. They reflect some of the deepest patterns of being that humans have experienced from prehistoric times on. This is not to say that myths and fairy tales realistically represent everyday life as individuals once lived it. Rather they reflect various "interior" levels of human experience, just as dreams do.

According to depth psychologists like C. G. Jung, the worldwide mythic motif of the questing hero embodies a universal pattern of human development known as individuation. "Individuation" means just what it says: It is the process by which a person becomes an individual, as opposed to remaining psychologically merged with his mother or the environment. According to Western norms, the more highly individuated an individual is, the better. To remain metaphorically attached to one's mother indicates immaturity. An adult child must move away from her influence and into the *world of men*.

Typically, most psychotherapists, following Freud, elaborate the process of individuation from an androcentric perspective. Each step shows what is necessary for a man to become capable of functioning according to Western conceptions of selfhood. That manhood and self-hood are interchangeable is abundantly clear in Freud's writing. In com-mon parlance, too, concepts of selfhood and manhood are frequently confused. Consider, for example, the words of a man just out of a job who must accept handouts from a food bank: "'I lose all my manhood to do this,' said Mr. Davis, 50 years old, as he carried two bags of groceries for his family. 'But what can I do? You have to eat.'"[3] As a woman, I know that given his situation I would feel the same devastating loss that Davis expresses. But having no manhood to begin with, it is impossible that I should lose it. In Davis's position I would say I was losing my *selfhood*. The fact that I would never say, "I am losing my womanhood," in this context shows how "selfhood" and "manhood" reflect each other in ways that "womanhood" and "selfhood" do not.

The problem with this unconscious association of selfhood with manhood is that it places women in an untenable situation. To date the most compelling insights into this difficulty have come from psychologist Carol Gilligan. In her book *In a Different Voice*,+ she points out that men characteristically seek separateness and self-containment; women do not. For women, community and relationship are more typical. Yet what is customary behavior for women has been ignored as a norm because it deviates from the supposedly universal norm designed on, for, and by men. Consequently, for a woman to follow the quest of the hero may not be simply to imitate men on a superficial level. It may even be to attempt to change ourselves at the very level of our being, the ontological level, as well.

If so, that means women trying to develop what is ordinarily called "selfhood" must seek to become something fundamentally alien to our very being—we must seek to become men. Women who choose motherhood for a period of their lives are especially ill-served by this quintessentially Western, "heroic" model of selfhood. Although heroic selfhood often resembles, may originally derive from, that of motherhood, essentially it opposes motherselfhood. No matter whether these two models are biological or cultural, an issue that may never be resolved, the negative effect on women of being held to the single, heroic model can be devastating. Awareness of the alternative motherselfhood is therefore extremely liberating.

CHAPTER 4.

Heroself

The hero who succeeds in his mythic quest achieves a very special gift. This gift goes by various names; it may be a plant of immortality or some magical object capable of satisfying all wishes. No matter what it is called in myth and fairy tale, in a psychological context this special gift is "selfhood." Speaking of the process whereby the hero quests for this gift of selfhood, mythologist Joseph Campbell says:

> The original departure into the land of trials represented only the beginning of the long and really perilous path of initiatory conquests and moments of illumination. Dragons have now to be slain and surprising barriers passed—again, again, and again. Meanwhile there will be a multitude of preliminary victories, unretainable ecstasies, and momentary glimpses of the wonderful land."[1]

As Campbell's words make clear, the goal of the traditional hero's quest, from a psychological perspective, is selfhood.

To the extent that achievement of selfhood is construed as the result of successful heroic questing, it is implicitly masculine. Consequently, selfhood, as traditionally defined, is extremely difficult for women to understand, much less experience for ourselves. Even without this gender complication, however, "self" is a complex idea. In fact, despite its common usage, the term "self" is just as difficult to define as the term "God" it has replaced in some contemporary theologies. Because "self" is so taken for granted it falls in the category of words whose meanings we tend to assume rather than prove. We all "know" what "self" is until we try to explain what it is we know. Books and books exist which examine numerous Western conceptions of selfhood. Yet in the broadest sense certain ideas typify the majority of them and influence the belief systems of most of us. First, that something called "self" exists has been and still is axiomatic for most Western thinkers. Although few of us can define it satisfactorily we nonetheless take "self," whatever it may be, for granted, much as members of Christendom in earlier ages took for granted the existence of God. For most individuals, self, one's own personal "I," is the starting point for any thought or action.

This has certainly been so ever since Descartes uttered his "*Cogito, ergo sum*" (I think, therefore I am). That famous utterance has also generated the assumption in Western thought that "reality" consists of two halves: self and other, variously referred to as subject and object, mine and not-mine, us and them, and so forth. Whatever the names of the two terms, one always represents the perceiver, one the "other." For many contemporary thinkers this Cartesian dualism, as it is called, blocks the progress of philosophical and theological thinking about such concepts as selfhood. This blockage occurs because we in the West have all been acculturated into a belief system which assumes this dualism of subject and object to begin with. Therefore we find it difficult to experience the world in any other way. After all, "you" get up in the morning, "you" brush your teeth, "you" eat breakfast. You are not the morning, your teeth, or your breakfast. Furthermore, it is not your cat, a ray of sunshine, or some disembodied spirit who performs those functions for you. Nor do those functions simply perform themselves; "you" have to be there doing them; they will not just happen on their own.

But wait, you may say. Sometimes it does seem as though they just happen. . . . Sometimes "you" do not seem to be there at all. Most people have experienced such "sometimes." But ordinarily such times remain the exceptions you tend to ignore in favor of the more accustomed situations in which "you" control. But who or what is this "you"? Is it your body? Your mind? Your soul, your spirit, or your psyche? All of them? Although many thinkers throughout history have applied themselves to these questions about the "you" of selfhood, they all refer to mysteries that cannot be fully answered.

In our own era, probably Freud's thinking most directly influences the way most of us answer them. His well-known division of self into ego ("I"), superego, and id ("it") is so familiar that most people now take these theoretical constructs for granted. We assume that these three subdivisions sufficiently respond to the question, "What is self," that no other explanation is needed. Most of us also take for granted Freud's distinction between the conscious and unconscious selves. These distinctions are now "facts," for many of us. We often speak, for instance, of our unconscious, our ego, our id, precisely as we do of our arms or legs. When we do so we treat Freud's *model* of reality as if it were the actual reality itself.

What Freud did was to create various terms that seemed to him appropriate for talking about emotional phenomena. As those constructs became generally accepted, his original purpose became subverted; from being models they became "realities" to the general public. Once an abstract idea becomes concretized in this way (or reified, as this process is known technically), it becomes an accepted part of everybody's thinking, but on a level different from that originally intended. This situation may be compared to a common television phenomenon. Many soap-opera fans become so involved in the doings of their favorite heroines and heroes that if one becomes ill, the fan may actually call or write the actress or actor to make sure she or he is all right. Whether it is a soap-opera character or a psychological construct such as the ego, when either is taken literally, a useful distinction in levels of "reality" breaks down.

As with the soap-opera characters who seem so real for many people, the notion that "self" and the different elements thought to compose it are artificial constructs is nearly impossible to accept. That is because our whole mode of understanding depends on the existence of this "self" to do that understanding. If "you," a self, have to exist in order to understand, how can it possibly be the case that this self is just a construct?

Help in understanding this difficult point comes from a tradition very different from any indigenous to Western thought. In the East, Buddhism asserts that "self" does not, in fact, exist. Self is an illusion created entirely by the senses. Although your senses do tell you that something you call "I" exists, your senses are wrong. The senses distort ultimate reality and so mislead you. Human experience, in this view, is basically empty. The content of experience is not actually there; it is the false creation of your mind and senses. In this view "self" is a delusion. To quest to actualize your "self," therefore, as Western thought teaches, is to move in precisely the opposite direction from the one which will free you from delusion. Instead, your goal is to see through the faulty construction of your senses to the emptiness beyond them. That way you may ultimately achieve the desired state of no-self or enlightenment. This achievement is exactly opposite from that sought by the hero of Western quest.

To look at this complicated situation in another way, for anyone imbued with Western understandings, the ultimate problem of existence is one's own death. At death the individual "I" ceases to exist. This cessation of one's own "I" haunts most Westerners, often to the point that we simply evade thinking about it. For Easterners imbued with Buddhist understanding, however, the situation is reversed. From their perspective the extinction of the "I" would be welcome. Unless an individual has achieved enlightenment during life, however, he will return to a succeeding life here on earth. From a Buddhist perspective the major philosophical problem, therefore, is not the idea that the "I," the "self," will eventually cease to exist. Instead, difficulty arises from the sensory delusion that such a thing as that "I" should be thought to exist in the first place.

Rather than desiring a self separate from everything that is nonself, the goal of a Buddhist is understanding what we would call "self" as being at one with the spaces, the nothingness, around him or her. In being at one with the environment, no separate "I" can exist to care about its unique "I-ness." Instead of an "outside" existing separately from the "I" and an "inside" constituting the "I," what exists is a single unselfbound consciousness. When that consciousness realizes that its consciousness too is but a delusion, it will have reached the next state. In this state one has finally achieved enlightenment.

By contrast, part of what makes "self" so complicated a concept in Western thinking is precisely its presumed separation from its surroundings. In fact, the quest of the hero, viewed from a psychological perspective, involves the quester in separating himself from his maternal world. Ideally, to succeed in his goal of selfhood he must become a totally separate individual. That means he must break away from his mother and the world of maternal values for which she stands. Instead, the hero-son must reach the opposing world represented by his father.

From a philosophical perspective, this separation is known as a Cartesian split. It is this separation which gives to selfhood its dimensionality, for self includes both inside and outside. But as we actually experience "reality," interior and exterior are not nearly as well differentiated as this Cartesian view implies. This lack of differentiation often means that the hero on his quest cannot tell if he is journeying outside or within, if the "monsters" he encounters are external or internal. Unlike a traditional rectangular house, for example, which demarcates a clear inside from an equally distinct outside, inside and outside intermix within the self. Consequently, the traditional Western inner-outer distinction blurs. An image that can help clarify this complicated blurring process which makes both the quest of the hero and the way of the mother so complex is the Klein bottle.

The Klein bottle is a figure drawn from topology, a mathematical field that focuses on special kinds of geometric configurations. A kind of three-dimensional Möbius strip, the Klein bottle is formed by twisting a continuous spherical surface. The neck of the bottle is bent so that it penetrates its own body. As a result, the whole remains a single continuous piece. It is impossible, given this construction, to point to any section which is interior or exterior. The two parts flow into each other in such a way as to make such traditional categories meaningless. Consequently, the image is extremely threatening to anyone who, like the hero venerated in the West, longs to be separately individuated from his mother. From the perspective of a mother vis-à-vis the child in her belly, however, this image is highly appropriate.

Theoretically, the condition of undifferentiated self roughly illustrated by the image of the Klein bottle should translate into the selflessness desired in the East. Logically, too, Eastern women should therefore be thought more capable of achieving the desired state of selflessness than men. Actually, however, this is not the case.

Although it would be unfairly oversimplifying to say that women in the West are faulted for the condition of selflessness so highly valued in the East just as their Eastern sisters are for being too self-deluded, it is difficult not to notice that the ideal in both systems is male! In the Eastern tradition of Buddhism, this ideal prevents a woman from achieving enlightenment because maleness is an essential attribute of the Buddhahood necessary to achieving it. It is thus impossible for a woman to achieve this state unless she first changes her body into that of a male! *The Sumati-sutra, Lotus, Vimalakirtinirdesa*, and *Pure Gift Sutra* all contain episodes in which a woman changes the female body in order to achieve the enlightenment of Bodhisattvahood.[2]

The opposing perspectives of the Eastern and Western views of selfhood show that the goals of the two traditions are markedly different. Whereas the Buddhist struggles for release from the illusion of self, the Westerner tries to realize that self, to bring it more fully into existence as an entity separate from its context. Typically, women in the West have been found deficient in self, being viewed as too dependent for truly separate selfhood. Conversely, in Buddhism, women are felt to be so mired in the illusion of selfhood that they are incapable of achieving enlightenment without first "becoming a man."

This demoralizing idea explicitly stated in Buddhist texts that only by becoming a man can a woman achieve such gifts as salvation, enlightenment, and selfhood implicitly colors traditional hero tales. These tales, whether traditional fairy tales or contemporary psychological theories, place women in an awkward situation. Instead of marrying the Goddess, as the hero almost invariably does, a woman becomes consort to an immortal. She then leaves earth for his supernatural abode. The implication here is that earth is not good enough; the supernatural world of heaven is better. This androcentric devaluation of earth, natural realm of the Mother Goddess, is nowhere more apparent than in these words of Joseph Campbell's as he points out that the Feast of the Assumption in both the Roman Catholic and the Greek Orthodox churches celebrates the mystery of woman being assumed into Heaven: "'The Virgin Mary is taken up into the bridal chamber of heaven where the King of Kings sits on his starry throne. . . . Oh! Virgin most prudent, whither goest thou, bright as the moon? all beautiful and sweet art thou, O daughter of Zion, fair as the moon, elect as the sun.'"[3] In the context of the quest of the hero, in which Campbell is speaking, this assumption is necessarily "good."

C. G. Jung likewise celebrates this assumption of Mary into heaven, claiming it gives "the feminine" its rightful place. But Mary's assumption is clearly a patriarchal vision. The ultimate realm here is heaven, abode of the male god. Assumption removes Mary from the natural earth, mythically associated in almost all cultures with women, and places her instead within a totally imagined territory. Assumption makes her like the male gods; it does not make them like her. Nor does it accord dignity and sacredness to her own realm—earth. Instead her assumption places her in the familiar pattern of the hero who earns apotheosis—elevation to divine status in the sky. Reversed thinking governs this pattern, whether it is applied solely to Mary or to mothers in general. Much as Mary incarnates in patriarchally adulterated form the far older prehistoric Mother Goddess, the hero also does. Unconsciously he has appropriated and adapted many positive elements of the mother image. But such appropriation and adaptation are never credited, presumably because they are not recognized as having occurred in the first place. After their incorporation into the hero, the image of the mother is subsequently redefined. Now she is seen as being inferior to the hero. Only through "becoming like a man" and ascending to Heaven does this image of the mother, once superior to all others in human thought, ever again achieve parity with, let alone superiority to, those of the father and son gods.

So it has been historically with the concept of the self in the West: A woman has been defined as lacking in self. Then she has been judged lacking because she does not possess the very quality which by androcentric definitions she cannot have in the first place. Historically, the issue of woman vis-à-vis selfhood, as earlier with possession of a soul, has thus placed us in a classic no-win situation. To be possessed of either self or soul we have had to become other than what we naturally are. We have had to "become men." This cultural imperative to "become men" devastatingly reinforces any fears troubling women who are considering the way of the mother for themselves.

CHAPTER 5.

Polytheistic Selves

The implicit assumption that self is masculine is not the only barrier to women's understanding of what "self" is in the context of Western patriarchal thought. An almost equal hindrance to such understanding is the belief that self is single. This belief seems to reflect the religio-cultural assumption that unity is better than multiplicity, that "one" is superior to "many." The problem with this assumption in terms of human selfhood is that for a woman who becomes a mother, selfhood simply is not experienced as a single, separate unit. Instead, selfhood for a mother is a relational mode of being. Such selfhood involves what would ordinarily be called two selves co-existing in such a way that they are almost one. The awkward term "binary-unity" indicates the predominant quality of this kind of selfhood which brings together as "one," the two "separate selves" of mother and child. As the two sets of quotation marks indicate, our androcentric language cannot adequately handle this selfhood.

The nature of this two-in-one kind of self-image becomes apparent by analogy. Imagine yourself learning to run a maze. The first time you run it, you will likely falter repeatedly and grow lost. The second time, however, you increase your speed and decrease your time considerably. By the eighth time you can run right through it with no hesitation whatsoever. The question is: What happens? Did *you* change? From all visible signs the answer is "no." You still look the same, feel the same, and weigh the same. Did the *maze* change? Again the answer is no. And for the same reasons. What changed is the relationship existing between you and the maze. Somewhat similarly, in the kind of selfhood characteristic of a mother, the "self" does not reside simply in the mother. Rather, an interrelationship exists between mother and child, such that the two together form a kind of interactive, two-in-one self.

But this two-in-one kind of selfhood does not at all fit the standard conception of self exemplified by the individuated hero. In fact, the very nature of his (more rarely, her) quest involves breaking away from this original bond. What he quests for is the unitary conception of self, generally assumed as "normal" in Western culture. Such selfhood is both expected and assumed to be single. Split selves are thought of as negative Jekyll-and-Hyde personalities. Multiple selves are labelled pathological like the famous Sybil of multiple personalities or the Eve of Three Faces. While it is undoubtedly simpler to function if you can assume one body equals one "self," what is the logic that also assumes that this is healthier? more normal?

The binary-unitary selfhood characteristic of mothers may be more understandable when it is considered in a psychological context that sees selfhood as multiple rather than single. Such a context emerges from the thinking of C. G. Jung. Sometimes this context produces what is called a polytheistic approach to selfhood. In the thinking of such proponents as depth psychologist James Hillman and mythologist David Miller, the construct ordinarily called "self" in the West is called Psyche instead. Psyche can be envisioned as a container that sequentially incarnates various "selves" or, more precisely, deities. Hence the term "polytheistic." This way of envisioning self is seemingly antithetical in all respects to that of Freud. Although this may be largely true, for purposes of distinguishing images of selfhood, it helps to collapse the differences between these two thinkers. Greatly oversimplified, what Jung calls "selves," or "archetypes," Freud called instincts. Thus, although we can readily imagine multiple instincts within a single self, to picture multiple deities suggests multiple selves instead of a single one.

Drawing heavily from Jung's theory of archetypal images, both Hillman and Miller radically reconceptualize the traditional Western unitary model of self. A key word in their thinking, as in that of all Jungians, is "archetype." In its general sense, an archetype is an original pattern. It can be applied to any context in which an original pattern exists. But the word has taken on a very precise meaning in depth psychology. As used there, "archetype" reflects the ancient premonotheistic roots of Western culture. Jung studied myths and tales from around the world and collected dreams and spontaneous images from numerous analysands, leading him to theorize that the psyche of every human being contains within itself various archetypal patterns. According to his theory, a particular pattern or archetype is originally empty. It does not become "filled," or particularized, until an individual encounters a figure, either human or fictional, whose qualities sufficiently match that pattern to activate it.

This theory and its elaborations by thinkers such as Hillman and Miller provide an explanation within "normal" bounds for those situations we all experience when we feel that "I" didn't do something we realize is logically attributable to the personal "I." Instead of assuming a single "I" (minimally subdivided into the Freudian ego, id, and superego, yet still considered a single unity) that is normally in control, the Jungian model posits an individual who functions more like an empty stage upon which numerous dramatis personae including the well-known questing hero sequentially take their turns. Although something called "I" exists, the hero—this "I"—is constantly doing battle with them. Sometimes he is overwhelmed by these differing characters, in which case one of them takes over and acts in his place. To translate into Freudian terminology, when this happens instinct, the id, wrests control from the ego, the "I." Thus, from a Jungian perspective, a woman behaving in a decisive, take-charge fashion in the business world can be described as incarnating the goddess Athene at that moment. When, a few hours later, she is harshly criticizing her male colleagues in a women's consciousness-raising group, she might be seen as Artemis. Still later, if she responds encouragingly to the caresses of her lover, she might appear to incarnate Aphrodite. And so on.

Superficially it sounds perfectly innocuous to assert that certain patterns of experience that reappear in the dreams, fantasies, stories, and art of human beings across time are archetypal. Yet great danger potentially attends such an assertion, particularly for women attempting to follow the way of the mother. If archetypes are built into the human psyche that means that these particular patterns are predetermined. Archetypal psychology therefore strongly suggests that both women and men are locked into certain ways of being as much through psychic predetermination as cultural conditioning. If so, the patterns of human behavior that most feminists, myself included, consider culturally induced, hence changeable, would be biologically unalterable.

To understand this serious issue more thoroughly it helps to compare these Jungian archetypes to colors on a color chart: red, orange, yellow, green, and on through the spectrum. Naming colors that fall in between, such as turquoise or red-orange, is somewhat arbitrary. Such naming involves individual judgment as to which of two colors predominates. You might, for instance, categorize as blue what your best friend considers green, unless you compromise on turquoise. The fact that the English language includes such a color name, however, allows us all to recognize a color that would otherwise go unnoticed. In the absence of such a name, turquoise would simply be lumped in with either green or blue, whichever one it most closely approximated. Similarly, the individual patterns known as archetypes can be useful if you see them simply as "markers" along a continuum of possible human behaviors, knowing that they, like the primary colors of the color wheel, are those which the eye of the psyche, like the eyes in the head, has a propensity for "seeing."

Aside from this danger that belief in archetypes will limit the possible range of human selves which might otherwise be perceived to exist, another problem makes archetypal psychology suspect to feminists as well. In Jungian theory these archetypes are models drawn from a patriarchal culture that has altered their earlier, matrifocal qualities. Therefore, it is difficult to imagine that they, or various interpretations of them, are any less contaminated than any other structures of received thought. After all, the classical Greek pantheon from which they are all drawn is a late development, brought to Greece by successive waves of patriarchal invaders: the Ionians, the Achaeans, the Dorians. Prior to their coming, goddess worship had been the norm. As Charlene Spretnak argues convincingly in *Lost Goddesses of Early Greece,* "The invaders' new Gods, the Olympians, differ in many ways from the earlier Goddesses."[1] Yet it is precisely these goddesses and gods of the Greco-Roman pantheon whose epiphanies within contemporary human psyches Jungian thinkers such as Hillman and Miller so frequently celebrate. Instead of being non-gender-specific appearances, these archetypes reflect patriarchal control of the symbol systems they are intended to help illuminate.

The result, for women attempting to discover our own authentic forms of selfhood, is somewhat like that in Aesop's fable about a foolish man and his son who set off for market on a donkey. At first, wanting to protect the donkey, they both walk and lead the donkey. The first passerby they meet along the way shakes his head and chuckles, "My, my, you foolish man, why do you walk when you have a fine donkey to ride on?" And so the man, feeling foolish, hops up on the donkey's back. The next passerby, too, shakes his head and chuckles, "My, my, you wicked man, letting your son walk while you ride, how can you be so cruel?" So the man hops off and changes positions with his son only to have the next passerby chastise him for walking while his son rides. Now they both ride, only to be castigated for abusing the donkey. In this way the permutations continue until the two end up carrying the donkey.

In the case of polytheistic, archetypal psychology, women are frequently maligned for being too erotic (Aphrodite overwhelms them too often), too shrewish (Hera), too man-hating (Artemis), and so on. Seldom is the balance just right. In addition to questioning the use to which these archetypal images are put relative to women, it is appropriate to ask, why did just *those* deities appear and no others? Why are those deities more valid than those of China, Japan, or aboriginal Australia? The answer that the latter belong to non-Western cultures and are not reflective of Western

archetypal thinking seems incongruously Lamarckian, hence highly suspect. Such belief seems far more likely to rest on culturally imposed views
than on any hypothetical characteristics supposedly innate in all individuals who share collective cultural or racial memories, as Jung asserted.

To believe that the particular goddesses and gods canonized in the
patriarchal Greco-Roman pantheon are the only possible psychic images
offensively denies possibilities for psychic expansion beyond just those
predetermined categories. Nonetheless, in the absence of a viable alternative, if these various caveats about archetypes are heeded, a polytheistic,
Jungian view can provide an extremely useful jumping-off point for ex-
ploring, expanding, and understanding those aspects of self for which the
Freudian model of ego, id, and superego does not as fully suffice. Such an
understanding of selfhood is also useful in considering aspects of self that
are undeniably multiple.

What neither this polytheistic, Jungian model nor the comparatively
unitary Freudian one adequately addresses, however, is the concept of the
"I," whether called ego, self, hero, or psyche, that is predominantly
relational. Characterized neither by strict unity nor by multiplicity, this
concept of the "I" is marked by a combination of both. This concept, so
badly needed by women following the way of the mother, is called the
motherself.

CHAPTER 6.

Motherself

"I praise and adore the mother."
—first line of the national anthem of India

The mother, like any other human being, is a physically separate person. Presumably, like the questing hero, she is also to some degree a psychologically separate person as well. Furthermore, given the prevailing world view of Western culture in which "self" is assumed to be singular, she must therefore hold some sort of unitary image of herself. But that image, in which she is a completely unitary self, differs greatly from the selfhood a woman comes to experience as she progresses along the way of the mother.

This selfhood, known as motherself, is a bit of a paradox for it contradicts our intuitive notion that selfhood is single. Furthermore, it also counters accepted belief that the instances in which selfhood is not single involve serial selves, in which the individual is governed first by one personality or archetypal god or goddess, then by another. Mother-selfhood, by contrast, involves a simultaneous two-in-one relationship, composed of mother and child. That mother and child may also be conceptualized as Mother Goddess and hero-son further complicates the situation. Even more confusing, the relational nature of this kind of selfhood means that it is constantly changing.

When motherselfhood first comes into existence, the relationship of its two component units typically is unequal. The selfhood of the mother, theoretically complete in itself at this point, is suddenly disturbed by the growing fetus within her. Just as the mother-to-be slowly grows accustomed to this extension of herself which is yet not herself within her own body, she must endure another alteration: The baby is born and is now physically outside her. Yet once outside, paradoxically, it demands more of her, and its physically separate selfhood merges more fully with her own. The paradox of this strange motherselfhood does not cease here, however. As time goes by, the mother grows more accustomed to this "extended self," and the more accustomed she becomes, the more that "self" pulls away from her, in the psychological process known as individuation. Furthermore, what is an instance of motherself for the mother is one of heroself for the child. Inevitably, the two are simultaneously one yet separate, attracted yet repelled. No wonder they have been envisioned mythically both as lovers and as embattled combatants, she the radiant goddess who turns monster without warning, he the beautiful hero-son who just as suddenly attempts to kill her. Indeed, this motherselfhood is often inwardly experienced as selfhood at war with itself. Mythically, it has frequently been portrayed that way.

To evaluate motherselfhood as good or bad is inappropriate. The same is true, of course, of its complement, heroselfhood. Both misleadingly imply something good, the one by the word "hero," the other (at least for some people) by the word "mother." While it is difficult to avoid unconscious evaluation with both terms, both should be thought of as neutral in and of themselves.

By definition the term "mother" is relational. Without having a child either naturally or through adoption, a woman cannot logically be called "mother." "Mother" automatically implies child. The obvious rejoinder is, "So does 'father.'" But *does* "father" function the same way "mother" does?

This tricky question of whether "father" and "mother" are equivalent terms must be explored if the concept of motherself is to be clear. Consider: Which two of these three couples belong together—a sow and a piglet, a woman and a baby, and a man and a baby? Do the sow and piglet more closely approximate the woman and baby than the man and the baby? That choice makes motherhood essentially sex-related and sufficiently different from fatherhood to transcend the barrier between animals and humans. But not everyone would answer that way. Whether "mother" must also be a female is usually not debated. Yet consider the experience of Teddy, a two-year-old raised primarily by his father.[1] In this family the mother works in an office while her husband works at home. One day two-year-old Teddy was showing family photographs to a friend of his parents. "Who's that?" the friend would ask, pointing first to one, then to another photograph. Teddy, beaming, would give his one-word responses. When asked to identify his father, he answered without hesitation: "Mommy."

Indeed, is "Mommy" the one who functions as mothers traditionally have done, staying home and actually raising the children on a daily basis? Or is "Mommy" the woman who gives birth to or adopts the child? These are perplexing questions.

Whether or not we choose to consider the possibility of male mothers, the term, "Mother," like the selfhood it generates, is nonetheless primarily relational rather than gender-related. Teddy's understanding of "mother," while amusing, has serious implications. Without trying to enter the mind of one particular child, we can nevertheless imagine some differences in Teddy's relationships to his parents that led him to categorize his father, Jon, with the other "mommies" he knows. It is Jon who stays home and takes care of Teddy on a day-to-day basis. Jon has fed, diapered, comforted, and played with Teddy since his birth; Jon cooks, shops, and cleans; Jon takes him to the park. In clinical terms, Jon is the primary caretaker. As far as the external, visible functions of a mother go, Teddy's answer is appropriate, although it leaves unanswered the larger question of why a man who functions this way is thought of as "Mommy," rather than as "Daddy," by his small son.

But the concern of a woman trying to decide whether or not to follow the way of the mother lies primarily with the internal identity of the person who functions as Mommy, with what constitutes her mother-selfhood. What is it that transforms *functioning* as a mother into *being* a mother and a motherself? In the case of Jon, who (except Jon himself) can say whether he sees and experiences himself as a mother, much less a motherself; perhaps only his small son sees him this way. But comparing the traditional transition of a boy into a man, hence a heroself, illuminates the similar process by which a woman turns into a motherself.

In tribal cultures the transition from boyhood into manhood constitutes a full transformation in the male's being. The ordeals he endures as an initiate are designed to prepare him for a total change of selfhood. Before initiation he is a child belonging to the women; afterward he is a man, belonging to the men. Because industrialized cultures do not conduct major ceremonies to demarcate childhood from adulthood, world views that totally distinguish these two conditions may seem strange. Although one may facetiously ask a teenager if she feels any different on her sixteenth birthday, who really expects an affirmative answer on this or any other birthday? But in tribal cultures the difference pre- and post-initiation is enormous. Cultures that conduct initiation rites view the initiate as a different person from the one he (or sometimes she) previously was. As anthropologist Victor Turner argues persuasively in *The Forest of Symbols,* during the time a novice prepares for his initiation into manhood, he is a nonperson.[2] As such, he exists in a liminal or in-between state: He is neither this nor that. He is therefore to be avoided as a threat to the otherwise ordered system in which all entities, human or otherwise, are clearly defined.

In this in-between state an initiate exists in the margins between childhood and adulthood, a condition for which, in tribal cultures, no specific name exists. Natural birth from the womb of the mother brings the initiate into his first existence. Initiation, his second birth, leads him into the very different, man-made world of culture. This time he is born from a male womb into a masculine culture:

> During the course of the painful rites. . . . the lads, at times, are given nothing to eat or drink but the men's blood. . . . The blood is poured over them also, as a bath. And so they are literally soaked, inside and out, in the good body content of the fathers, which has been drawn in almost incredibly great quantities from the men's arms and subincision wounds. The men jab the subincision scars of their penises or slash the insides of their arms, and the blood pours forth. . . . The blood is physical food, like mother's milk, but spiritual food also (which the mother's cannot furnish) . . . truly man's food, the amniotic fluid and energizing force of the alchemy of this frightening yet fascinating crisis of the second birth.[3]

Like a young male initiate, a woman newly experiencing motherhood metamorphoses far more radically than she can possibly anticipate beforehand. Her nine-month liminal period of waiting cannot entirely prepare her for this enormous transition in selfhood. The physical changes and discomfort of pregnancy pale in the face of full-blown motherhood. Once she realizes her total responsibility for another human life, a woman's transition is complete. It takes but an instant for such realization to occur:

> It was still winter when I went into the hospital. Complications prevented my release until early May, two weeks later. And then I was warned not to leave the house for yet another two weeks. That was almost June. I walked outside, alone. It was the first time I had been by myself since the baby was born. Having been extremely ill, I was a bit shaky. The sunshine made me blink. All around me the trees were green. Seeing them, I shook my head. How strange: the last time I had been out like this, all by myself, the branches were bare and the sky was gray. Now everything was bright blue, sunny, and very green. I shook my head again, wondering how and when this had all happened. I hadn't seen it. As I started to cross the street, I stopped. First I looked left; then right: something I hadn't done in years. I felt compelled; it wasn't just me anymore. In fact, it felt like I *wasn't* a "me" anymore. Janie was back there in her crib waiting. It was as if *I* was back there, too, and yet here at the same time. It was a terrible feeling.[4]

These words express the young woman's shock at discovering she is not a "me," a single self, anymore. In her words, which so vividly describe the experience of a mother as opposed to that of a hero, this woman exactly captures the shift from individual self to motherself. Like all extreme changes of being, this transformation cannot be appreciated easily by one who has not experienced it.

The process whereby the selfhood of a woman becomes mother-selfhood may be likened to that whereby a tribal boy becomes a man. Both are marked by a set of horrific ordeals. For a woman, these ordeals begin with her awareness of the baby in her womb. Slowly, as the fetus grows bigger, it increasingly interacts with its environment—the body of the mother. Physically this interaction starts even before the mother can actually feel a baby as such inside her, when the embryo disturbs the woman's accustomed hormone balance. A sufficiently severe disturbance may nauseate her, causing her to suffer from morning sickness. Then, as the fetus grows, the woman experiences distortions of her body. Her belly sometimes becomes so distended that her stretched skin actually hurts. Extreme distention may even permanently disfigure her with unsightly stretch marks. Excessive distortion of her body shape may cause severe back or chest pain by throwing her body out of alignment. In the last trimester of pregnancy, leg swelling and increase of blood pressure may also trouble her.

Even more upsetting for some women than these physical symptoms is the awareness of something alive inside. Much as a woman may welcome pregnancy, the sensation of something moving inside her—something that is not precisely herself—may strongly discomfort her. To see the ordinarily smooth surface of her belly suddenly undulate through no action of her own may even occasion panic. Here she is, a person in her own right. Yet she can no longer control the motions of her own body. To have another creature inside herself—it is as if she had become the burrow for some unknown little animal who sleeps, wakes, and attains nourishment within her body at will. Just who or what does that make her, herself? Something is consuming her own nutriments. Something is taking over, colonizing her body.

Once the baby is born, this colonization assumes less physical form. Instead of usurping her body, now the child demands all her time. Always, always the baby needs something. It is hungry; it has a bubble and needs to be burped; its diaper is wet; it is tired and wants to be rocked to sleep; or it is wide awake and wants to be played with. A mother may not mind such hard work, but these demands never cease unless the baby is sleeping. And at first it only sleeps two or three hours at a time. Then it awakens, howling for breast or bottle.

With such unceasing demands on her time, a new mother constantly feels tired. The extent of this perpetual exhaustion is perhaps nowhere better captured than in the following episode from Gail Godwins's *A Mother and Two Daughters*, in which a mother and her two sons are reminiscing about a wish to help other mothers she expressed when she was a very young mother herself:

> . . . Leo laughed aloud. "You said you were going to leave a big quiet house with bedrooms, where mothers could go and have naps while the children were right next door in another house, watching movies and things."
>
> "Oh Lord, was I that transparent? How awful! What did you all *think* when I said that?"
>
> "You were tired an awful lot," said Leo. Then he added politely, "Not that you were *always* tired."⁵

Often such extreme fatigue as this excerpt suggests is the most outstanding memory a woman retains of her years of early motherhood. This inordinate fatigue closely parallels the enforced sleep deprivation typical of the period of a young male's preinitiation ordeals. With constant interruption of what is scarcely "her" time now, the mother of a young child feels enslaved to its life rhythms. It is almost impossible to think her own thoughts without some intrusive demand of the baby's intervening. For these reasons, in the early stage the binary-unity of mother and child that constitutes motherselfhood is often negative for her.

When the negative aspects of this new motherselfhood outweigh the positive, what is ideally a loving symbiosis may turn hostile. Like the mythic hero battling what he construes to be a monster, the mother may likewise demonize her child. For instance, if a woman's accustomed state of being, in which she is free to think or daydream as she pleases, is threatened, she may forget herself and attack her child. Infuriated at its perpetual crying, which no amount of feeding, burping, walking, or diaper-changing will appease, she may shake it angrily, screaming, "Shut up"; sufficiently provoked, she may even hit the child or throw it up against a wall. Now the battle is on. Anything to keep this squalling antagonist quiet. Its constant, grating cries cannot be ignored: It rasps so irritatingly that something must be done to stop it. Such crying penetrates the barriers of any self within hearing distance. As an intrusive weapon, the baby's squawking is as capable of eliciting a mother's great fury as it is her tearful concern. In this battle the mother may feel that she is fighting for her very existence.

In a very real sense, a woman struggling with this new selfhood connected with motherhood *is* engaged in a life-and-death struggle. As with the tribal initiate whose old self must die before his new man-self can be born, she must relinquish her accustomed self in favor of her emergent motherself. If she does not, her baby may die or at the least fail to thrive. Yet if she does, she may feel as if she were dying.

Even the way we typically use the term "mother" indicates how this is so. Most mothers are "Mother" or any of its diminutives such as Mama, Mommy, Ma, or Mom, all with a capital "M." That makes "Mother" and all its variants extremely personal. As such it is neither an abstraction nor a generalized word as "mother" with a small "m" may be. This personalization of the word is entirely appropriate, so long as it is kept within the bounds of what Mother is to her children. Some women, however, are "Mother" in just this fashion to their husbands as well as their children (as sometimes their husbands are Daddy to them). Women who delete their given names this way at home, making themselves "Mother" to spouse as well as children, very much abdicate their personal identities in favor of that of the Mother Goddess.

Theologically, this process whereby self is abdicated is known as "kenosis," an emptying out of self in order that godhead may take its place. On a global scale, Mother Theresa exemplifies this phenomenon. All the poor of the world are her children. Closer to home, most of us know women who delight in mothering all the neighborhood children as well as some of the adults. These are women to whom anyone can take problems and receive a comforting, sympathetic hug. Entering the home of such a woman is like going home to Mother. She typically urges everyone to eat, as Mother probably once did. When she entertains formally she usually bustles around, refilling everyone's plate, lest anyone go hungry. Because she is so warm and welcoming, people seldom realize how little they really know her. She may know others' troubles, but they often assume she has none. It is she, of all the neighbors, whose sudden divorce is the most shocking. "Never in a million years," says everyone on the block. "Anyone but Alma." "Being Mother" for such a woman means perpetually placing the needs of others before her own. In this common image of Mother as the perpetual self-sacrificer, we see the death of the self that a woman new to motherhood most fears.

Fortunately, however, the woman who wishes to pursue the way of the mother need not go to such an extreme. Allowing the Mother Goddess to take over completely is neither the way of the individuated hero nor authentically the mother's way. Motherselfhood always involves some sort of balance between what can be termed a woman's "own" self and that of her child. In the situation of a woman who is "Mother" to everyone, none of her "own" self remains. This situation involves complete absence of any selfhood at all. The personhood of the woman is swallowed up as she accedes to the wishes and demands of those around her.

There is yet another extreme that can destroy the delicate balance of the binary-unity. In this situation, individual selfhood and true mother-selfhood are both swallowed up. This time it is not the Mother Goddess who overwhelms the mother, however: It is her child. This kind of overwhelming of the mother by the selfhood of her own child, masking as motherselfhood, fools many people, including mothers themselves, into mistaking it for the real thing. It is often lauded in popular thought as the selfless essence of motherhood. But being overwhelmed by the selfhood of the child is anything but appropriate for either mother or child. Simultaneously it effaces the person of the woman who happens to be a mother and overvalues that of the child. Neither "self" benefits from this imbalance.

Both extremes destroy the requisite balance of "selves" in mother-selfhood. A more appropriate balance is suggested by the words of the woman who says, "I am a mother." By her statement, "*a* mother," she indicates that she also considers herself to be other things as well: a teacher, a writer, a tennis player, whatever. Hence she is preserving part of *her*self, not just relegating her entire being to her role. In no way does she imply that "mother" is her sole identity. For her, being a mother could mean as little as that she gave birth to her children and then handed them over to a nurse who has assumed primary responsibility ever since. In this case no motherselfhood occurs; she simply retains her original level of single selfhood. But it could also mean that a woman enjoys her children but also finds great satisfaction from other components of her life such as work, spouse, and various avocations. In her case, the binary-unity may not be operative at all, as in the case of a woman who bears children but then relinquishes them, either by putting them up for adoption or by giving them completely to the care of a nanny. On the other hand, the binary-unity may be functioning when it should be—when she is in her mother role—but not to the extent that her separate "I" role is entirely effaced.

The words "I am a mother" can also mean that a woman is an adoptive mother who raises but did not give birth to her children. From such a statement it is not possible to tell how much of the woman "mother" occupies. "Being mother" for a woman who can speak of being "*a* mother" is not nearly as dangerous to her underlying individual self-hood as it is for those women who allow "Mother" to engulf them. It may, however, lead her to reject motherselfhood and thus to distance herself from her children. The trick, for a woman, is to negotiate the difficult way of the mother in such a manner that she does not lose her selfhood either to the Goddess or to her child. At the same time, she must not repudiate motherselfhood.

To help illustrate the difference between being a "me" (a self) and a mother, a trivial comparison may help. I recall once trying to decide when I was a young mother of three small children whether to get a dog. When my neighbor's dog had six puppies, my children immediately begged for one, to my neighbor's delight. How could I say no? I did not know how piteously a newborn puppy howls for its mother all night long. By the time he stopped this routine he had begun chewing the furniture. Meanwhile, I had discovered that training a puppy makes toilet-training a child seem easy. But I could get rid of the puppy. . . . That is the difference for most women between being a mother and a nonmother. The mother is always a mother; the dog-owner can cease being a dog-owner at any moment.

Women indoctrinated with patriarchally oriented literature—necessarily most women in Western cultures—will find the disparity between the two kinds of self-image disturbing. How the figure of the hero wars with that of the mother! Finding a child appended to her self-image, instead of feeling like an addition to her selfhood, may well feel more like an amputation than a gain. Instead of "her" needs, it is now "their" needs or "its," a far different orientation. As a result of such dual consciousness, a mother often feels confused as she experiences what she mistakenly thinks is loss of self. Her mistake is commonly buttressed by her surrounding culture because, patriarchally speaking, women are frequently believed to be lacking in selfhood anyway.

She may find herself frequently torn, uncertain what to do. If she is at school, where she has longed to be for years, she finds herself wondering, "What are the children doing? Are they all right? Do I dare stay for this special lecture on Sartre, or should I go home?" And if she skips the lecture, she finds herself pacing fretfully: What on earth possessed her to rush home? She can see that her children are happily involved in their own projects, completely oblivious to her presence. Neither way entirely satisfies her. Even if she knows her children are well provided for, she wants to be where they are, sharing time with them.

A contemporary divorced career woman named Anita, interviewed for an article in the September 1985 issue of the *Ladies Home Journal*, reflects this dilemma when she "confesses that she is not as free as she appears. For instance, she has often canceled plans to go out with friends at the last minute when Caroline wants her home—not because her daughter wants to do anything special or appears upset, but simply because she needs to know that Anita is there."⁶ Yet what about a woman's own needs? Often she acts like a two-headed creature, a kind of Siamese twin, who cannot simultaneously satisfy the demands of both heads. She is neither one nor the other. She is simultaneously mother and individual self and this makes both her mode of "self"-understanding and her way of being in the world extremely complicated. This perpetual ambivalence differs so greatly from the single-minded purposiveness of the unitary self-image that it contributes to a number of widespread beliefs about women: Women are more neurotic than men; women are less capable of sustained effort; women are less capable of success; women always place family before career.

Many arguments focus on these beliefs. Men use them to denigrate women; feminists dismiss them as being entirely without basis in reality. The truth lies somewhere in between, reflecting the underlying identity structure of the particular woman in question. To say that all women are _____ filling in the blank with a specific quality is obviously foolish. Some women possess certain stereotypic qualities, others do not. To say no women are _____ is just as absurd. What needs examining is not the women but the qualities and the underlying system of ideas that values women negatively. For instance, to call a woman neurotic because she has difficulty choosing between the needs of her unitary self and that of her combined mother-child self is to misapply the concept of self. It is rather like faulting a peach for lacking the smooth skin of a nectarine.

From my own experience I know what it is to disappoint the unitary self, hence to feel I have done nothing whatsoever all day when, in fact, I have made two family meals, cleaned up after both, tidied the house, made the bed, shopped for groceries, addressed, stamped, and licked close to a hundred club-related envelopes, driven one child to the orthodontist, and helped drill another on his French verbs. On a day like that *my* needs are unfulfilled. Yet is the day I leave the house to teach an eight o'clock class before my youngest child goes to school, grade forty papers, teach a second class at three, attend a special Jung seminar, and write three rough pages of my dissertation any better? On that day I arrive home at six o'clock, exhausted, with no dinner yet planned, and a nagging feeling that, despite my personal exhilaration, I have nevertheless missed something—a few hours interacting with my children, talking to them, listening to a tale of what Chris said to Cynthia, playing a game of Pitch, or just being there to hug them when they came home from school. Anne Tyler illustrates this phenomenon in her novel *Celestial Navigation*. Mary is a young mother alone with her small daughter, Darcy. Mary's life revolves around waiting for her married lover to call her, now that she has left her husband:

> On the nights we go out I put Darcy to bed early and ask Mrs. Jarrett to keep an eye on her. Then John and I go to dinner someplace and talk, although half my mind, of course, is always back with Darcy. . . . When Darcy and I are alone I think about John; with John, I think about Darcy.[7]

When weighing the competing demands of the unitary self-image of the hero against those of the binary-unity of the motherself, it is important to understand that motherhood is not a static, once-and-for-all state of being. It is an evolving process. It is perhaps only when its evolutionary character becomes apparent to a woman that the benefits of mother-selfhood become apparent. As one elderly woman puts it, "Never forget what an important force for growth and transformation in her life a woman's children are."[8] Although it is customary to think of a mother as a point of departure for her children, it is just as important to reverse the relationship. The mother-child relationship is reciprocal, not just when children have grown to adulthood, but even earlier. This reciprocity can work in many ways. A fifty-year-old woman tells of an especially meaningful instance in her life. Her eighty-eight-year-old father had been dying for several months in another state, about two hours away by plane. Early one Christmas Eve Day she received a call to come immediately. For that evening she had invited forty people, family and friends, to a special dinner before midnight mass. Her four children, ranging in age from fourteen to twenty, all urged her to leave without worrying, and immediately assumed all the preparations. There was no question but that they would manage successfully.[9] In so doing, they necessarily assumed the "mother" role. Another woman tells of receiving word late one evening when her husband was away that her favorite aunt had died. Unable to repress her sobs, she told her three children, aged about eight, eleven, and thirteen, about her loss. Without the least self-consciousness, the three formed a small protective circle, twining their arms round her in a communal hug.[10] In this situation, too, the children were quickly able to reverse the customary relationship to play mother instead of child to their own mother.

In *A Mother and Two Daughters*, Gail Godwin describes just such reciprocity within the mother-child relationship. Lydia, one of the two daughters, has arranged a special visit to a local television studio for her fifteen-year-old son, Leo. The show about to air as they arrive is a local talk and cooking show. The hostess, taking an immediate liking to Lydia, invites her to become a guest. On the air, they discuss historic anecdotes from Lydia's hometown. Driving home, Lydia asks her son what he thought of her spur-of-the-moment television debut. Leo asks: "'You cared what *I* thought?' 'Well, of course,' Lydia said. It was true, she *had* thought first of what Leo would think; and then the others, too, but Leo was such a perfectionist. 'Of course I cared. Don't you care what I think about you?" After a moment, Leo said, 'I guess I do.'"[11] Here the reciprocity is not that of role exchange, but of mutual concern for the opinion and respect of the other, a factor too often overlooked by mothers who do not develop true motherselfhood.

More long-reaching in its impact is the following instance. Marie, a woman about fifty, ascribes the resolution of her midlife crisis to insights she gained from her children.[12] Forced to relocate just as she became an empty nester, she found the transition more difficult than anything she had previously faced. In her words, "I felt trapped." For months she tried to find a way out of her pain. One day as she wrestled with it, she thought of her son, then twenty-one, whom she describes as "very definitely his own person. He knows what he wants and he gets it, not by imposing on others, but by quietly pursuing goals that matter to him regardless of what others think of them. It occurred to me that if my son could find a way, surely I could. I began to think about the kind of person he is, and I recognized traits we have in common. It only stands to reason that some of what he is comes from qualities I possess and passed on to him." And so it seems that the binary-unity of motherhood does allow for an interchange of roles not often enough appreciated.

Another woman extends the reciprocity of the mother-child relationship still further when she says, "I wish I had had the opportunity to grow up in the family I created instead of the one I was actually born into. I think it would have been very satisfying. Sometimes I feel a bit awed by what my husband, along with our children, and I have been privileged to create." For her, the reciprocity of mother and child reaches the point of wishing she had been child to her own self.[13] With her wish to be child to her own self, this woman expresses the underlying meaning of the motherself. If women can only learn to "give birth to ourselves," we will have countered the "birth" from the fathers which patriarchy automatically imposes on all of us. And in giving birth to ourselves we automatically fulfill the promise implicit in the term "motherself": Symbolically we are simultaneously mother and yet child to that mother; we are also simultaneously mother to the child we physically gave birth to. Such is the complicated nature of motherself.

PART II

The Way
of the Mother

CHAPTER 7.

A Mother's Story

If a society existed in which the way of the mother were the norm, tales of mothers would predominate the way tales of heroes do in cultures throughout the world. As it is now, we tend to take mothers for granted while we glamorize heroes.

Our earliest ideas of what a hero is generally derive from books, movies, and TV shows, rather than from daily life. Fairy tales commonly inculcate a child's earliest understandings of heroes if he or she is lucky enough to grow up in a family in which reading or storytelling occurs. By contrast, daily life experience with one's own mother more commonly establishes understanding of motherhood. From that initial difference stems a major, continuing difference in most people's general understanding of the two terms. According to that understanding, heroes:

1) are somewhat removed from "real-life"
2) are better than "ordinary people"
3) are revered
4) are to be admired and emulated
5) are typically male
6) are those with whom most individuals automatically identify
7) are brave
8) function as models for others
9) earn their rewards, though not necessarily their punishments, through their own actions
10) bring good fortune to communities
11) act as the main characters in their particular worlds
12) save people from harm

The corresponding attributes of a mother give her equally great power. Yet this power of the mother is simultaneously both familiar and strange. It is familiar because we all know it from the very deepest sources of our being, from having been children to mothers of our own. But it is also strange because we have all been acculturated to believe in the greater power of various competing patriarchal images of power—those of the hero, the son, and the father.

These competing patriarchal images are particularly evident in the Christian tradition, where the figures of son and savior hero coalesce in Christ. Furthermore, for most Westerners of either sex, the concept of power as sacred force is bound up almost exclusively with the male father god. Whether such connection is overtly and formally "believed" in or not, it nonetheless so permeates our culture that it informs the belief systems of total secularists as much as it does those of practicing Jews, Christians, and Moslems.

One way to understand the apparently great difference between the two figures of the mother and the hero is to note that he is "framed" while she is not: He is placed in the confines of a myth or legend. But what would the mother look like if she too were given a frame?

This is what the image of "mother" might become were she, like the hero, framed positively in a traditional type of tale.[1] Once upon a time, long before Eve and Adam, there lived a beautiful young bride who was so ill every morning that she could barely get out of bed. Just one month ago she had married a handsome, blue-eyed, dark-haired prince, who loved her very dearly. Both were deeply distressed by her morning malaise and consulted many court specialists about it. But none was able to cure her.

One day a very old woman hobbled up the palace steps, volunteering her opinion. She looked the young woman over and nodded her head three times as she held one forefinger to the side of her nose. "Yes," she said, "I know your problem."

The fair young bride looked at the old woman, waiting for her to continue. "Please tell me," she begged.

"If I do, you must promise to perform three tasks."

"Oh! I will, I will," promised the young bride.

"All right then, here is what you must do: For thirty days you will suffer malaise every morning. But then you will awaken on the thirty-first day feeling better than you have ever felt before. At that time your belly will begin to swell. Do not be alarmed, that is a necessary part of your condition. This is what you must do to cure it: First, you must produce human life out of your very own body. Second, you must nurse that life for one full year, again out of your very own body. And last, and most difficult of all your tasks, you must teach that human how to survive on its own. When you have completed all three tasks successfully, send for me and I will return. Then, and only then, will I reveal to you the secret of your distress." With these words the old woman disappeared.

The poor bride was so startled by the Wise Woman's words that she almost forgot to wonder at her sudden disappearance. "Oh me, oh my, whatever am I to do?" she asked herself. "How is it possible for any human to produce another human life out of her own body? This is an impossible task she has set me. And even if I should be able to perform that feat, how could I possibly complete the remaining two?"

Weeks and months went by and the young bride swelled and swelled, just as the old woman had predicted. At last she reached a point where she was sure she must burst. One night soon after she awakened, startled, and began to moan softly.

The poor groom, frightened out of his wits, called for his aged granny, who came immediately.

The old granny took one look at the bride and banished the groom from the palace. Lo and behold, when he returned some hours later, he heard the sound of crying. Knowing full well that his wife rarely cried, he was puzzled. But when he entered the bedroom, he was astonished to see a tiny human, much like his wife, but far, far smaller.

"Look," she beamed, "The first task: I have produced life out of my own body, just as the Wise Woman predicted."

A year passed. During this time, the mother, as most people, including the groom, now called her, fulfilled her second task. Miraculously she fed her child with a rich white liquid that flowed copiously from her breasts.

NOW BEGAN THE HARDEST TASK OF ALL. . . . Such "framing" of the mother makes more vivid the underlying similarity of function common to mothers and heroes. Observing the mother set apart within a distant realm highlights her natural capacities. Suddenly natural maternal qualities appear as the miracles they actually are. Yet most individuals take these first stages of motherhood for granted because pregnancy and childbirth "simply happen" during the natural course of events. Possibly only the last of these tasks seems at all "miraculous." Raising a child to be a reasonably self-sufficient member of society no longer can be taken for granted as perhaps it could in less complex societies.

At the point where this story breaks off, then, what might it say? Consider a male-oriented hero tale for comparison. In such a tale, the hero typically must journey to some other world. He may reach the land at the bottom of the ocean, the place east of the sun and west of the moon, or the well at the bottom of the world.

Now consider the means by which a mother-to-be accomplishes her first two tasks: swellings and openings. First her body swells. Then the mouth of her uterus opens. When it enlarges sufficiently it provides a birth passage for the baby. When the mother's breasts swell and her nipples open, milk passes out of her body to nourish her child.

In keeping with the formal requirements of repetition in fairy tales, what subsequent "swellings" and "openings" would allow the young woman to complete her final task? "Swelling" signifies that a transformation of "place" is occurring. In its original flatness, the belly of a woman is not particularly noteworthy. But with its swelling it dominates a woman's figure. Then a woman seems nothing but belly. Observers see in her solely the mother-to-be, forgetting that she may also be teacher, movie-goer, gardener, traveler, human being. She belongs now to an entirely different category of being. This is a point made abundantly clear in prehistoric fertility images like the well-known Venus of Willendorf.

But swellings are obstacles as well as signs. As with mountains, how does one circumvent them? The ability to create holes or openings in otherwise insurmountable circumstances distinguishes the hero from others. If the hero is a mystic, he recognizes hidden passageways; invariably he finds ladders, bridges, and openings to transport him, when necessary, into some other, nonordinary, space. If he is a mundane hero, he recognizes the appropriate helping figures to guide him. This recognition occurs, for example, in the Grimm's fairy tale, "The Water of Life." In this tale the two older brothers, in contrast to the heroic youngest, fail to recognize the helping figure for what he is. For the older prince the meeting takes place like this: He sets off "and when he had ridden some distance he came upon a dwarf standing in the road, who cried, 'Whither away so fast?'

'Stupid little fellow,' said the Prince proudly, 'what business is it of yours?' And he rode on."[2] With only slight variation, the pattern is repeated by his middle brother. By contrast, the youngest prince, the hero, varies the pattern by his behavior:

"When he also met the dwarf, and the dwarf asked him where he was hurrying to, he stopped and said, 'I am searching for the Water of Life, because my father is dying.'

'Do you know where it is to be found?'

'No,' said the Prince.

'As you have spoken pleasantly to me, and not been haughty like your false brothers, I will help you and tell you how to find the Water of Life.'"[3]

Toward the close of the story, too, when the two false brothers attempt to claim the hero's betrothed, they both fail to react correctly to an appropriate sign. Instead of a helping dwarf, it is now a golden road leading to the Princess, which they fail to recognize for what it really is.

Both of them refuse to ride *on* it, fearing to mar it. By contrast, the hero "came out of the wood to ride to his beloved, and through her to forget all his past sorrows. So on he went, thinking only of her and wishing to be with her, and he never even saw the golden road."[4] In this case the false brothers pick out the wrong sign: gold, the sign of wealth, rather than the Princess, emblem of love.

By *not* riding on the gold, the two brothers reveal their true motive: desire for wealth. In doing just what his brothers do not do, the hero unconsciously reveals his love of the princess. So preoccupied is he with thoughts of her that he never even notices the gold lying beneath his horse's hooves. In this particular context gold functions deceptively; it is a false sign. By being oblivious to it, the hero automatically discovers the right opening, the path leading to his love. For a mother, too, such "heroic" ability to read signs, act upon them correctly, and "find openings" is essential.

What happens when a mother acts according to this ability? Spotting the telltale "swellings" and creating the necessary "holes" to surmount or penetrate them occurs in various ways. For Serena, a mother at midlife, discovering the appropriate sign takes place rather dramatically.[5] Off and on for months Serena says she has felt as though she were swimming. This "swimming" feeling puzzles her. She says, "I haven't been swimming for years except on an occasional vacation. Why should I keep feeling like I'm swimming now? Even as a child it was never my favorite sport, although I always enjoyed it." Serena recognizes that this feeling means something significant to her or it wouldn't be repeated so insistently. But she is unsure what. Apparently unconnected to this "swimming feeling," certain less well-defined feelings also nag at her. "It's as if I should be doing some things that I'm not doing, but I don't know exactly what. I can't really describe what they are at all. I just know I want to be doing things that I'm not doing. I have a bad feeling that if I were to die today I would say I haven't really lived out my life. I seem to just wait for something to happen. Only I don't know what that something is. I also don't think waiting is the right thing to do."

One day, however, Serena awakened exhilarated. "I was actually joyful at 6:30 in the morning! I sat at the breakfast table and as I finished my toast and coffee peace and joy simultaneously engulfed me." When pressed, Serena admits that these feelings probably were not quite so sudden as she now thinks they were. She had recently been extremely tense, having lost her last child to college: "I had never expected the empty-nest syndrome to affect me, of all people. I'm so busy with my career [as a university reference librarian] that I always assumed not having children around would be a relief. Instead, nothing seemed right after Katy left. At night I was so restless I sometimes couldn't sleep. That's not like me at all. Then my stomach began bothering me. Suddenly I began wondering why I was working at all. It's not financially necessary, but I have always loved my profession. One day I just decided to quit. At first I didn't feel any better. But slowly I began painting, potting plants, going to matinees, doing things I hadn't left time for in years. The day before I experienced my intense joy I spent the entire evening reading a guide book to China. It's hard to describe, but suddenly I knew *I am living my own life now.*"

From the perspective of a secular theology, Serena's discovery constitutes salvation. To be saved, in secular terms, is to live one's own life rather than one prescribed by someone else. That sounds simple. But learning to live a life authentically one's own represents a salvation as difficult to achieve as the kind more traditional theologies promise.

As in Serena's case, what one wants is often deeply hidden. Learning to recognize swellings of interest and then discovering how to satisfy them is a major task. Not only must a woman do it for herself and her child, she must also teach her child to do it for itself. When the mother functions this way, she strongly resembles the hero she is otherwise often battling. Like him, she is a culture-bringer. To understand the importance of this function in the repertory of the mother's tasks, consider what the world is like for an infant: Everything in the world is as new for a baby as it would presumably have seemed to human beings in the earliest stages of their development. A person who acculturates a baby into the ways of its world performs exactly the same function as the heroic culture-bringer of myth. Few would argue that some mothers perform this task more fully than others. Rejecting mothers may not perform it in a positive sense at all, although one can argue that the "culture" they inculcate is one of deprivation in which the repeated message is "no." When your mother once told you: "No, dear, you mustn't point and make loud comments about someone who is fat, it isn't polite; you might hurt someone's feelings if you do," or when she taught you how to tie your shoelaces, or pointed up to the starry night sky and outlined its constellations, she was bringing culture to you as surely as Maui did for the ancient Polynesians when he stole fire from the keeper of the underworld.

It is perhaps in this role of culture-bringer that a mother is most controversial. Like any culture-bringer, she may transgress against the goddesses and gods in performing her role. A case in point is the Greek culture hero Prometheus who stole fire for humanity against the express wish of Zeus. For his hubris he was punished horribly: Bound with brass chains to a rock in the Caucasus Mountains, he endured the daily pecking out of his liver by an avenging eagle sent by Zeus. For a mother in a patriarchal context, "transgression" is invariably defined in one way. She is a sinner against those "gods" otherwise known as men.

But within a gynocentric context she may transgress as well. In her mother role a woman can mold human life as she desires. How tempting to try to live her child's life instead of letting the child do so. Of course a mother wants only the best for her son or daughter—the best schools, the best opportunities, the best friends, the best neighborhoods. The list is endless. But does she also honestly concern herself with her child's happiness?

As culture-bringer, a mother treads a very fine line. If, on the one hand, she (and/or the father) fails to make any plans whatsoever for a child, simply letting it grow as the child itself chooses, she is guilty of withholding her own wisdom. On the other hand, if a mother decides what is best for her child even against its own wishes, she deprives it of a chance to live its own life. At this point a woman's own self-image may intervene negatively. A mother who totally arranges her child's life risks eclipsing its separate selfhood. Conversely, a mother who uses her child to live out her own life for her vicariously is guilty of sacrificing her individual selfhood to his. In so doing she essentially effaces her own separate being. What is necessary for both mother and child is the kind of selfhood the awkward term "binary-unity" implies. She and the child must co-exist in a reciprocal relationship much like that of pregnancy. But now what was previously physically within and seemingly part of the mother—the baby—is outside. In the mother's role of culture-bringer and creator of her child, creation involves not primarily one separate self or the other but both combined. This is a very different conception of selfhood from that of the single heroself.

At a still deeper level, a mother functions not just as a culture-bringer but as a savior as well. Every day she "saves" her child by providing for all its material and emotional needs. She feeds him, changes him, bathes him, plays with him, rocks him, comforts him, holds him, loves him. If she glimpses the baby as he tries to swing a leg over the edge of his crib, she runs to catch him before he falls. When the baby is a little older she snatches him from in front of a car just as he starts to dash across the street. She rushes him to the hospital when he drinks some of her imported French perfume. And when he contracts measles, she bathes him in cool water to lowers his 104degree temperature. In all these roles a mother is functionally indistinguishable from the hero she otherwise so frequently opposes. For any woman trying to decide whether or not to follow the way of the mother, realizing this functional similarity of mother and hero should be highly reassuring. Nonetheless, a woman making this important decision probably wonders, What does it actually *feel* like to be a mother? What distinguishes it physically from being a hero?

CHAPTER 8.

Being a Mother: A Body Mystery

Being a mother immediately suggests birth. But it relates to *giving* birth, not to being born oneself. This distinction, seemingly so obvious, demands attention. Worldwide, this difference informs symbol systems otherwise vastly different from each other. *Being* born is everywhere celebrated in myth and ritual; *giving* birth is quite another matter. Often it is simply ignored. From this major difference emerged the hero, who quickly eclipsed the mother who bore him.

Although we encounter the birth of the hero in story after story, no attention is paid to his mother's experience of giving him birth. Mary is the most venerated mother in Western culture, yet nothing tells of the actual birth itself, even in popular thought. The Shearmen and Taylors' pageant and the Weavers' pageant in the Coventry cycle of plays dating from 1534 come close; both show Mary pregnant. But both emphasize a male issue: Joseph's assumption that he has been cuckolded. Not until an angel tells Joseph what happened does he return and beg her forgiveness. But absolutely nothing here or in other plays in the cycle tells of Mary's actual experience of pregnancy. A play that comes a bit closer is the *Ludus Coventriae,* which shows Mary having no pain in childbirth. Here the major stress is an argument between the attending midwives, Zelony and Salome. Neither one can believe that Mary and the baby are not only clean but also undefiled by this event, which in Jewish tradition ordinarily necessitated ritual purification. While the play gives some sense of Mary's impregnation and pregnancy, it says nothing of the birth itself. Is this because Mary, unlike any other mother before or since, was spared (or denied) the pain of childbirth? Only in some popular oral traditions does Mary become a woman of flesh and blood. For instance, interviews of Roman Catholic women in the area of New York City once known as Italian Harlem reveal beliefs that Mary menstruates.[1]

The mother's experience, whether she is as venerated as Mary or as ordinary as the woman next door, is not part of the hero's life. Therefore, in Western culture her experience essentially vanishes. Part of the reason may be a common difficulty imagining time before we came into existence. After all, the world only comes into being for any individual at birth or, more precisely, at the dawning of consciousness. Combined with our inability to believe in a world apart from ourselves is fear that such a world may actually have existed. If each individual is the center of the world, how can the world possibly have existed when we ourselves did not?

In a patriarchal context this egocentric desire to make the world "my" world often turns into a dangerous disavowal of woman. Typically, the experience of the mother has been demonized: She is the fearsome monster against whom the hero must struggle. In contemporary tales this mythic struggle is overtly psychological. An episode in John Rechy's *This Day's Death* makes the battlelike aspect of this ancient struggle between the hero and his mother particularly clear. The protagonist wonders:

> *Is she moving toward siege?*
> Why always in terms of war? . . .
> *"I'm dying!"* she cried frantically.
> It was those two words that enflamed his anger. She had lain in the dusky darkness of her room all day. Suddenly the world seemed to shrink for him into one black smear through which he saw only her dark glasses. In that second—which was all at once a continuation of that long winter day of dying—he wanted finally to bring it all down. "You're not sick!" he shouted at her. "Goddamnit, stop it!"
> "I don't want to be sick!" she gasps, her hands clawing at the air. "You think I'm responsible! *What do you want me to do!"* . . . "I—. . .!" she started.
> And that word turned into a long, long scream. . . . Against the labor demanded to bring them all to life, the blood shed to thrust out those new lives, leaving an emptiness within her which nothing could fill. A cry for the savage pain of flesh ripped from flesh with a part of her soul. Torn flesh rebelling to be free from her, to assume—her remaining son, her daughter, her torn flesh—a life of its own apart from its source—her womb. Her.[2]

Like this contemporary story, mythic tales in which the hero is swallowed by a monster also implicitly demonize the mother. In them we hear about the struggle of the hero, who is "good," against the monster, who is "bad." The story of Jonah is a good example:

> And the Lord appointed a great fish to swallow up Jonah; and Jonah was in the belly of the fish three days and three nights.

> Then Jonah prayed to the Lord his God from the belly of the fish. (Jon.1:17-2:1)

We hear only of Jonah's distress, nothing whatsoever of the monstrous fish. This discrepancy is natural if we think of the swallower only as a fish or monster. But that is exactly the problem. From the hero's patriarchal perspective the one who contains him is *always* a monster of some sort. From a gynocentric perspective, however, the one who contains is a woman. Like the hero, woman-as-mother experiences her own set of ordeals. First she is penetrated, "taken," or "known" by her lover; subsequently she is colonized by a growing fetus. These birth-related events are always envisioned through the eyes of the hero in traditional tales, never through the eyes of his geneatrix. This is so even if the hero, as sometimes happens, is a woman. We therefore re-experience the birth of the hero in story after story; almost never do we encounter that birth described from the perspective of his mother.

And yet from a gynocentric perspective the way of the mother, not the quest of the hero, is the norm. Her way markedly counters the quest of the hero. If you are a hero, you experience your body extending itself and moving through space. By contrast, if you follow the way of the mother that relationship turns inside out, making you or your body function as space for something else. In the dominant patriarchal context this way of the mother is not immediately familiar territory the way the quest of the hero is. In fact, it tends to disquiet most people a little. Patriarchal thinking teaches both sexes that the way of the mother is *not* positive: It is always the way of the "other." Anything we know of her way we know from the perspective of the hero.

In fact, anything officially sanctioned by Western culture comes to us from the vantage point of the hero. That is because both sexes automatically experience space within the hero's mode. Everyone enters and leaves containers every day: rooms, houses, automobiles. Some people consciously prefer cozy, enclosed places to wide-open ones; others prefer just the reverse. And some people scarcely notice their interactions with surrounding spaces. It may take a dramatic event like a climbing a mountain to make them reflect on their spatial needs.

Such a climb, particularly one which allows scrambling among rocks, shows that an important, generally unrecognized need is being fulfilled in the process. Perhaps the hiker begins by climbing an expanse of fallen rock. She may have to crawl. Only by grabbing for saplings can she retain her footing. Then she must forge through, rather than over, some of these rocks. Unless she turns back, she must drop about five feet to slither through a two-foot opening. How satisfying to conquer and slither. The pattern is vaguely familiar. This closeness of body to rock and soil deeply satisfies. But what need is this that ordinarily does not even seem to exist?

How like being born and becoming an individual is squeezing through the tight-fitting rocks and then "conquering" a mountain. This pattern of bodily compression and extension need not be construed reductively. Reductive thinking, as the words imply, reduces a condition to a single, predetermining factor, thought to constitute its entire meaning. For example, Freud is frequently accused of reducing everything to sex. To say of the rock climb that it symbolizes rebirth could be to engage in reductive thinking. But not necessarily. The terms can be looked at reciprocally: If birth is the first meaningful life event for any individual (an assertion difficult to contradict), then logically some subsequent events will repeat or slightly vary it. Over time, a pattern of such birth and individuation events accumulate in every person's life. Certainly much religious imagery is predicated on this assumption. To look at such repetitions and say, "Oh, that's merely a repetition of birth," is to speak reductively. But what if one sees the entire pattern adding up to a kind of serial birth? Then the original birth is enhanced. Birth now becomes one of many such meaningful experiences. Instead of being reduced, the experience is actually enlarged. The original birth then inaugurates an incremental pattern of meaning. Indeed, this pattern is one of the major motifs underlying the life quest of the hero. In leaving home the hero adds to the pattern of leaving his mother's womb. In moving away from home, he repeats the subsequent step of individuation. Conversely, in every encounter with a containing individual or circumstance, he (or she) repeats the motif of containment within the womb.

We are all, women and men alike, familiar with numerous variations on the hero's relationship to interior and exterior spaces. His quest is full of thrusts forward and outward and struggles against prolonged confinement in various containers, whether castles, caves, prisons, or the bellies of beasts. What remains mysteriously unspoken of is this same birth story in all its variations told from the perspective of those spaces themselves. It is a truism to say that experiencing something *inside* oneself is very different from being inside something. To swallow is not at all the same as to be swallowed. Nonetheless, in this context it needs saying, for we hear comparatively little in myth and literature about what it is to contain something inside ourselves. And yet a whole gynocentric way of being exists from within those spaces themselves. For example, what is it like for the whale of Eskimo legend to contain the trickster-hero Raven? Or the Celtic monster known as the *peist* to contain the Irish hero, Finn MacCool? Aside from John Gardner's retelling of the Beowulf story in his novel *Grendel,* very few works present the story from this, the monster/mother's, point of view.

In its primary form, the way of the mother begins, of course, with insemination. A woman does not know at the time if one particular act of love will actually lead her into the way of the mother or not. What she does know is the thrust of her lover's penis into her vagina. He is inside her thrusting, thrusting, in and out, in and out, sliding against her vaginal walls. This process increases in speed and intensity until one or both come to orgasm in an explosive burst of liquid.

What was clearly outside is now in. Yet her lover is inside her only a portion of the way she imagines possible. She does not always feel the full extent of his thrusting. Mostly she feels his entry across the threshold of her body. This is her counterpart of the first ordeal of the mythic hero's quest—his journey across a threshold into an alien world. There at the opening of her vagina she feels her lover's presence most strongly. But once he is beyond her clitoris, there exists for her, as for him, a trace of unknownness. As long as he touches her vaginal walls, she knows he is there. But if he does not touch them, something appears lost inside. A tiny swimmer seems to be drowning in her depths unbeknownst to her. This feeling reverses the hero's experience of the same phenomenon. According to psychologist Norman O. Brown, for the male this situation resembles that of "the little man in the enormous room."[3]

For a woman to be penetrated is therefore fully as mysterious in its way as penetrating her is for a man. He is there, and yet she does not always feel him. Like the seed he may implant, his presence is not always palpable. And that is a discomforting feeling—something is there or may be there, yet a woman does not necessarily know it through her own bodily sensations.

The moment of birth reverses this original, somewhat mysterious, pattern of insemination. Where it was thrust, thrust in order to implant, it is now thrust, thrust on the part of the mother to deliver the baby. Despite their reversal from each other, both involve interior, as opposed to exterior, experiences. In purely physical terms, bodily interiority is the primary attribute of the way of the mother along which a woman must travel in her effort to attain motherselfhood.

Notwithstanding its innateness in women and, in its fullest form, especially in those who have already experienced childbirth, is it possible that interiority can be experienced in some way by men? Or by women who are still deciding whether or not to become mothers? In fact, it is. Just as members of both sexes naturally experience extensionality, the physical essence of the quest of the hero, both also experience interiority. The way this interior quality of the way of the mother can most easily be known, nonsexually, to those who are not themselves mothers is through eating. Though we seldom stop to think of it as such, eating is just as mysterious as birth. You take a substance totally alien to yourself, such as a potato, put it into your mouth, chew, swallow, and lo and behold, it becomes trans- formed inside you. Now it is part of you. By this act of eating, you have altered dead material into live. In a sense you can be said to have brought it back to life. Every time you ingest a substance you therefore fulfill the promise of alchemy: you create life out of the lifeless. Metaphorically, you relate to that substance in the mode of a mother. You are the space, it is the "hero," so to speak, entering your body. For once, however, "the hero" is silent. You as eater do not stop to think what "it" feels like, although if you did, your knowledge of hero stories would enable you to imagine it far more easily than most people can imagine the complementary way of the mother.

Despite this nonsex-specific activity of eating which theoretically allows everyone to know the physical pattern of the way of the mother, a mystery still remains. Our cultural assumptions have taught us that as heroes we can see ourselves: We know what our hands, feet, torsos, and heads look like because we have observed them directly in the mirror. We have also observed the bodies of others. But as interiors we are unknown to ourselves. If we have studied anatomical charts we may have a gener- alized sense of body interiors, but not our own. Even X-ray, tomogram, CAT scan, and fluoroscope do not reveal our own interior surfaces directly to the naked eye. Our interior remains as mysterious, possibly more so, as anyone or anything else's interior for us, for we have never seen the body interiors of others unless we are physicians, undertakers, or ghouls.

Yet we can still "follow" the food with our senses to know almost immediately what is happening, just as we can know the terrain around us when we are in the hero's mode. For instance, when we climb over a hill, we know immediately through our senses whether the slope is sharp, springy, squishy, smooth, hot, cold, warm, barren, or densely vegetated. But we are less immediately aware of our interior spaces, so we know less about our bodily responses to what we ingest. Nonetheless, if we consume something sharp, we feel stabbing, particularly if the object lodges in the throat instead of passing on. If we consume something too rich or too acidic, we suffer heartburn. And if we consume something gas-producing, we experience flatus.

After eating we carry within ourselves the contents of the meal. Where we felt empty before, now we feel full. If we have overindulged we feel uncomfortably bloated, an experience comparable to the first few months of pregnancy. If we see the surface of our abdomen ripple or feel a bubble of gas, what we experience is very like the kick of a fetus against the belly.

In this situation we experience ourselves as an enclosed universe, housing all the contents of our bodies. We might be likened to sentient vessels. In contrast to the hero role which impels us to wander, either following or creating a path, in this "mother role" we need go nowhere; we contain within ourselves all the diversity we require. In the hero role we relate to a world external to us, extending and thrusting our bodies along its surfaces and into its crevices in order that we may know it. In this mother role we *contain* the world: Everything that is, is within. Yet paradoxically in both cases the "I," the individual's personal consciousness, generally remains "outside." In either mode of being, the "who" or "what" of the "I" remains partially separate from its "world."

This separation common to both modes vitiates the commonly held belief that woman is "other." "Otherness" is clearly present in both cases. And in both it relates to the body. It does not relate to what a woman, like a man, cannot help separating out as her "I" (except in those rare mystical instances where her "I" and her body do *not* split apart). Whether she is pregnant, birthing, eating, or digesting, a woman is ordinarily aware of a "me" to whom those conditions are occurring. But this "me" is neither identical with these conditions nor fully aware of what constitutes them. Her awareness of mystery is separate from the mystery itself. This situation renders the bodily interiority of the mother's way as "other" in feeling to a woman as the external world of the hero is to him in his quest. In *both* modes the habitual relationship is characterized by separation. Only in rare moments of mystic communion does that separation disappear, allowing a woman and her body or a hero and his surroundings to become one.

But historically, within patriarchy, woman as well as man has been confused on this point. This confusion arises primarily because for hundreds of years received wisdom has automatically identified woman with the body, man with the mind or spirit. Generally speaking, educated women have decried this split that seemed to make women inferior and simply identified with men, enacting the role of the hero and ignoring the mysteries of body and otherness. By masculine logic, that is the only possible response; women, like men, are simultaneously body, mind, and spirit. And for both, the processes of body interiority remain equally mysterious. But instead of ignoring this mystery, women must learn to recognize it, placing it correctly as a *body* mystery, not a woman-only mystery. Just as extension of the body in space physically characterizes a hero, this body mystery, with all its difficult-to-grasp interiority, constitutes the physical essence of being a mother.

CHAPTER 9.

The Mother's Call

The irresistible appeal of the body mystery of the mother, characterized by interiority, is its sexuality. Indeed, it is the sexual aspect of a woman's interiority that precipitates her call to the way of the mother in the first place. By contrast, the hero's quest typically begins with some sort of call to adventure. Ordinarily his call comes in the form of an encounter, often by chance. Whatever its form, the call characteristically leads him to realize how thoroughly he has outgrown his familiar life pattern. He may find himself in a dark forest where he meets some form of the underworld serpent, universally common to mythology. Or perhaps he spots the equally common world tree believed to be the center of the universe. Then again he may simply hear an underground spring, another ubiquitous mythic symbol suggesting the mysterious forces of life.

But whereas little boys in traditional Western cultures have customarily grown up identifying with the heroes of adventure stories, their female counterparts have, until very recently, been presented with a very different pattern. The young women about whom they read did not at all follow the sequence of development ascribed to male heroes. Almost exclusively, it was males, not females, who were called to battle pirates on the high seas, confront outlaws in the Wild West, or track lions in the jungles of darkest Africa. By contrast, the only call to which women were traditionally exposed was very different; it was sexual.

While sex typically forms *part* of the adventures of the hero, at least in adult-oriented tales, it is rarely his *entire* adventure. Yet for women, until very recently, it has frequently been so.[1] In male-oriented adventure stories, if female characters figure at all, they exist simply to be "taken." Most often they are passive figures who appear solely for the male's pleasure. This is not the case in stories geared to young women. Especially in romances,whose popularity continues even in the "post-liberated" 1980s, women characters are the main focus of attention. But for these female characters physical adventure is entirely subordinate to capturing (or being captured by) the right man. The difference between the two orientations is immense. Where male readers have absorbed multiple images of heroes—men of action—to identify with, female readers of traditional serious and popular literature have almost exclusively encountered images of women as rather passive creatures overwhelmed by love.

For both hero and woman (the parallel term "heroine" is inappropriate here because it connotes a creature more restricted than the context demands) the call, whatever its form, signals a coming transformation. Sometimes it is a quite literal call. This is the case for Paul when he is still Saul of Tarsus. As he journeys on the road to Damascus he hears a voice calling him, "'Saul, Saul, why do you persecute me. . . . rise and enter the city, and you will be told what you are to do'" (Acts 9:4-6). At other times the call is so disguised that it is scarcely recognizable. Then it appears little more than happenstance. It occurs this way in the Grimm's fairy tale of "The Blue Light," for instance. The circumstance that brings it about is an encounter of the hero, a wounded ex-soldier, with a witch. In return for three nights' food and lodging, the witch exacts a promise. The soldier must perform a special task: On his last day he is to retrieve an ever-burning blue light from the bottom of a dry well behind the witch's house.

In obedience to his promise, the soldier does as the witch demands. Nearing the top of the well, light in hand, he is startled when she reaches out for the light. Fearing that she means to grab it and leave him in the well, he refuses to relinquish it. This unexpected maneuver so enrages the witch that she simply lets the soldier fall back down while she stomps off muttering imprecations. From this seemingly random incident arises the subsequent adventure and resultant transformation of the soldier into hero and king.

An archetypal call to adventure of this sort is rooted in a context that understands the world religiously. Automatically a call implies the existence of someone or something to do the calling. To be called therefore necessarily implies something other than oneself to do the calling. That someone or something must be somewhere "out there" or at least separate from oneself. Consequently, the concept of being called differs greatly from that of willing to do something. *You* do the willing. That makes you the agent in any action you take. But if you are called, you are the passive recipient of some sign which then leads you to act. The idea of a call for either hero or woman is therefore connected to a traditional, religiously understood world. That means that "the call" radically diverges from the secularism characteristic of our age: the idea of "being called" clashes violently with the belief that willed actions, often symbolized by technological "advances," invariably solve problems.

The call signals a coming initiation into a new state of being. Generally speaking, initiation is considered positive. Typically it eases young people through tremendous life changes, most often those that end childhood and begin adulthood. For traditional males initiation means leaving the world of their mothers and entering that of their fathers.

In tribal societies, from which myths originally emerged, infant males typically spend their time within the world of their mothers. In the largely communal structure of a tribal setting this maternal world normally includes many mothers, not just separate units composed of individual mothers and their own children. Otherwise this exposure to mothers does not differ significantly from that of post-tribal children even today.Although post-tribal children may perhaps experience more frequent contact with men, it is still primarily women who provide childcare throughout the world. At whatever age tribal males enter into adulthood, however, they physically exchange the original world of the mothers for the very different one of the fathers. Now the youths discover the men's secrets, participate in the hunt, memorize the sacred lore of their tribe.

By contrast, tribal women never leave the world of their mothers. This is so even in virilocal cultures (those in which a woman leaves her childhood home and moves into that of her husband). Naturally, the women in her husband's home are individuals different from the women she grew up with, but the structures of the women's world itself will remain the same. Thus initiation for a traditional female has totally different meanings from those imparted to her male counterparts. For a woman, in fact, the transformation signaled by the call may well be negative. Whereas a genuinely new world typically opens up for the male hero, for a female such renewal may not occur at all.

In myth, fairy tale, and romance the patterns become more complex. But basically the world of the hero still opens up while that of the woman remains relatively closed, leaving her still in the realm of the mothers. This happens when a young woman's initiation into sex is authorized by the community as a whole, either through marriage or tolerance of premarital sex. Such communal authorization allows a young woman's world to remain comparatively unchanged. But sometimes, as when communal authorization is lacking, her world actually diminishes. In this case a woman's call, rather than being creatively transformative for her, is disintegrative. Until the late 1960s, in most industrialized cultures, only marriage could legitimate sex for a woman. Consequently, if a woman answered the sexual call illicitly, rather than experiencing the stasis of her legitimate sister or the creative transformation of her hero-brother, she usually felt her world disintegrate.

The most disintegrative transformations typically occurred in cultural contexts that highly valued female virginity. Such contexts were common, for example, throughout rural and small-town America until as recently as the early 1960s. In high schools in these cultures everyone knew who was "doing it" and who was not, just as everyone knew who the "good girls" and the "bad girls" were. "Doing it" might be okay if the guy was a long-time steady. But promiscuity definitely placed a young woman beyond the pale of respectability. She might have guys hanging around her all the time, but she would not necessarily be asked to the Junior-Senior Prom.

So fraught with danger was "going all the way" that heavy petting more typically substituted for complete sexual fulfillment in pre-pill days. Consequently, for many women the initial meaning of the sex to which they were called was forbidden pleasure. Seeing how far she could go without being caught, initially by watchful adults, subsequently by pregnancy, added to many a young woman's sexual activity an allure not innate to sexual intercourse per se. As a result, the call to sex often became associated with great danger. To fall from "good girl" status to "bad" was to risk eternal damnation. Socially, "bad girls" simply ceased to exist. An episode in the novel *Kinflicks* dramatizes the way a young woman of pre-pill days could lose her accepted high-school social status:

> Standing in front of a microphone singing, dressed in a tight black straight skirt and a low-necked rayon jersey and ballet slippers, was Maxine "Do-It" Pruitt, my best friend from the first to the fifth grades. In the sixth grade we had gone our separate ways, me to become a left tackle and then a flag swinger, and Maxine to become "Sausage: Everyman's meat," as a moralistic girlhood book had warned us.
>
> Maxine's hair, which had been a dirty blond in the fifth grade, was now strawberry blond and was teased into cascades of ringlets that made it look as though her neck would inevitably snap under the excess bulk. She had also been transformed from a stringy lanky kid into a warm soft voluptuous young woman with huge breasts that were molded by her bra into bulletlike projectiles.[2]

Any woman or man who came of age in small-town America in the fifties recalls one or two Maxines—those young women who distinctly no longer figured in the rigid hierarchy of high school society, having succumbed too flamboyantly to the call to sex.

In such a cultural context a young girl was very aware of her virginal status. "Now I am this," she might think to herself, meaning by her vague "this" all the qualities that she thought of as herself: "I am clean, I am whole, I am *me*." It is unlikely that she would have encountered ancient teachings of the Church Fathers linking virginity with wholeness, yet her inner sense of herself might have suggested an unconscious connection to ideas such as: "The image of the virgin body was the supreme image of wholeness, and wholeness was equated with holiness."[3] Such imagery partly resulted from the inexact anatomy of the day. It was thought that a hymen completely sealed a virgin's body, hence she was an unbroken vessel. In thinking, "I am me," a young woman reflected similar understanding, for "me" typically names the separate self. To "do it" was to "give herself" to someone, to be "taken" by him. Whether or not she consciously reflected on these metaphors of sex, a young woman automatically would absorb some of them from her surrounding culture. No one could miss the distinctly different attitudes accorded presexual and sexual women. One false step could indelibly alter who and what *she* was. To follow the call to sex and "do it" was to lose forever the self she now was.

The immensity of this particular distinction between virgin and nonvirgin has become almost extinct in all but isolated patches of late twentieth-century American society. Now it is difficult to reexperience that world view in which the invisible line separating virgins from nonvirgins mattered so intensely. To cross that line was to lose forever a self one had always been. To wake up a beetle, like Gregor Samsa in Kafka's *Metamorphosis,* could occasion no larger a dislocation of self.

Such a total transformation of self wrought by loss of virginity occurs vividly in Stephen Crane's story of "Maggie, A Girl of the Streets." In girlhood Maggie "blossomed in a mud puddle. She grew to be a most rare and wonderful production of a tenement district, a pretty girl."[4] But then she meets her brother's friend Pete. Inevitably they begin stepping out. Just as inevitably she succumbs. When Maggie tries to return home afterward, her mother says, " 'Lookut her, Jimmie, lookut her. Dere's yer sister, boy. Dere's yer sister. Lookut her! Lookut her!' "[5]

The entire population of their tenement house, overhearing, comes to observe the fallen Maggie. Her brother, Jimmy, turns on her, " 'Well, now, yer a hell of a t'ing! ain't yeh?' he said, his lips curling in scorn. Radiant virtue sat upon his brow and his repelling hands expressed horror of contamination."[6] Maggie has no choice. She must leave. Losing her virginity transforms her entire life. Only one possible choice remains to her: She must become a whore. For Maggie, initiation, rather than opening life up, closes it off forever. To be a whore in that place at that time is to be placed totally beyond the acceptable limits of society.

Today, however, in postmodern cultures of the Western world, the kind of jolting transition of self once occasioned by a woman's call to sexuality has almost entirely reversed itself for many young women. Instead of guarding their intact virginal status, many now rush to alter it, as if losing virginity rather than preserving it were the most important act of their lives. The following recollection well exemplifies that change. Alice, an extremely attractive, amply endowed woman, who came of age in the late sixties, says, "I was convinced that something was wrong with me. By nineteen, I still hadn't slept with anyone."[7] Determined to change her virginal status, she accepted a weekend-long date with a smooth-talking college senior who had been chasing her throughout her entire sophomore year. "I didn't even like him. But I was sure something was wrong with me, so I decided to try sex with someone I didn't like. That way whenever I did meet the right man I wouldn't disgrace myself by not knowing what to do." However one evaluates Alice's decision, her attitude about virginity is worth noting: "Something must be wrong with me."

Feeling that "something must be wrong with me" because of continued virginity at age nineteen exemplifies an important negative shift in the meaning of sexual initiation for many contemporary young women. To feel that "something must be wrong with me" is to experience pressure in what has previously been a very private area in many eras of Western culture. Once almost nobody would have known if a person of either sex or any age were lacking in sexual expertise. In contemporary Western culture, to the extent that multiple partners are still common despite health risks, relatively large numbers may find out. Consequently, for a woman, "being good," sexually speaking, now often contravenes what "being good" meant before the pill. Now she must be as talented in her lovemaking as she is in the kitchen, at the office, on the dance floor, and on the tennis court. "Will I measure up? Will I do it right? Will I do all the necessary things?" These are relatively new worries for most women. They help shift the emphasis of sexual meaning away from concern for another person to worry about how a woman measures up relative to other women. In turning competitive, sex changes its meaning. Where it was once a private, often idealized human experience whose nearest, generally unrecognized analogue was Holy Communion, it has now turned into one of many competitive sports. As a game, sex loses much of its specialness. Now technique matters most to many people in the West, especially those who came of age after the pill gained acceptability. What used to be almost universally a highly charged rite of passage for women has now degenerated for many into a competitive event. That change drastically alters the meaning of a woman's call to the way of the mother.

Highly illustrative of this desacralized, meaningless sex that now often results when a woman responds to the call is a scene from "The Fire Sermon" section of T. S. Eliot's *Waste Land*. In it a tired, bored typist permits, without desire, the caresses of her carbuncular male dinner guest.

After he completes his unwanted but unreproved lovemaking and leaves, she scarcely even knows that he has gone. She thinks, "'Well now that's done: and I'm glad it's over,'"[8] as she automatically smoothes her hair and plays a record. What was once one of the most meaningful of all possible human actions has become for her just another ho-hum bit of tedium.

Both these extreme variants of a woman's call to motherhood—the one to strict premarital virginity, the other to early loss of virginity—fall short of most women's needs. Both misplace their own emphases. Neither is chiefly concerned with the personal well-being of the individual woman. In opposite ways, both close off life rather than opening it. In this sense they are calls to a kind of death rather than life. Both situations, in opposite ways, threaten to subordinate a woman's life to biology. When enforced virginity is the cultural norm, the sexual aspect of a woman's mysterious bodily interiority is so deeply meaningful that only strict prohibitions can keep it in check. Any sexuality that manages to escape these prohibitions is therefore immediately demonized as something evil. The woman, as bearer of this evil, is consequently stigmatized. By contrast, when promiscuity is culturally acceptable, sex easily becomes routinized, hence finally meaningless.

Both these extremes of the call reflect patriarchal rather than gynocentric values: Both deflect attention away from the goal of genuine selfhood, whether that authentic to the hero or to the mother. Instead both extremes focus exclusively on the sexual status of the woman involved. Inevitably within patriarchy this status cannot be neutral; automatically it comes complete with moral evaluation. Almost always in pre-pill Western culture a virgin was "good," a nonvirgin, unless married, "bad." In the early days of sexually liberated Western culture, the valuations essentially reversed. In neither case does the individual woman particularly matter. Nor is *motherhood,* supposedly the result of women's sexuality in pre-pill culture, of real concern. Instead, what matters is *how* a particular young woman relates to men. Such preoccupation with her virginal or nonvirginal status necessarily ignores the selfhood of the woman.

This major shift in the drama of sexuality from enforced virginity to permissive sexuality inevitably alters the nature of the mother's call for some women. What was once so deeply meaningful a part of every woman's life as to be a truly sacred event (even if more often demonic than divine in outcome) has now become desacralized into a mere routine for many, in the way that Eliot's lines so clearly dramatize. To think of sex as a gift, as once was the case, is scarcely possible in a society where it is so readily available on an impersonal basis. Although one might conceivably give friends confined to the city a box of lovingly collected seashells, one would scarcely give such a present to neighbors at the shore. What was precious within a rigid, and often even oppressive, framework rapidly loses its former value once the surrounding sanctions are eased. Freedom from the oppressiveness of the old system is truly liberating. But simultaneously losing the deep meaning attached to sexual relationships is not. Only a balance between the two extremes can truly open up a new space for women.

The drastic difference in meaning between "before" and "after" in Western culture is completely reversed for many women. Instead of being valued, virginity, as in Alice's case, is viewed with some degree of horror. Possibly, like her, some women who feel stigmatized by their virginity may find that losing it enhances their sense of self. But many more risk overemphasizing sex so much for its own sake that they may sacrifice selfhood to the superficial excitement of indiscriminate sexual encounters. Such encounters may then victimize them as much as social ostracism for sexual behavior did their sisters of an earlier generation.

Both these extremes deviate from what is supposedly the mother's call. Ideally, a truly gynocentric call to motherhood does not subordinate the sexual act to its product, making sex "dirty" unless engaged in purely for the sake of reproduction. Nor does it subordinate the product to the act, making reproduction totally irrelevant. Instead, it makes a woman consciously note the interconnection between this act of love (or sex, as the case may be) and that outcome: a child.

Today a woman can control her maternal destiny to an extent that just a generation ago would have appeared utopian. Superficially such ability to control counters the entire notion of a call. A woman's ability to choose whether or not to have children technologizes a formerly sacred occurrence. Actually the situation is not so simple. A woman may simply decide "I want a child" in much the same way she wants a car, a house, a diamond bracelet, or a schnauzer. She may want it "to give me the love I've never had from anyone else." In such instances the idea of motherhood as sacred calling undeniably disappears. But the situation differs essentially for another kind of woman. This woman welcomes the profound change in her own being necessarily effected by motherhood. For her the call, in an era of choice, unquestionably signifies approaching self-fulfillment unlike any other. In accepting a genuinely gynocentric call to motherhood, she accepts a challenge to become a new sort of self. As this new self she will bring new life into existence. When appropriate, she will even *willingly* subordinate her own needs to this new life. It is this willing choice of a different self that constitutes the true call to the way of the mother.

This ability of women to choose for ourselves whether to become mothers also makes the way of the mother extremely threatening to patriarchal values. As long as men controlled and defined the permissible levels of women's sexuality, the way of the mother could be idealized, sentimentalized, or trivialized as men chose. But now that women can decide consciously whether to accept the call, it becomes a very powerful instrument for our own self-definition. Implicit in the call is the threat that women can now control our own destinies almost without reference to men. This threat is too devastating to be admitted in all the bitter arguments against abortion, adoption by unmarried women, and out-of-wedlock motherhood. Just as terrifying for upholders of patriarchy is the fact that a woman can now reproduce without permanently relying on one man legitimated to "protect" and "support" her.

Not only does this new freedom to choose mean that a woman can now readily "use" a man sexually to conceive a child primarily for herself, it also means that love for a man, whether actual or pretended, no longer need determine a woman's path to motherhood. Even a child conceived in absolute loathing of the male partner may be chosen by a woman. The fetus produced by a love affair gone sour, revenge at a man, or even rape need not be aborted, put out for adoption, or raised in hatred. These perhaps unlikely contingencies and all the other significant changes in the way a woman can now freely relate to her sexuality redefine the way of the mother. It is now a very different path from the one patriarchy once exclusively defined. Misused, a woman's new power to control her choices can become an instrument of retaliation against men. Used wisely, however, her power can be a very satisfying entry into the space patriarchal thought perceives as lying on the other side of the threshold. This is, of course, women's own truly gynocentric space.

CHAPTER 10.

The Threshold

Sexuality is, without question, what leads a woman to begin her way of the mother. In either idealized or demonized form, it characterizes the space into which the hero of traditional tales must venture on his quest. This place is known as the space beyond the threshold. Because of its sexual connotations, this threshold motif presents an especially grave challenge to women attempting to follow the way of the mother. Consequently, it is extremely important to look closely at this concept which figures so prominently in every quest.

After a traditional hero has accepted his call to adventure, his quest proper begins when he crosses a threshold. This crossing leads him into an area of great power, a sacred space of some kind. A good example of this motif occurs in the Grimm's tale of "Sleeping Beauty," when the hero penetrates beyond the protective briar hedge surrounding the enchanted castle. Until his coming, this hedge has always entrapped would-be heroes on its thorns. But for the true hero, the briar hedge "was covered with beautiful large flowers which made way for him of their own accord and let him pass unharmed, and then closed up again into a hedge behind him."[1] This realm into which the hero penetrates is sexually charged. Undeniably, as indicated by the thorns, it is also an area of great power, even of danger.

In some stories this place beyond the threshold appears less appealingly sexual, more overtly threatening. This is so in "the Realm of the Mothers" in Goethe's *Faust*. Faust speaks of the place in dread, asking Mephistopheles the way. Mephistopheles replies,

> No way!—To the Unreachable,
> Ne'er to be trodden! A way to the
> Unbeseechable,
> Never to be besought! Art thou prepared?
> There are no locks, no latches to be lifted;
> Through endless solitudes shalt thou be drifted.[2]

These two realms—that of the Mothers and that of Sleeping Beauty's enchanted castle—represent opposing androcentric attitudes toward women's sexuality. Respectively, they embody the negative and positive faces of the interior, sexualized sphere of intense power into which the hero must enter. No matter what combination of these two faces he encounters, the patriarchal hero will find here two interconnected themes: *women* and some *other* world. This other world varies enormously from the one natural to the hero in his everyday existence. In patriarchal thought, woman and "other world" coalesce to typify the place "beyond the threshold." This is so whether the threshold opens into space, some sort of underworld, or the unconscious.

Not only does the threshold separate two very different worlds from each other, it also symbolizes a woman's sexuality as it is perceived in patriarchal thought. As symbol of a woman's sexuality, the threshold motif vividly condenses the traditional patriarchal control of woman's sexuality. A woman is initially "protected" by her father and brothers to assure her "purity." They then give her over, "undefiled," to the suitor of their choice. From now on her suitor-turned-husband guards her sexuality. The woman's preferences are seldom considered. If she does not wish to function as a "threshold" for the "right" male, her wish is considered aberrant. She is unnatural if she eschews the heroine role. Surely she must long to have her space entered that she may be "rescued" from her "sleep," a common folkloristic image for unawakened sexuality.

But often a woman quite obviously does *not* view a would-be entering male as her savior. Instead she sees him as an intruder she wants nothing to do with. This theme clearly underlies the Grimm's tale of "The Twelve Dancing Princesses." Every night the twelve beautiful princesses of the title are locked into their bedroom by their father, the king. But every morning he notices a curious fact: Their shoes have been danced to shreds. To solve the mystery of this strange phenomenon, he announces a contest. Whoever can solve the mystery may wed the princess of his choice and reign after the king's death. Whoever fails after three successive attempts, however, must die. Many try, and many fail. Finally, a poor soldier who has been advised by a typical helping figure of fairy tales, a wise old woman, tries his luck. Forewarned that the eldest princess will lace his wine with sleeping powder, he lets the draught run into a sponge hidden beneath his chin. When the twelve get up, he follows. The youngest sister, sensing danger, repeatedly expresses her unease: "'I don't know what it is. You may rejoice, but I feel so strange. A misfortune is certainly hanging over us.'"[3]

From a patriarchal perspective such pains as the soldier exerts for the hand of the princess mark him a hero. This kind of exertion is part of the ordeal essential for achieving hero status. Anthropologists point out that such contests for a bride commonly reflect matrilocal cultures wherein men, not women, leave home to live with the family of their spouse. However, even in such matrilocal societies, the husband, not the wife, "rules." This is so even when, as here, she, not he, is born of royal blood.

Psychologically, in patriarchal thought, this same theme of winning the bride symbolizes the process by which a man achieves true selfhood. Winning the bride shows that he has overcome a series of inner obstacles representing the repressed "feminine" side of his nature, which previously hindered him from attaining his goal of deep selfhood. Psychological analysis of this sort presents women with a problem. This is yet one more way that male-controlled symbolism turns woman into the object of man. Such a view of selfhood requires woman's selfhood to be created through the agency of a man. For a man to achieve his goal of selfhood, a woman must be "rescued," that is, abducted, if necessary. According to the patriarchal mystique, not just *any* man can do this. Only those men capable of achieving full selfhood or hero status can. But the patriarchal perspective asserts that the "right" man, a man of heroic stature, will invariably succeed. That perspective automatically renders woman passive. *Her* selfhood can only come into being at the behest of the right man. Belief that it is actually the *duty* of the man to form the selfhood of his bride has inspired many men, especially in Victorian days, to play Pygmalion. Consequently, the intrusion (or rescue, depending on whether one's perspective is gynocentric or phallocentric) of the hero into female space far exceeds mere physical penetration.

Ultimately much more devastating to women than physical intrusion are the intangibles involved in the hero's crossing of the threshold. In the quest of the hero this threshold motif also symbolizes patriarchy as a system of thought, language, values, and actions constantly penetrating gynocentric space. These intangible intrusions immensely complicate a woman's journey along her own way of the mother.

Symbolically, woman and woman space are both purely "other" for man. Woman is the opposite, the unknown who is almost never presented, as are men, as an "I" in her own right. In the case of Sleeping Beauty, this otherness wholly attracts men. In the case of Goethe's Mothers, it terrifies them. In either case, however, woman is so alien to man that she appears to belong to another species than he does. If this other species were equivalent no harm might result. But "alien" also implies "inferior."

A woman acculturated to patriarchal understandings of "reality" may unquestioningly accept this view that woman is "other." For her, permitting male intrusion into her space is "natural," and submitting to males is what she does. But some women sense a discrepancy between their own experience and the "officially" accepted view of reality sanctioned by patriarchy. For them, existence is split. On the one hand, a woman who feels her own experience split off from that defined by patriarchy experiences herself as an "I" trying to live out her own life; on the other, that "I" absorbs patriarchal projections. In their varied legal, economic, social, familial, and sexual permutations these projections counter the shape of the life she tries to call her own. Repeatedly, she is caught between these two experiences of selfhood. Part of her feels that a genuine "I" wells up from inside herself. But another part seems to be nothing but a patriarchal encrustation composed of elements not truly her own. These elements reflect what patriarchy teaches a woman she "should" be. This kind of split often badly confuses a woman.

Despite its seeming negativity for a woman, however, the threshold motif, rightly understood, is as critical to the way of the mother as it has always been to the quest of the hero. For both mother and hero the space on the other side represents a mystery that must be successfully dealt with before their respective quests can proceed. For a woman that means the threshold must be explored as a motif with meanings appropriate to her own gynocentric perspective. These meanings bear no relationship to androcentric interpretations which view woman and threshold as interchangeable objects existing purely for the pleasure of the penetrating man. Instead, they are meanings that help a woman discover who she is on her own terms.

CHAPTER II.

The Other Side of the Threshold

Women now have other options besides the traditional passive waiting for Mr. Right, so typical of the woman's threshold role in a traditional heroic quest. We can now make conscious choices about our sexuality. No longer must we automatically be symbolized by the threshold. Seemingly, in the way of the mother, no exact counterpart to the hero's threshold crossing exists for a woman. There are several reasons for this apparent lack. To the extent that the space beyond the threshold is traditionally woman's own interior space, a woman's entry here seems problematic. Because of its sexual nature, a woman's entry into this space is taboo: It severely threatens accepted patriarchal assumptions of a heterosexual norm. At the same time, to simply reverse the accepted imagery of the space beyond the threshold and connect it with male sexuality so violates the nature of the metaphor that it doesn't work. Labeling this space "male" for a woman not only contravenes patriarchal patterns of behavior, it simply does not fit the myth of the way of the mother. First of all it is *not* male space; it is woman's space. To say that it *is* male space a woman enters when she crosses the threshold is to reverse the meaning of woman's own interior space and mislabel it. On the other hand, if a woman *does* enter some other space, such entry removes her from her own internal journey and places her into an external one instead. This journey takes a woman out of the mother pattern and places her right back in the androcentric role of the mythic hero. In that case the space she enters means something entirely different. It is external space, usually referred to as public space. This is not to say that such entry into male space should never occur. It should and it does happen frequently. But when it does, a different pattern obtains. Hence different meanings occur as well.

The importance of understanding this distinction cannot be over-stressed. Its importance has nothing to do with the well-known fact that traditional stories seldom show women heroes setting off and entering male space. That is a different issue. Rather, its importance concerns an entirely different fact: The biological basis for this particular metaphor, in which men penetrate and women are penetrated, prohibits neat substitution whereby women and men can reverse roles using this same motif. If this biologically based motif were seldom employed, this distinction could be ignored. Unfortunately, however, this is not the case. This motif of the necessity and right of males to penetrate female space is a root metaphor of patriarchal thought structures. Its relationship to gynocentric experience must therefore be considered with great care.

In traditional tales, once the hero has crossed the threshold, he finds himself in a very different space, "a dream landscape of curiously fluid, ambiguous forms, where he must survive a succession of trials."[1] From a woman's perspective, of course, this space the hero enters is her own. That the hero will look around this space and gain important new insights is a major part of his quest. But what about the woman whose realm he has entered? What she sees and experiences when she herself looks into it will depend greatly on her perspective. Will she "see" with eyes and "hear" with ears conditioned to patriarchal imagery? If she does, what she is likely to hear is a patriarchal distortion of her sexuality. Or will she resolutely push aside those negative evaluations and allow her own experience to stand on its own?

According to Joseph Campbell, "the idea that the passage of the magical threshold is a transit into a sphere of rebirth is symbolized in the worldwide womb image of the belly of the whale. The hero, instead of conquering or conciliating the power of the threshold, is swallowed into the unknown. . . ."[2] The unknown of which Campbell speaks is precisely the interior of the mother, the fearsome creature into whom the hero passes on his quest. The interior aspect of the mother is one of the most central qualities of her motherselfhood.

This bodily interiority that so terrifies the archetypal hero remains a relative mystery to most people compared to their understanding of externally visible body parts. Sadly, this is as true for women as it is for men. Even the fact that women as a class experience our anatomy more interiorly than do men as a class does little to alter this circumstance.

Nonetheless, women's interior experiences of being sexually penetrated, pregnancy, and giving birth all "speak" to us if we can just learn to "hear" what these experiences tell us. Ordinarily we are cut off from this bodily speech. This is so because we are frequently denied direct access to our own experiences. Such denial occurs in two ways. One way is predominantly physical, as when we are drugged in childbirth. The other is largely symbolic. Symbolic denial of women's experiences occurs because, given the patriarchal symbol systems responsible for the tools we all use to create concepts, we lack language appropriate to the deepest meanings of our interiority. While we may feel and experience our interiority, expressing it therefore often creates insurmountable difficulties.

To express interiority women must sometimes translate it into an alien, insufficient androcentric language. To speak of ourselves in terms of our interiority we must turn the traditional categories of existing language inside out; such inversion makes creating speech appropriate to our experience of interiority difficult. A second problem even more significantly hinders women from understanding our own experience of the motif androcentric thinking terms "being in the belly of the whale." This is the problem of official patriarchal norms. These norms reflect extensionality rather than interiority. How threatening for a woman to discover that she "deviates" from these male-determined norms. To deviate is to "be a monster."

A related problem for a woman whose value system has been thoroughly androcentrized is that interiority as a mode of being lacks the status of heroic extensionality. Interiority is considered inferior to extensionality. For all these reasons—language, valuation, and status—women have historically kept our interiority largely "silent."

Nevertheless, despite these androcentric linguistic, conceptual, and evaluative emphases on extensionality, women do experience our interiority. Most commonly we experience this quality which automatically gives us an inside view of what lies beyond the threshold—the interior of the belly of the whale—through being penetrated. Typically, such penetration occurs through sexual intercourse, often referred to as "being known." In the symbol systems of heterosexual patriarchal cultures, into which we are all born (even if we subsequently try to reject them), "being known" belongs strictly to woman. She is the receiver of the penis. This is a "fact" we take for granted. What being known may mean to any individual woman we largely ignore. Patriarchy teaches women and men alike that taking in the penis is a mimetic act. By taking into herself the body of the male, a woman "consumes" him. By her coupling, female with male, she thereby mimics the ancient ritual sacrifice by which the bloodthirsty Goddess receives a sacrificial victim. Woman in coitus is the archetypally devouring female who invariably engulfs the male hero.

This idea of woman as devouring female occurs worldwide. In folklore the relevant motif is known as the *vagina dentata*, the toothed vagina. An indication of the power this image commands is apparent from the many stories in which it appears. One such is a myth from the Ticarilla

Apache Indians of New Mexico.[3] Once upon a time, according to this tale, only four women in the whole world had vaginas. These were the daughters of the fearsome Kicking Monster. These four "vagina girls," as they were called, had the form of women, with all a woman's body parts, but they were actually vaginas, living in a house full of vaginas. Naturally enough, this house attracted men from everywhere. But each man who ventured near was kicked into the house by Kicking Monster, never to be seen again.

One day, the hero, Killer-of-Enemies, outwitted Kicking Monster and entered the house on his own. All four vagina girls ran to him, longing for intercourse. He fended them off, asking them questions that he might learn the secret of the men's disappearance. "We ate them up because we like to," said the girls. When he found out what had been happening, Killer-of-Enemies told them they must first take some medicine made from sour berries. Then he would have intercourse with them. The sour medicine ate away the strong teeth of the vagina girls, leaving them unable to consume their victims from that day on.

All the many extensions of this darkly negative patriarchal image of woman as the toothed vagina—the castrating mother, the devouring witch, the monster into whose belly the hero must go (as in Jonah and the Whale)—represent a powerful means by which men have traditionally robbed women of the positive experience of our interior mode of being. Instead of experiencing our bodily interiority for ourselves as a valued modality of being, we have been denied immediate access to it; patriarchal interpretations have been thrust (often quite literally) in the way of our own understandings. By these means we have been taught that our female mode of sexuality is evil. Such labeling robs us of our firsthand experience.

Interiority, though similar to being penetrated, differs from it. Interiority is the condition of a body's insides. Being penetrated, by contrast, is what a woman feels when something enters her. Ordinarily, of course, she is unaware of her interiority *unless* something penetrates it and thereby brings it to her attention. The two conditions therefore overlap. Nonetheless, interiority is always part of a woman, whereas penetration is intermittent.

Unlike a woman, a male hero typically knows the "contents" of interiority as something *outside* himself. Those contents are other and they belong to another. They are not he himself, nor are they part of him. But a person who symbolizes interiority, a woman or a biologically male insertee, is known as the awesome mystery or terrifying stigma of interiority itself. She (or he in the case of a gay male) is the insides turned out, showing herself in all her glory or hideousness, depending on whether the perspective is gynocentric or patriarchal. Even if, as is sometimes the case, those "insides," are defined, not as nothing, but as *something*, they are thought simply to mask the underlying nothingness of interiority. In Western patriarchal thought "thingness" or substance is positive, "nothingness," negative. Each is so by definition. Therefore, woman within patriarchy is automatically connected to nothingness.

But "nothingness" is a slippery concept. One of its definitions involves a linguistic shift of meaning. "Nothing" in its primary sense means absence or negativity. Secondarily, however, it means a condition of utter insignificance. Hence it becomes depreciated in meaning. This connotation, however, is not inherent in the first meaning of "nothingness." Consequently, to say that something is "nothing" need not automatically imply a condemnation of it. Nonetheless, a woman growing up in an androcentric culture early learns to associate the nothingness or negative space of her sexual organs with a "negative" valuation as well. Yet this correlation merely reflects linguistic assumptions of Western patriarchal cultures. It is *not* part of her inherent body condition.

This symbolic shift in the meaning of "nothingness" from absence of content to lack of goodness forms a very significant part of the meaning attached to women's interiority from a patriarchal perspective. Nothingness becomes evil in the predominant religious tradition of the West, the Judeo-Christian complex. Traditional religious visions of negativity can be placed in two categories. First is *absence* of good, a form of nothingness. In one pattern of thinking absence of good is automatically defined as evil. That means that God, the highest good, stands at the apex of a system whose opposite is *absence* of God. In this system of thought, damnation equals distance from God. The farther away a sinner is, the more he is damned. Although "Hell" may name the "place" of this distance, Hell possesses no value in its own right; it is simply a place from which God is absent. Applying the logic of this view to a woman's interior space, her interiority is not "evil" in its own right; it is simply lacking relative to the "norm" of male extensionality. Where a man possesses a penis, she has only an opening—a nothingness. Consequently, as thinkers from Aristotle to Freud have contended, woman is an incomplete man, a man lacking the essential attribute of full humanity, a penis.

A contrasting thought structure pictures evil as a principle in its own right. In this case, evil is "positive." This is not to say that it is "good." Rather, evil exists apart from, and without reference to, good. In this view a counterpart to God exists: the Devil. And his abode, in contrast to Heaven, is Hell. Unlike the Hell in the first system, this one possesses characteristics of its own. While this Hell, too, is envisioned as being far away from God, it is feared primarily for qualities unique to it. Characteristically it is a place, conceived as a dark interior, filled with unspeakable abominations. It stinks of sulphur and brimstone. Its contents all arouse unpleasant sensations: extreme heat and cold, sliminess, unbearable thirst-inducing dryness, and so forth.

An equivalent split between absence and "thingness" belongs to the masculine/feminine polarity characteristic of symbolic, logical, religious, and social organization in the West. On the one hand, interiority is viewed as nothingness, as absence, as a condition whose very lack of nameable attributes renders it nearly impossible to grasp. Hence it remains a perpetual mystery. Analogy places women, because we lack a penis, at a great distance from men. Our "evil," in this view, depends on our great difference from man, who mirrors God.

The logic of the opposing position may also be applied to interiority, however. In this case interiority is viewed not as lacking a principle in its own right. Rather, its "contents" serve as its substance. Consequently, the inner organs and their secretions, rather than the space they help define, become the "stuff" of interiority. Now woman is judged not by her lack, but by the "disgusting" nature of her interior.

It is obvious that both women and men have bodily interiors. But in the dominant symbolism of our culture women, by virtue of our sexual anatomy, are connected to interiors, as men are by theirs, to exteriors. As a result, all the repugnance patriarchal thinking attaches to various orifices and their effluvia, whether sexual or not, concentrates primarily on the vagina. Unlike the phallus, which Western culture venerates as an object of beauty, the vagina is generally considered unclean, smelly, ugly, evil, slimy, even dangerous, as in the image of the toothed vagina. (Even greater "evil," of course, attaches to the anus of those, such as gay males, who use it as a surrogate vagina.)

Seemingly the meaning of interiority is sufficiently demonized in the process which defines woman as a vaginal "opening into Hell." Not so. A woman is further demonized by patriarchal interpretations of the sexual relations which bring men into contact with women's interiority in the first place. From a patriarchal perspective, to be the insertee rather than the insertor is to be degraded. Somewhat disconcertingly, considering the sexual behaviors of its members, nowhere is this distinction more apparent than within some male gay subcultures. According to many male homosexuals, the determining factor in labeling another man gay is not whether he engages in sex with another man. It is whether he plays the passive role. This means that many homosexual men who only fuck without allowing themselves to *be* fucked or who allow fellatio to be performed on them without reciprocating define themselves as "straight." In the argot of gay speech, such men are "butch." It is solely their "nellie" (feminine) counterparts who are homosexual.+ Only the partner who is "like a woman" is degraded!

This distinction may strike heterosexuals of both sexes as self-deceiving, even ludicrous. Nonetheless, it helps elucidate the symbolic nature of interiority that lies beyond the threshold as it is understood by at least some males acculturated to a patriarchal context. Clearly the male homosexual view of maleness correlates to the traditional image of the hero as one who knows, who "inserts" his (or her) body into the "nothingness" of space. By contrast, "femaleness" is being known, is space itself. What remains to be seen is just what this condition of being known means to a woman and how she can give voice to it.

Often a woman struggling with this difficult task of giving voice to her own gynocentric experience needs assistance. Like her counterpart, the questing hero, she may require intervention from a supernatural helper. Otherwise she may find herself unable to proceed appropriately along the way of the mother.

CHAPTER 12.

Supernatural Help

Like the hero on his quest, a woman often needs help at a critical point along the way of the mother. To develop eyes and ears gynocentrically attuned to the meanings inherent in her interior space she must have such help. Otherwise she cannot orient herself in this region which, though it is her own, nonetheless feels so strange that she cannot get her bearings. What she sees when she is wearing the customary blinders of androcentrism looks totally different from what she will now see without them.

In the case of the hero, the help needed to negotiate the space beyond the threshold (which is also the space within the belly of the whale) comes at the behest of a supernatural helper he may have met at the outset of his journey. Typically this helper will be a wise old woman or man, sometimes a helping animal. For a woman attempting to follow her own gynocentric way, the way of the mother, such help, to be effective, must come from a source relatively uncontaminated by patriarchal thought. Otherwise she will simply see her space as patriarchy teaches both sexes to perceive it. Persephone, despite her abduction by Hades, provides just such an appropriate helping model for a woman.

Unlike the typical heroine of patriarchal culture, Persephone refuses to be "rescued" by a lover. Her story begins innocently enough: She is playing in a field of flowers with the daughters of the god Oceanus. Suddenly Hades appears and drags her off to his underworld kingdom. There she is to reign as his queen.

The loss of her daughter so saddens Demeter that she immediately starts searching for her. Disguised as an aged mortal, she goes to Eleusis where she accepts lodging in the household of a woman named Metaneira and her husband, Celeus. Demeter refuses Metaneira's offer of wine, asking instead for a potion of meal and water mixed with soft mint. This potion (κυκεων) subsequently becomes part of a communion ritual to commemorate the sorrows of Demeter within the Eleusinian Mysteries. Demeter, still disguised as a mortal, becomes nurse to Demophoon, the son of Metaneira and Celeus. By day she feeds the child ambrosia, by night she anneals him in fire to make him immortal. But one evening Metaneira, glimpsing this strange treatment, protests. So angered is Demeter by this response to her well-intentioned ministrations, that she leaves the household. Before doing so, however, she reveals her true identity, instructing the people of Eleusis to build a temple to Her: ". . . I myself will teach my rites, that hereafter you may reverently perform them and so win the favour of my heart."[1] So saying, Demeter metamorphoses out of her loathly, human form into the radiant beauty of deity and departs. In the morning, Celeus bids the people of Eleusis to construct an altar and temple to her. This story explains why her rites are subsequently conducted primarily at Eleusis.

During the following year, Demeter, still mourning Persephone, causes the nourishing earth to wither. Zeus tries repeatedly to dissuade her from her course, but until he forces Hades to release Persephone he fails. Before releasing Persephone, sly Hades feeds her some pomegranate seeds. She, unaware that consuming even a morsel in the Land of the Dead ever after forces the consumer to return, accepts them. That is why Persephone must perpetually dwell for a third of each year in Hades.

Because Persephone's story strongly violates accepted patriarchal standards it is appropriate for helping women understand the meaning of our own interiority. Persephone is one of very few female figures admitted into the canon of patriarchal literature for whom *marriage and husband* signify the underworld. Furthermore, in marked contrast to typical patriarchal heroines, Persephone's *positive* world remains the original world she knew, that of her mother, the fertile earth itself. Ordinarily patriarchy reverses these categories, connecting the world of the mothers to the loathed underworld.

Most women only indirectly discover what should be universally recognized as our primary space. This recognition reverses what we have been patriarchally acculturated to expect. Instead of realizing that this space exists for us from the start, we typically come to it indirectly, as do men, through the stories, rituals, and thought patterns of androcentric cultures. Thus, women, like males, read of the hero's crossing a threshold into a "zone of magnified power" protected by threshold guardians, beyond which lie "darkness, the unknown, and danger."[2] Reading of such exotica, knowing they are symbolically connected with ourselves, is all part of what makes women perpetually "other," not just to men but ultimately and more dangerously to ourselves.

In this strange land of woman's interior space three major themes intertwine: woman, sex, and death. In patriarchal thought women and death are equally unknown and mysterious. Woman as "opposite" to man is mysterious much as is death, the "opposite" of life. The third theme, sex, enters in because for men the voyage into the unknown realm of woman is naturally enough effected by its means. Sexual intercourse is often considered a "little death." Persephone, as one well acquainted with death, therefore provides women with an excellent model for understanding this realm.

Persephone's role as a supernatural helper for women attempting to understand the space beyond the threshold is also appropriate for another reason. Unlike most women in myth or history Persephone repeatedly chooses her mother and life among the living in preference to her husband and queenship of the dead. In contrast to all the thousands of women who end up supposedly living "happily every after" with the hero who "rescues" them, Persephone earns the right to divide her time between the two realms of life and death. At that, she spends but one-third of each year with Hades, the "hero" who tried to "rescue" her from earth! Persephone, indeed, seems to possess the secret of balancing life between the two antithetical realms of patriarchal and gynocentric space. This ability eminently suits her to function as a helping figure for women struggling to achieve such knowledge for themselves.

Just what then can a woman learn from Persephone? What is the nature of her great secret?

The secret Persephone can impart concerns a peril commonly attributed to this strange woman-realm beyond the threshold. In traditional hero tales this peril is called enchantment. In the story of Ulysses, for example, enchantment occurs when Circe turns his men into swine. But a counterpart also exists for women. The nature of this counterpart is what Persephone can share.

Specifically, the counterpart centers on the patriarchal mystique that whereas sex for a man may result in the negative condition of enchantment, for a woman it is salvation. The secret Persephone can impart does not necessarily dispute this notion. But it does imply that the gynocentric meaning of sex for a woman differs significantly from its common patriarchal interpretation.

Over and over women are told by the cultural assumptions, stories, and clichés of patriarchy that sex, enacted properly, with the "right" man, will solve all our problems. So dominant is this belief, particularly in contemporary American culture, that almost every ad and commercial exploits a variant theme: Sex saves. Only "sexy" products sell. If sex is a panacea for selling lifeless objects such as cars, how much more truly will it save humans! Especially is this so for women. After all, sex, imprecisely equated with love, has traditionally been touted as the be-all and end-all for woman.

But is sex salvific in precisely the way the patriarchal mystique insists? The myth of Persephone does not read as if it were so. Otherwise that story would not so flagrantly flout the better-known, patriarchal pattern. In fact, in Persephone's story, the categories patriarchy values actually invert. Instead of "rescuing" her, Hades "abducts" her. And instead of staying there in his space with him, she leaves him for nine months a year. Furthermore, in her story, it is *his* space which is "other," not hers; *his* space which is the "under"world, hers which reflects the light of day.

The patriarchal mystique plays with the ambivalent notion of enchantment. On the one hand, enchantment refers to ecstatic admiration; on the other, it means to be moved by charms and incantations. The patriarchal mystique also makes enchantment and sex appear interchangeable. The fact that Persephone "eats" in the realm of Hades certainly suggests that sharing sexuality with another person sometimes becomes an enchanting or, more precisely, an ecstatic experience, ecstasy simply being another term for enchantment, when enchantment is viewed positively.

Ecstasy refers to being taken out of oneself. It is associated primarily with the Greek god Dionysus, whose appearance so inflamed his followers that they would drop whatever they were doing to follow where he led. But just as the ecstasy-producing gift of the vine, for which Dionysus is famous, endangers those who indulge too heavily, so does the ecstatic gift of sexual union. In both cases, the danger centers on two themes: deception and dependency.

Ambiguity therefore governs ecstasy, whether vine-induced or sexually effected. In the case of sexual ecstasy, dangerous deception exists for a woman who believes sex can solve all her problems. At the heart of this deception is the "place" a person "is" or "goes" during coitus. Popular belief holds that the ecstatic relationship takes lovers out of themselves. It is thought to bring them into a single entity larger than either self alone. As a result, so popular wisdom insists, they actually do become one.

The model for the union sexual ecstasy is thought to create is obvious: mother and fetus. Just this kind of close relationship connects the growing organism to its maternal surroundings. But Persephone is wise. She knows that the sexual union which allows men symbolically to return to the womb is not really experienced that same way by women.

In patriarchal thought, the ecstatic experience of sex is believed to accomplish two mutually contradictory ends. On the one hand, sexual union is touted as "return to the womb." Clearly that metaphor is androcentric. Sex cannot logically be return to the womb for a woman. She *is* the womb. On the other hand, in the way myths often become twisted, the hero also functions as a kind of mother for the heroine. In "saving" the woman he protects and nurtures her. The masculine mystique holds that everything will be all right for a woman once she is "rescued" by him. In its overtly sexual form, this mystique asserts that through sex with the man she loves, a woman will be fused in a way that suits her presumed woman-need for union.

The first of these interconnected themes—that sex is return to the womb—focuses on the experience of the hero. For him, the experience of crossing the threshold obviously symbolizes penetrating a woman's vagina with his penis. Symbolically, by such entry, he is the infant reversing the process of birth. As such, he engages in the familiar perilous voyage common to the mythic quest of the hero. In this motif the woman functions as both part and whole—she is both womb and mother.

The other two themes interwoven into this patriarchal mystique of sex as salvation—that the hero is a kind of mother and that the hero "saves" the woman—both focus on the experience of the woman. But her experience is presented from a patriarchal, not a gynocentric, point of view. These themes assert that the woman needs rescue by the man. She must be "carried away," "swept off her feet," "taken care of," and "saved" by him. The first two of these metaphors, "to be carried away" and "to be swept off one's feet," are both sexual. The latter two, to be "taken care of" and "saved," are maternal. Combined, these metaphors eroticize the male with maternal connotations, giving to women this message: "You will simultaneously be sexually stimulated and taken care of."

So far the mystique appears innocuous enough: Both partners in the act of sex symbolically become as children. But mythically, in the case of the hero, this sexual realm represented by women is always overtly connected to great danger. Consequently, he knows from the accumulated lore of patriarchal culture that he tarries there at great risk. For a woman, however, such warning is not given at the mythic level, although traditionally it has been given to unmarried women in everyday life. But the difference between the levels of mythic and everyday "reality" matters greatly. The danger a woman is warned about is moral and practical: If she engages in casual sex she will become "loose" and she may become pregnant. The danger the hero is warned about exists in an entirely different realm: Should he tarry too long in a condition of sexual ecstasy, whether licit or illicit, he might never "return." His separate selfhood is thereby endangered.

Yet for a woman this "same" tale is connected to just the opposite ideas: to comfort and rescue. If she gives in to ecstatic sex with her partner, she will "live happily ever after." Why should the "same" experience be considered dangerous for one partner, salvific for the other? To understand this important difference necessitates looking more closely at the way ecstasy functions.

Despite the patriarchal mystique that celebrates it as a model of union, sometimes ecstasy actually *excludes* the other person instead. This "little death of the bed," as the seventeenth-century metaphysical poets referred to coitus, actually separates individuals just as much as it unites them. To describe ecstatic coitus as union therefore fails to capture the entire experience. Instead, it is a momentary union leading to an equivalent, equally momentary extinction. This process reverses, and greatly condenses, that of being born.

Being born involves emerging from nonexistence into an extended state of unity with the mother before existence as a separate individual occurs. Birth eventuates in selfhood; coitus, carried to the point of ecstasy, results in momentary selflessness. Consequently, to say precisely what happens or where ecstasy takes place, or where it takes any given set of lovers is not possible. The "what" of ecstasy is mystical, hence incapable of precise description. But when ecstasy occurs intensely enough, lovers are known to black out. A model for this kind of "union" might therefore more appropriately be drawn from sleep.

A woman may say to her lover, "Let's dream the same dream tonight so that we can stay together while we're sleeping." But while she may say and wish it, she cannot actually make it happen. Somewhat similarly, when her lover and she "merge" in coitus, they simultaneously fall into their own, necessarily separate, ecstasies. The union they experience when they are out of themselves can take place because their bodies have merged as closely as two separate bodies can. But the union *itself* is also a dissolution. As such, it takes each lover beyond individual ego consciousness. But what it unites them with is not precisely the other person. It is variously nowhere, or unconsciousness. This can be thought of as the realm of Hades. If a woman is unconscious and her lover is unconscious, they are "dead." Certainly they are not exactly one. Instead, each has been taken to a separate, private world.

Understanding this situation is especially important for a woman trying to examine the nature of motherselfhood because coitus traditionally embodies the ideal for selves trying to dissolve in union. That model is all well and good, but it is unevenly applied. In patriarchal thinking, women are often chided for existing in precisely this condition of relational selfhood. One of the "problems" attributed to women by patriarchal psychology is that we are thought not to develop selves sufficiently separate from those of our mothers and subsequently our lovers. That is to say, we are faulted for developing a kind of selfhood which exactly reverses that of motherselfhood, so necessary in our role of mother. Yet at the same time, women are brought up believing that our deepest needs for selfhood can *only* be satisfied by passively accepting union with a strong, "rescuing" male to whom we now relate as once we did to our own mother. The patriarchal ideal for what we "should" be therefore reflects an internal inconsistency that places us in a double bind. If we do not exhibit the kind of separately individuated selfhood the hero represents, then in the world of heroes we are faulted for insufficient selfhood. At the same time, if we do not privately succumb (licitly) to the repeated "ecstasy" implied by a permanent sexual relationship, we are faulted for betraying our "passive," "dependent," "feminine" nature.

Sexual union, pushed as a desirable goal for salvation, is therefore yet another way patriarchal ideology shapes a woman to the image of its desire. Taught that sexual intercourse is the means by which this supposedly desirable union occurs, a woman often craves it. (She will presumably crave it also for biological reasons, but those reasons are legitimately gynocentric, not androcentrically imposed.) Sex, not for what it is in and of itself, but for what she has been taught that it is—salvation from her problems, a kind of drug or panacea—will surely lead her to the "salvation" she longs for. Only if she dares look long and hard into her self does she realize that *she,* not sex, not the hero, nor even union with the hero, is the genuine salvation she seeks. This is a hard lesson for a woman to learn.

Even Persephone repeatedly has to relearn this lesson that sex is not salvation for a woman in the way patriarchy teaches that it is, for in the ignorance of her youth she tasted of the fruit of her lover's realm. Consequently, she finds herself evermore lured back there. The attraction of ecstasy is too strong to resist. No matter that she spends most of her time on earth in the light of her own gynocentric space. She is still drawn back irresistibly time and again by the promise that heterosexual love will "save" her. If it is herself a woman wants to be "saved" from, yes, sexual ecstasy may work. But if it is herself she wants to save, sexual union rarely accomplishes this promise.

By no means does the lesson of Persephone suggest that sexual intercourse is something a woman engaged in the quest for motherselfhood should avoid. Far from it. A woman can scarcely follow the way of the mother without it. What Persphone does allow a woman to see, however, is the pernicious *meaning* frequently attached to sexual intercourse from a patriarchal perspective. This is the belief that sex can "save" a woman. Believing that this is so often leads a woman into great danger.

Deluded by this belief she may actually engage in and maintain a relationship harmful to her. Or she may become a love junkie addicted to multiple relationships, convinced that her new lover is the rescuing hero no previous lover could match. Instead of assuming responsibility for her own problems, she looks to sex and the lover who provides it to "rescue" her. As long as she operates on the basis of this belief she remains in the underworld realm of Hades. But if, like Persephone, she is able to escape to the light of day in her own space, she can gain sufficient distance from this patriarchal mystique to understand that ultimately only *she* can save herself.

Yet Persephone also teaches something else: She does not give up on sex or her lover—she simply views both realistically. She neither rejects men nor remains subject to them and the allure of sexuality they represent. Instead, she maintains a balance between the two worlds, always reasserting the primacy of her own gynocentric space for herself. This is the secret the story of Persephone can teach a woman trying to decide whether or not to follow the often perilous way of the mother: A woman need not give up her own space; in fact, she should not do so in her quest for motherselfhood.

Having come this far, a woman must now take the next step along the way of the mother: She must learn what it means to experience the ordeal of pregnancy.

PART III

Ordeals

CHAPTER 13.

Pregnancy

"Reproduction is not just a handicap and a cause of second-class status; it is an achievement, *the* authentic achievement of women."[1]

Traditionally the hero is tested in various ways before he can complete his quest. He may be given an impossible task such as finding the water of life, or he may be asked a seemingly unanswerable question like that posed to Oedipus by the Sphinx. The counterpart to such ordeals within the way of the mother most often occurs during pregnancy.

This view of pregnancy as ordeal is well expressed in the words of the narrator of Marilyn French's *The Women's Room:*

> Pregnancy is a long waiting in which you learn what it means completely to lose control over your life. There are no coffee breaks, no days off in which you regain your normal shape and self, and can return refreshed to your labors. You can't wish away even for an hour the thing that is swelling you up, stretching your stomach until the skin feels as if it will burst, kicking you from the inside until you are black and blue. You can't even hit back without hurting yourself. The condition and you are identical: you are no longer a person, but a pregnancy. . . . You look forward even to the pain of labor because it will end the waiting.[2]

On the other hand, pleasurable anticipation of the baby may, over the course of nine months, outweigh anxiety at the present responsibility the gift of pregnancy entails. This is particularly likely if the baby results from a truly joyful sexual communion: "With all the pain of it, I long for the wonderful thing to happen, for a tiny human creature to spring from between my limbs bravely out into the world. I need it, just as a true poet *needs* to create a great undying work."[3] More often, however, the attitude of a pregnant woman falls between these two extremes of abhorrence and joy, reflecting her anticipation, on the one hand, her feelings of apprehension and insufficiency, on the other: "If I could only *feel* the child! I imagine the moment of its quickening as a sudden awakening of my own being which has never before had life. I want to *live* with the child, and I am as heavy as a stone."[4]

The way a woman conceptualizes her pregnancy is critical to this time of testing. For some women being pregnant feels like the natural condition of woman. Such women may even consider pregnancy, as opposed to the baby, an end in itself. Slowly growing larger and clumsier feels positive. This is the way she *should* feel. She scarcely minds when her ankles swell. Even when the baby grows so large it pushes against her diaphragm she barely complains. She is one of the lucky ones for whom pregnancy fulfills her sense of self. In this state, she has achieved a condition she has been waiting for all her life. It makes her joyful. Mary, a highly maternal woman in Anne Tyler's novel *Celestial Navigation,* exemplifies this attitude: "Motherhood is what I was made for, and pregnancy is my natural state. I believe that. All the time I was carrying Darcy I was happier than I had ever been before, and I felt better. And looked better. At least, to myself I did."[5] But a serious question must be asked about such a woman. Is her joyful attitude authentically her own response? Or is it a response she makes because patriarchal thought tells women we "should" be mothers, that motherhood is our true function, destiny, and highest fulfillment in life?

A woman taught, as women in most cultures worldwide traditionally have been, to obey and to please others, particularly men, may not know what she genuinely feels. She can far more easily identify what she has consistently been told she *must* feel. Therefore all the "joy," "naturalness," and "rightness" of her pregnancy may be false emotions. She may just assume she *should* feel that way. Consequently she assumes that she actually does. On the other hand, a woman who has always doubted tales of "the joys of motherhood" can probably assume that any joy she feels is genuinely her own.

In contrast to the woman who experiences pregnancy as a fulfilling, joyous event is the woman who feels it, instead, as a liminal state: As a liminal state, her pregnancy places her outside both heroselfhood and motherselfhood. Pregnancy experienced this way is not a fully satisfying state in and of itself. Such an experience of pregnancy feels very different from its joyful counterpart. In a liminal state a woman is no one, existing nowhere. She is not sexy, not slim, not really a person. She is more like a cow or some odd-shaped, nameless creature. Feeling that she is neither this nor that, she cannot wait to be "herself" again. This "thing" inside bothers her. It is something foreign to her, not herself at all. And when it quickens she feels extremely squeamish: Something is moving *inside* her. She cannot help but imagine a small, furry, vicious animal caught there. This imagined feeling makes her body alien. It locates her sense of "self" somewhere else. If she is not this pregnant cow, this bloated creature with the small kicking animal trapped inside it, *she* must be something else.

This way of thinking makes a woman's body something other than her "self," and so her pregnancy comes to seem like an alien experience, an illness, rather than a natural part of a woman's life. Pregnancy is something unnatural happening, but it is not happening precisely to her*self*. She feels separated from herself as she grows heavier and heavier. Even if she manages to hold her weight down, she feels heavy. Her stomach pulls her down, down, down. Her back aches; her legs swell. Sometimes the pain in her chest from the baby's pushing up against her diaphragm constricts her so intensely that she cannot lie down. Instead she must sit the night out in a chair, propped by pillows in order to breathe. Much more of this discomfort and she will cease to exist. Whatever she thinks of as her "self" will be completely swallowed up by this dreadful pregnancy.

Rather than living in the present time, accepting her condition of pregnancy, a woman may dissociate herself from the whole messy affair. When she does so, she actually misses a part of her life. This phenomenon of an individual missing out on her actual life by escaping to another, not her own, commonly characterizes fairy tales. There it is known as "the supernatural passage of time." Italo Calvino presents a fine example of this motif in his translation of an Italian folktale called "One Night in Paradise."[6] The tale centers on two young men who pledge that no matter what, the first to marry will choose the other for his best man. But just before one friend marries, the other dies. The groom, undeterred, calls his friend back from the grave. The dead man immediately jumps out to perform his promised role. In so doing he reveals nothing about life in the next world. Throughout the day the groom, avid for information about his friend's new existence, dares not enquire. Just as the dead man readies himself to jump back into his grave, however, the groom nerves himself to ask. Thereupon the dead man invites him to see for himself. After viewing only some of the many marvels of Paradise the groom suddenly recalls his bride. Upon his return to earth, he finds himself not in the town he left but in an entirely strange city. The bishop recalls vaguely the tale of a groom who disappointed his bride some three hundred years ago by jumping into his friend's grave on his wedding day. Hearing these words, the groom dies on the spot.

For the groom in this story, curiosity about the hereafter ostensibly causes him to miss living his own life. Yet the tale can be interpreted another way. It also dramatizes a reluctant bridegroom's avoidance of his "real" life—marriage—in favor of continued male fraternity. Similarly, an expectant woman may so dissociate herself from her pregnancy that she misses this important time of her life. It is as if pregnancy were not actually happening at all. Her reasons for such dissociation may not relate simply to physical discomfort.

When a woman is pregnant, other people looking at her think she embodies the essence of femininity. After all, there she is, a visible reminder of the primary purpose of sexuality. Her skin glows and her breasts enlarge. Yet she also grows heavier and her belly protrudes ever more awkwardly. In contemporary Western culture such heaviness is seldom regarded as sexy. During pregnancy, as throughout motherhood, elements of the familiar virgin/mother/whore triad militate against any associations with sexuality. Expectant women and mothers are not "supposed" to be sexy. A woman who thinks this way and feels her very being threatened by existing as a "nonsexual creature" can scarcely find pregnancy rewarding. Rather it will be a condition to be gotten through as quickly as possible.

But if a woman experiences pregnancy as a condition positive in its own right, without considering potential male devaluations of her sexiness, it becomes an extremely meaningful part of her life. In this case the day-to-day changes she experiences assume the kind of importance that the stages of a male hero's quest traditionally have done.

From deep within herself she may feel awed by what is happening. "Here is life. I feel it moving inside myself. Something within me is pushing, pushing, expanding the very configuration of my body. Where I was flat, now I am convex. The baby is exerting pressure against me. I watch: My body accommodates, slowly, slowly stretching to allow for this other human being inside me. And look how my breasts, anticipating my infant's needs, have likewise expanded. I look in wonder at what my body is doing: One egg and one seed—just one of each—and all these physiological changes are taking place. And it is *my* body which is letting it all happen! As I watch, the baby kicks. I can even see the outline of a foot or a leg. I watch as my belly changes shape, the way a field of grain ripples in the wind."

The quality of interiority, so central to the entire way of the mother, particularly marks this stage. As mother-to-be, a woman is the one whose body moves, stretches, conforms to the shape of the embryo inside her. She is the one who responds to the needs of that inner creature. She brings it forth when the time is right, her body expelling it from her womb into the world outside herself. There it, too, must now exist, as a separate individual in its own right. Her body; *her* body, has permitted all these changes.

Whatever a woman's attitude, certain well-recognized signs indicate her approaching transformation. She may feel some nausea, swelling of the breasts, and general malaise. The lack of the sign of blood, however, most clearly identifies her condition. Usually it is not until she misses her period that she truly recognizes her changing state for what it is. Though she may ignore one such miss, she cannot deny the significance of two. At that point she can choose: She must now either accept as definitive this call to motherhood or seek unequivocally to refuse it.

If a woman chooses to accept her suspected call to motherhood, her first task, after spotting the appropriate signs and guessing that she is pregnant, is to call a doctor. Even if pregnancy delights, seeing the doctor may alarm her as she contemplates the pelvic examination awaiting her. If she is young and newly married, she may have had only one such exam before. Perhaps recalling it makes her shudder. If her doctor is male, going to him may cause her deep pain. Once again she must place herself in a position of inferiority to a man. Who can help feeling humiliated, lying feet up and spread apart in stirrups, vulva exposed to view? Trussed like a chicken, she must allow him to poke and prod her insides at will.

Gathering courage, she will arrive on the appointed morning. Perhaps she has forgotten that others will be here too. Seated beneath a Kathe Kollwitz mother-and-child reproduction, she sees other women in various stages of pregnancy. One has a belly so large that it will surely burst. Either that or the woman will deliver on the spot. That grotesquely protruding belly suggests that late pregnancy may hurt. That thought hadn't occurred to her before. So thinking, she averts her eyes. Is it fear, loathing, or deference to the stranger's right to privacy that makes her do so? Not everyone here is visibly pregnant. Perhaps some are waiting for other reasons? Can they tell why she is here? She may not know yet what she wants the world to think.

"Mrs. Hatfield." She puts down, unread, a copy of *Time* magazine to follow the nurse down the narrow hallway. "And how are we this morning? Let's see, it's Julie, isn't it? Take this cup and give me a urine specimen. Remove all your clothes. Slip into this gown leaving the opening in front. When you're done, open the door and go into room A."

She feels herself shaking. From her armpits cold sweat drips. From afar she seems to be watching herself perform her nurse-assigned tasks. That was bad, but it is even worse on the table. Feet in stirrups, legs wide apart, she winces as the obstetrician, briefly introduced by the nurse, pokes hard. It hurts. That awful, cold metal thing: Why can't it be warmed first? And why a rectal? And a blood test? With each new intrusion of fingers or steel her humanity shrivels a bit more. Like the hero whose ordeal transforms him to stone, she feels immobilized. Yet for the sake of her unborn baby she must—she tells herself—submit to these indignities.

She may leave the doctor's office unsure how she feels despite the physician's best efforts to reassure her. This is but the first of many, many such visits. Now once a month, soon twice, eventually once a week she must return. She sighs, not at all ready to accept what lies ahead.

If a woman is lucky, of course, she will be able to choose from a variety of medical practitioners. She may opt for a midwife or a woman physician, choices now readily available in most communities in Western cultures. Just having such choices gives her some control over what is properly her own function.

Some women, however, instead of actively participating in their prenatal care, choose not to acknowledge their pregnancies at all. Instead of consulting any sort of medical personnel, a woman who refuses the call may deny her symptoms completely. In Anne Tyler's novel *Morgan's Passing,* a married woman realizes with horror that her lover may have impregnated her:

> "I am seventeen days overdue. . . . Of course, it could be a false alarm. . . . I'm not the slightest bit morning sick. And I would be, don't you think? I was terribly sick with Gina."[7]

Such a woman may act as if she were merely gaining weight. Refusing to wear maternity clothes, she simply puts on larger sizes of regular wear. When it is time to deliver she may allow herself suddenly to give birth at home or be rushed to the hospital for a "totally unsuspected birth," as happens to a character in another of Anne Tyler's novels, *Earthly Possessions:*

> . . . she got fatter and fatter, and had more trouble moving around. She tilted at each step, holding herself carefully like a very full jug of water. She grew listless, developed indigestion, felt short of breath, and started going through the Change. She was certain she had a tumor but would not see a doctor; only took Carter's Little Liver Pills, her remedy for everything.
> One night she woke up with abdominal spasms and became convinced that the tumor (which she seemed to picture as a sort of overripe grapefruit) had split open and was trying to pass. All around her the bed was hot and wet. She woke her husband, who stumbled into his trousers and drove her to the hospital. Half an hour later, she gave birth to a six-pound baby girl.[8]

An extreme variant of this situation occurs when a woman going to the toilet "discovers" she is having not a bowel movement but a baby.

For the woman who chooses to deny pregnancy, absence of blood brings no joy, only terror. Every hour on the hour after her twenty-eighth day she dashes to the bathroom, imagining the surge of hot blood. Having occasionally been late by as much as three days she is not yet *too* concerned. "Dear God," she prays, "Please: if only you don't let me be pregnant, I'll never do it again." Surely low in her back and pelvis she feels the familiar dull pressure of impending menstruation. That must be what aches now. But no, it is only her imagination.

In its most extreme form, passive denial of pregnancy becomes active rejection. Abortion results. The woman who chooses abortion has traditionally been castigated for her choice. As the increasingly militant behavior of antiabortionists in the United States attests, opprobrium still attaches to that decision for many women. In a patriarchal context the issue invariably focuses on the rights of the fetus and its presumed "personhood." By this reasoning the mother recedes into the background; she is merely a vessel for containing life. But turned around and viewed from the woman's point of view, this issue involves a choice between two totally different kinds of self. When a woman chooses to abort, her major concern is "saving" her own life. To bring into the world another life when she may not even be sure she can handle her own seems irresponsible. She is trying to nurture the kind of unitary self that the figure of the hero typically represents. She is not yet ready for the very different demands that the binary-unitary selfhood of motherhood requires. Until a woman is ready for it, motherselfhood appears horrifying. Undeniably it militates against the unitary self, sometimes even "killing" it.

A seldom-drawn parallel helps clarify this aspect of a gynocentric perspective on abortion. A man is walking down a street late one evening. Suddenly, from out of the shadows a stranger jumps him. The victim considers himself well within his rights to punch his assailant hard. Even if the mugger falls to the pavement and cracks his head, the intended victim feels justified. He is simply acting in self-defense. By his action he protects himself from the kind of potential catastrophic change in selfhood that severe bodily harm or death would occasion. Why should he hold back, risking his own present selfhood in favor of that of his attacker? Of course he should save himself even though he may actually kill the strange man in the process.

A young woman who wishes to abort may feel herself "threatened" by a future child in much the same way. Perhaps she is a young woman like Delia, almost eighteen, about to graduate from high school. Delia plans to attend a select college before going on to medical school. Until she met David, she rarely dated. "But David was special. I never planned to go all the way. I don't think he did either. It just happened. We were watching television at my house. Mom was out and. . . ."[9]

Delia could have the baby, of course, and give it up for adoption. "But that would mean telling Mom and Dad. It would kill them. Maybe they wouldn't even let me go on to college. In that case I might as well have the baby and keep it. I simply can't tell them. I don't know how I'm ever going to make all the necessary arrangements though." Delia says she will go to anyone, anyone at all, just to terminate her pregnancy.

What could a girl like Delia do with a baby at her age? What would happen to her? To it? She could never support it. She readily admits that "much as I thought I loved David before, now I know that I don't really want to *marry* him. And no one I have ever known lives on welfare. That simply isn't a possibility for me." She says that if she closes her eyes she sees herself living "in one tiny room with a camp cot in it, a crib, and a hot plate. That's all. Roaches crunch under my feet every time I walk across the room. And there are mice, too. I hear them in the walls. Once in a while I even see one." She shudders. "And the walls are peeling and cracking. A large stain covers part of the pink and white wallpaper in one corner. I'm only seventeen. How can anyone ask me to give up my whole life? I might as well be dead as live like that."

Her name might be Tina or Margaret or Patsy, her age anywhere from twelve to fifty, her skin any color. No matter. If she chooses to abort she is choosing to retain one kind of self while saying no to a very different one. She wants to actualize dreams of her own on her own behalf, not to postpone them in favor of living vicariously for a number of years. If she is young like Delia she wants some life now. If she is fortyish, married, already a mother of several grown children, like Tina, she wants to consider her own needs for a change.

On the other hand, she could be even younger than Delia and feel quite differently. She could be Judy, a striking fourteen-year-old from an abusive family, who has been sexually active since she was twelve.[10] Judy not only does poorly in school, she hates living at home. As she sees it, a baby will rescue her from both. A baby all her own, she insists, will love her. She can play with it, change it, feed it, and take it out in a stroller on nice days. Welfare will provide for them both, so she won't have to work. For Judy no true call exists. She just imagines it does. In a year when her baby is running her ragged by crawling and walking into everything, while her friends are all talking of their dates, she may begin to understand this fact. Right now, however, motherhood is nothing but love and games to her.

The woman who, unlike Judy, feels compelled to choose abortion, seldom experiences it lightly. Despite frequent rhetoric to the contrary, few women see abortion as easy birth control. Rather, it is a kind of amputation. Abortion removes something whose existence simultaneously threatens yet forms a new part of a woman's very selfhood: "She had deliberately not counted the months but she must have been counting them unawares, must have been keeping a relentless count somewhere, because this was the day, the day the baby would have been born."[11]

Such pain over the baby who might have been receives no ritual recognition in our culture. But in Japan a very different attitude prevails. Instead of demonizing abortion and stigmatizing women who choose it as does the Judeo-Christian tradition, Japanese Buddhism recognizes abortion as a deeply disturbing part of some women's lives. To help a woman acknowledge her anguish over choosing not to bear a child who might have been, common practice permits her to place a special statue at a shrine. This statue represents Jizo, a Buddhist bodhisattva especially dedicated to the care of children's souls. Such statues commemorating dead fetuses may range in size from a few inches to about a foot. They resemble abstract human forms lacking specific features. Rows and rows of them stand at shrines, rather like gravestones in a cemetery. Placing one of these figures in its appropriate setting allows a woman to acknowledge in ritual a painful experience that our own culture largely passes over in silence once the abortion has been performed.

Gail Godwin dramatizes the deep anguish that abortion typically causes a woman in our culture through her character Cate Strickland Galitsky in *A Mother and Two Daughters*. Twice married and twice divorced, the fortyish Cate displays the kind of profound pain such "amputation" occasions as she tells her sister about her experience:

> "I had an abortion. Don't ever have one if you can help it. Not that I regret my choice. I think it's every woman's right to have the choice. But just try to be careful so you won't have to make the choice. Though, God knows, I thought I *was* being careful, . . . It hurt my soul more than it did my body. And I don't mean that in any religious sense. I mean it just hurt my soul deep down."[12]

Besides coping with the pain she feels inside herself a woman may also have to fend off challenges from others. For Cate that challenge comes in the form of a woman who follows her from the clinic to talk her out of the abortion:

"She'd pick out a likely candidate, and then follow her out on the street and introduce herself as a sort of liaison lady of the clinic who volunteered to answer any *questions* you might have about . . . what you were going to go through the next day. . . . I couldn't resist asking her what motivated a woman like herself to do what she did. She explained to me, in her pleasant, well-modulated voice, that she'd had a religious experience the day of her miscarriage. When she'd gone to the bathroom to stanch the flow of blood, a perfectly formed little baby about the size of a mouse had dropped into her pants. She washed the blood off and was just cradling it in her hands, marveling at all its fully formed parts, when . . . IT SPOKE TO HER. According to her, it said, *'It's too late to save me, Mother. But save the others.'*"[13]

To have to counter gratuitous advice of this sort from self-appointed spokespersons of God makes the ordeal of abortion just that much more painful.

As full of despair as the woman who chooses abortion is the one whose story almost exactly reverses hers, the woman who spontaneously aborts. Instead of rushing to the toilet fearful of finding no blood, she rushes there afraid that she will. Each extra day increases hope. But always, always something happens. "What is wrong with me?" she wonders, sure that if she only knew the right secret she could manage to bear a live child. She longs to experience the condition so many of her sisters abhor. She would love to become ever larger and larger as the months of her pregnancy unfold. Strangely, only recently has the depth of the kind of loss this woman endures been fully realized:

> Recognition that a pregnancy loss is as much a form of bereavement as is any other death, and that it must be mourned, is recent. In the past, miscarriage, ectopic pregnancy (in which the ovum develops outside the uterus), stillbirth and even relinquishing a baby to adoption were treated as incidents to be quickly forgotten.
>
> That attitude typified the personal experience of Dr. Robert J. Echenberg, an obstetrician and gynecologist in Bethlehem, Pa., who is medical consultant to a support group for families that have suffered such losses. "I did not know until I was in my teens that I had an older sister who was either stillborn or died after birth," he said. "No one ever talked about it. A few months ago, I learned that my grandmother still lights a candle for that child."[14]

Occasionally such loss proves more than a woman can bear. Something inside her refuses to accept the actuality of her situation, and in compensation, she creates a surrogate child. A poignant example of this phenomenon occurs in Gail Godwin's short story, "Dream Children." The nameless protagonist, who has recently lost a child during childbirth, "meets" a "dream child" almost every weekday evening when her commuting husband is away in the city. She believes that the child's dreamlife brings him to her:

> He always wore the same pajamas, a shade too big, but always clean. Obviously washed again and again in a machine that went through its cycles frequently. She imagined his "other mother," a harassed woman with several children, short on money, on time, on dreams—all the things she herself had too much of. The family lived, she believed, somewhere in Florida, probably on the west coast. . . . They never spoke or touched. She was not sure how much of this he understood. . . . Perhaps he never remembered afterward, when he woke up . . . in a roomful of brothers and sisters. . . . He loved her. She knew that. Even if he never remembered her in his other life. [15]

Not surprisingly, a woman so afflicted, or one who is barren, is unlikely to sympathize with the complaints of her fertile counterparts. How she wishes to look like they do, feel those internal pressures, have shapeless, swollen ankles, worry about her weight. She would sell her soul to carry a live baby to term.

It may take years, but eventually, if the call to motherhood persists strongly enough, the infertile woman may adopt. While not precisely the same entry to the way of the mother as pregnancy and childbirth, adoption too is a process, an ordeal. Instead of frantic calls to the doctor, her ordeal necessitates making them to the adoption agency. Rather than endless pushings, pokings, and probings at her genitals and abdomen she must endure thrusts by strangers into the intimate details of her life. Is she married? Do she and her husband attend church or temple? How much money do they earn? Has either of them ever been arrested? How old are they? The list of questions unfolds endlessly. By the time she finishes with the caseworker's repeated visits she is exhausted and a little bitter. "They would never interfere this way with even the least qualified 'natural' mother," she complains to her husband. "Why must *we* be so minutely scrutinized? Is it a sin to be infertile?"

Whether a longed-for baby comes through natural procreation, adoption, or some form of artificial insemination, probably no ordeal of the mother's way provokes so much anxiety as waiting for it to arrive. Prior to this time, a contemporary Western woman will ordinarily have lived much like her male peers, her selfhood that of the woman who attempts the quest of the hero. Statistically, like many males in the West, she will have completed high school. She is even slightly more likely than they to have attended college. Like them, she will probably have worked outside the home at least for a while. With the time of waiting for her baby, however, she enters a totally new phase of her existence in which she is apt to question much that she once took for granted. The self she has always been will be irrevocably changed once the baby comes. She will never be exactly the same self she has previously taken for granted she is. She will be a new self entirely, a motherself. Besides the physical changes effected in her body over these nine months, emotional, mental, and spiritual changes will take place as well. As a function of these other, nonphysical aspects of pregnancy, a woman typically finds herself reassessing her values, her life, her sense of herself as a woman. Such questioning constitutes one of the major ordeals of a woman progressing along the way of the mother.

CHAPTER 14.

Womansins

> "While I was walking through that
> crowd with the policeman, I kept think-
> ing of my name: Evie Decker, *me*. Taking
> something into my own hands for once. I
> thought, if I had started acting like this a
> long time ago my whole *life* might've
> been different."
>
> —ANNE TYLER, *A Slipping-Down Life*

Those for whom access to the mother's way occurs without struggle may miss the point that it is a gift, seeing in pregnancy not grace but doom, even damnation. While gifts are generally construed as gains, some place on the recipients an obligation so heavy that the gift becomes a burden. To be given either kingship or motherhood is frequently just such an ambivalent gift. Pregnancy is often felt as one of the major ordeals for a woman following the way of the mother. As such, it is a counterpart of various difficult tasks required of the hero on his quest: retrieving the plant of immortality from the underworld, spinning straw into gold, disenchanting the paralyzed victims of the wicked witch.

Pregnancy may be experienced negatively because it challenges a woman's very sense of identity. Suddenly now she wonders not just who she is but who she will become. What sort of mother will she be to what sort of child? She has time, over the course of nine months, for judgmental self-interrogation in a way she would not have if childbirth more closely followed impregnation. This nine-month period allows her to focus on such issues if she takes the time and chooses to do so. Of course, she may decide instead to continue her previous schedule as if no major life change were occurring. In that case, she misses a valuable, naturally built-in time period in which to assist in her own self-transformation. For the woman who does avail herself of this opportunity, pregnancy is a particularly apppropriate time to confront the issues of womanhood to which it so obviously relates. This inner aspect of the ordeal of pregnancy may begin like this. A disturbing voice may tell her such things as: "Women are inferior to men; women don't try as hard; women are less intelligent than men; women are silly; women are more emotional than men; women are irrational; women are more neurotic than men; women are not trustworthy; all women want is a good lay; women in power are more tyrannical than men; women don't make good team players; women who get ahead sleep their way up; women belong at home."

Then the testing voice may ask, "To what extent are you, too, guilty of thinking in such stereotypes? Do you not sometimes make a special case for yourself? Do you not sometimes see some other women as guilty of incarnating those negative images, separating yourself out as 'the special one,' the privileged exception that makes you queen bee?"

A woman at this stage of the mother's way may find such internal questioning extremely discomforting. Where has she felt this same kind of unease before? Perhaps years ago, when preparing for Holy Communion, no matter how carefully she had confessed, she always felt sinful. And that is how she feels now. Hearing this voice makes her wonder if the androcentric "virtues" might not be gynocentric "sins."

Religionist Valerie Saiving was the first to deal with such "womansins." In an essay dating from 1960, "The Human Situation: A Feminine View," she points out that "the temptations of woman *as woman* are not the same as the temptations of man *as man*."[1] The sins of pride and will-to-power, so characteristic of patriarchal males, fall in a very different category from those more typical of women. The womansins she singles out are "triviality, distractibility, and diffuseness; lack of an organizing center or focus; dependence on others for one's own self-definition; tolerance at the expense of standards of excellence; inability to respect the boundaries of privacy; sentimentality, gossipy sociability, and mistrust of reason—in short, underdevelopment or negation of the self."[2]

Developing the rich potential of Saiving's essay, Judith Plaskow expounds it further, along a sin/grace axis.[3] Plaskow explicitly demands change in traditional patriarchal theology to acknowledge women's very different experience. She is careful to stipulate that she is writing about woman's experience out of white, Western, middle-class life. Besides shaping her own perspective, these qualities also color the ideas of the two seminal male theologians against whom she plays off her ideas, Paul Tillich and Reinhold Niebuhr. Plaskow carefully analyzes the aspects of human experience that Tillich and Niebuhr choose to develop in their respective theologies. Both choose exactly those qualities more commonly associated with men than with women in our society. Aspects they either ignore or regard as secondary are more typical of women. Plaskow grants the universal applicability of Tillich's ontological definition of sin as aliena- tion. She points out, however, that once Tillich leaves the level of highly abstract language to illustrate his contention, his examples more fully reflect men's than women's experience. As for Niebuhr, Plaskow counters his view that sin is always an active turning away from god toward self. This view ignores a sin common to many women: Women more fre- quently turn away from *both* God and self. To call this kind of turning away by the traditional word "pride" does not appropriately name the sin.

In my own thinking I have previously worded the problem of wom- ansin somewhat differently. Near the close of *The Sacred and the Feminine,* I quote this Hasidic parable:

> Before his death, Rabbi Zusya said "In the coming world, they will not ask me: 'Why were you not Moses?' They will ask me: 'Why were you not Zusya?'"[4]

For too long women have followed a pattern of trying to be "Moses" instead of "Zusya." Womansins are the various ways we fail our own particular "Zusyahood." We must wrestle with our particular sins of avoiding authentically gynocentric selfhood by first recognizing them, then admitting them, and finally trying to stop committing them. Within the way of the mother this struggle complements the period of testing integral to the quest of the hero.

Of all the ways of avoiding authentic gynocentric selfhood, one particular womansin dominates at all stages of the way. Many women allow their lives to be mediated rather than living them immediately in their own right. This mediated fashion of living assumes two forms. In one a woman allows patriarchal norms in general and her own spouse in particular to dictate her behavior. In the other she "lives" her life through her children. Both forms indirectly, but severely, harm human life. In the first case the woman primarily victimizes herself, although secondarily and indirectly her spouse also suffers. In the second, her children may suffer more. Both forms of mediated life negatively reflect patriarchal injunctions to women to "obey" men, particularly fathers, brothers, husbands, and sons. To ask permission for every act of life is to avoid direct responsibility for it. To allow others to control her like this is to enact the Nuremburg syndrome: "I was just obeying orders."

If at the end of her life a woman thinks, "I never had a chance to go back to school; I never took a job outside the home; I never dared ask if I could go to Europe with my church group because I knew 'he' wouldn't let me," then she sins doubly. She first sins by not finding a way to do those desired things; she again sins in blaming "him." This does not mean that a woman "sins" if she fails to actualize every single desire. But certain wishes call to a particular woman so persistently, ultimately matter so deeply to her, that she must heed and try to realize them.

Amy's experience is pertinent. Amy is a highly intelligent, elderly woman who constantly bemoans her interrupted high-school career.[5] After her junior year, her father made her work full-time to help the family. Undeniably, in those Depression days, the daughter of an impoverished immigrant family had little choice. To defy her father would have been to risk banishment from her family. This was almost unthinkable for a "good girl" in those days. But what is hard to understand is Amy's refusal to earn a high-school equivalency diploma in adulthood. Once her own children were grown she could easily have done so without disrupting her household routine. At that point, however, she excused herself by saying that her husband would not like it. But what would happen just because he did not like it? Would he throw her out after thirty-five years of faithful marriage? If so, is he really the kind of man with whom she wants to share her remaining years? Surely Amy is sinning deeply against her own deepest self in not fulfilling this aspect of her life.

In talking to Amy one repeatedly confronts a wall whose erection (the metaphor is intentional) is incomprehensible. When asked, "Why don't you get your diploma now?" she invariably replies, "It's too late for me now. I didn't know any better." That answer is baffling. Why does she not say, "I will begin it today"?

Amy's case typifies the failure of many women who refuse to become Zusyas. So many women's desires are not impossible, do not demand tremendous sacrifices on the part of others, would not profoundly alter the existing patriarchal system whose imagined collapse so terrifies many individuals of both sexes.

A coda must be appended to this discussion of the sin of not assuming responsibility for fulfilling one's own desires and needs. This coda develops the theme of blaming others when one's own desires and needs remain unsatisfied. In Amy's case, she still speaks bitterly of her father's unchallenged decision to yank her out of high school just one year short of graduation. Other, more subtle kinds of blaming as a cover for abdicating responsibility trap countless more women. How often does a woman find herself at loose ends? Perhaps going out would alleviate her boredom. But she does not know exactly what she wants. She says to her husband, "Pick something for us to do." He, not knowing any more than she does what would please her at this moment, chooses what would please him, perhaps a movie. While his wife still does not know what it is she does want, she definitely knows that sitting in the dark without speaking for two hours is not it. She may either go to the movie and then complain later, or she may complain now. Either way, she is blaming someone else for her own inability to figure out what *she* wants.

In this same cluster of sins in which a woman fails to realize her full gynocentric selfhood falls self-deprecation—that is, putting oneself down—and not taking oneself seriously. Sinners in this category are often heard to say, "Oh, I don't do anything; I'm just a housewife." If they do have either vocation or avocation, as most individuals do, they may speak of either almost as deprecatingly. Claudia illustrates this point perfectly. She is a woman who was unable to attend art school at eighteen as she longed to do because her father refused to subsidize anything but a traditional liberal arts education. Unlike Amy, however, Claudia finally did fulfill her educational dream once her last child entered junior high school. She even continued beyond her undergraduate degree to earn an M.F.A. as well. Because she was such an outstanding student, she was asked to teach a course following her graduation. Meanwhile, she had won several fellowships and exhibited works in numerous juried competitions. Yet when asked what she does, she replies, "Oh, I'm just an adjunct." And this is a woman aware of women's issues!

Another common womansin is asking permission of one's husband before venturing anything even slightly out of the ordinary. Undeniably, common courtesy suggests that anyone living closely with others should alert living companions, including children, as to their general where-abouts. But that is not the same as repeatedly asking, "May I?" Although this same trait is not sex-specific, it is far less common to hear a man ask his wife, "May I attend a trustees' meeting this evening?" than to hear it from a woman. Possibly early distinctions in etiquette for girls and boys cause some of this difference. If so, such permission-asking is simply an exter-nalized code for masking patriarchal dominance with something called "politeness."

Perhaps no womansin is quite so harmful as that of allowing another person to turn oneself into an object. This is not exclusively a womansin. It happens whenever a culturally dominant individual sees a culturally de-fined "inferior." The "superior" person seldom sees his "inferior" as a fully human being like himself. Instead of seeing before him another person whom he would naturally address as "you," he sees an "it." If the cultural definitions of "superiority" and "inferiority" are strongly embedded in both individuals, the "inferior" may then see herself through the "supe-rior's" eyes, rather than through her own. In the case of a womansin, the participants will necessarily involve a woman vis-à-vis a man. The woman now becomes an object not just to him but to herself as well. Her dehumanization is therefore twofold. It is occasioned first at his instigation, then again through her own collaboration in the process. She may not even realize that it is occurring. It happens something like this: Anna is at home one morning writing to friends.[6] Unexpectedly the doorbell rings. She groans. Unwashed breakfast dishes dirty the kitchen table and last night's paper, unemptied ashtrays, and snack trays clutter the living room. Worse, she herself still wears her nightgown and slippers. Uncomfortably aware of these factors, she opens the door. There stands Mr. Amoretto, her dishwasher repairman. As he looks at her, she "sees" what he sees: a slovenly housewife lounging around doing no work. The more she sees what he sees, the more her own will dissolves. Instead of resuming her interrupted letter writing, she begins cleaning the kitchen. That is what she "should" be doing. She feels ashamed. She prides herself on being good at whatever she does—housework, mothering, volunteer work, nursing. But ordinarily she works in her own way. Now she has been "caught" by a man she knows to be gossipy. Undoubtedly he will not only remember what he has seen, but spread it in great detail as well. Even if he does not, she feels "found out" by his having seen. "I am not this way," she thinks, knowing that she is, but that she is also many other ways as well. Yet all Mr. Amoretto can see at the moment is her deficiency. Therefore, that is what she must "be."

What Anna is not aware of is the larger significance of what is happening to her. Here she is, caught between two conflicting frames of reference: the conventionally accepted one backed by patriarchal norms, and her own which she has never actually articulated to herself, hence scarcely recognizes. Instead, what she experiences is her deviation from the culturally imposed ideal. She *should* be neatly dressed by at least 9:00, let alone 10:30, every morning; her dishes *should* be washed or at least off the table; her house *should* be clean. And she *should* be doing visible work to accomplish these tasks. Having *not* done any of these things, she primarily experiences negativity, her absence of production. This negativity translates for her into failure. She is *not* a good housewife. What she fails to consider is her *own* frame of reference, existing within gynocentric space, in which a counter set of values prevails. It is *this* failure which constitutes her sin, not the fact of her unstarted housework. This failure to recognize her own frame of reference is the central issue of her immediate existential situation. But what she actually values has not been formalized, much less sanctioned, within patriarchal space. Her valued objectives belong to no monolithic category such as "housewife." Instead, they remain inchoate, scarcely formed within her own mind. And within the minds of countless other housewives, similar personal codes remain unnamed, therefore largely unrecognized. This lack of naming is central to our problem. In the patriarchal structure Anna *has* a name: housewife. Within her own she has none.

Named "housewife," despite the fact that she distinctly thinks of herself as both more and other than that, Anna nonetheless wants to be a good one. This is where part of her confusion lies. Having learned early to be an achiever, patterning herself after the model of the male hero, she finds it difficult to do or be anything without doing and being it well. This is so even though she views her present "named" role ambivalently. At one level she feels that having to tell people she is "a housewife" both trivializes and demeans herself; at another level, however, she feels the role itself is essential. She likes a nice house, kept relatively neat and clean, run in an orderly fashion. She likes to present a good appearance by wearing well-cared-for clothes. Furthermore, she loves her husband and children. Surely she owes it to them as well as herself to do these things?

Yet inside she senses counterstrains. "I want to . . ." Often that is as far as her thinking progresses. It is not anything specific exactly. . . . And yet she does want to do something. Once Anna was a nurse At the time she liked her profession, but having been away from it for over ten years now, she is not sure she wants to resume it. She would really like to paint. But she does not dare think about that kind of thing. Painting is not the same in her mind as "doing something." She can easily say, "I am a mother; I am a housewife; I am a nurse." But a painter . . . ? Because she really is not one. And maybe she never will be. But there are things she would like to set down in some medium. She sometimes likes to just sit and think, too. But how can she possibly say, "I am a thinker"?

What is happening to this woman epitomizes womansins: These are largely sins of omission rather than commision. Parts of her are simply floating by, unable to come into full being because she has no culturally defined way of grabbing onto them and placing them securely within a named or easily nameable framework. The only models most women can conceive are just that: models. Models are visible, are named, are already in existence. But most women are also personally aware of just the opposite: not-ness. What Anna wants is not visible, has no model she is aware of, no name she can think of, therefore, essentially it does not exist. Consequently, she lives in a sort of two-tiered state. On her surface she fulfills, as best she can, the roles for which her culture does have names: mother, housewife, spouse, Girl Scout leader, Sunday School teacher, ex-nurse.

But underneath she lives in a state of vague, unarticulated desire. She wants, but she cannot state what it is she wants. Unfulfillment is the name for this particular kind of otherwise unnamed emptiness.

A woman must face the fact of her colluding with her oppressor, of accepting, living in, and maintaining patriarchal atttitudes and interpretations of reality. Because Western culture still dichotomizes between subject and object, knower and known, women often feel as though we cannot function without being torn apart. Symbolically, to be woman is to be object, the one known, rather than subject, the one who knows. To survive, a woman must also learn the male way of being subject, of knowing others. But the conflict is always there: Be feminine, women are told repeatedly. Or: You don't want to be mannish, do you?

How can a woman balance these conflicting demands? This question, chronic for a woman throughout her life, becomes acute when she copes with such issues as whether or not to have a baby and how to manage the demands of her life apart from the demands of motherhood. How can she even know who or what constitutes her "I"? Who or what that "I" is *supposed* to be? For a woman the "is" and the "ought" always conflict. Their conflict, which rages on the boundary between gynocentric and patriarchal space, partly accounts for the difficulty a patriarchally acculturated woman undergoes when she tries to define herself authentically. From infancy she is taught to be a "good girl." Being a "good girl" may not differ in kind from what her male counterpart is taught, but it is definitely different in degree. He is considered "good" and obedient if he learns to do and think for himself. That does not mean he can freely "betray his class" by espousing Marxism if he is heir to millions or challenge the family faith by joining the Moonies if he is Episcopalian. But it does mean that he is typically allowed and encouraged, often even expected, to behave far more independently than she is. When his adventuresomeness leads him into mischief, it is characteristically glossed over with the phrase, "Well, boys will be boys." (What young woman has ever been indulged with an equivalent, "Well, girls will be girls"?) He is often encouraged to have sexual encounters, to get drunk, to become somewhat rowdy at times.

But a woman is expected to do as she is told. When she does, she is rewarded with approval, reinforcing practice of a habit that leads directly to the sin most difficult of all her sins to recognize—that of being a "good girl." It does not matter what particular culture she is raised in—being a good girl always amounts to obeying patriarchal strictures. In childhood it means obeying adults without questioning them or talking back, even if she knows they are wrong. In adolescence being a "good girl" generally acquires the more specific meaning of avoiding sexual trouble. At its roots, being a "good girl" means perpetuating patriarchal values.

Being a "good girl" may lead a woman to live out a life other than her own. Instead of buying the clothes she wants she hands over her paycheck to her parents. Later, when she is married, being a "good girl" leads her to defer to her husband's wishes. If he wants to invite a group of male friends to dinner, she unquestioningly prepares and serves the food without sitting down with them. If he receives a promotion requiring relocation, it does not occur to her to say no, even though she dreads uprooting herself or her children. If Johnny has Little League, she refrains from taking an afternoon literature class so she can drive him back and forth to practice.

The obedience she exhibits in playing out her "good girl" role is often matched by the sin of subservience. Together, these sins add up to what Saiving refers to as "underdevelopment or negation of the self." Subservience differs from obedience because a woman can obey someone else, as a soldier for example does, without doing so in a servile manner. The subservience of a woman often approximates the "shuffling" of an Uncle Tom. Both are strategies adopted by culturally defined "inferiors" to get through life without attracting punishment from powerful oppressors. But until consciousness raising evolved, a woman, unlike a black, often had few or no relationships that permitted shared awareness of oppression. This was especially true if she never went away to school or camp where she might develop the kinds of close friendships conducive to such sharing. Therefore, she essentially lived out her "shuffle" all the time. To the extent that the "shuffle" seemed not just part of her but her normal self, she would not have been conscious of doing it. Such a woman could scarcely even imagine acting out the "bad girl" role of the young immigrant girl in this passage:

> She used to open the envelope and take a few dollars for herself if she needed it. [She] would come home at 12 o'clock—This was terrible, especially for the Italian people. The neighbors would gossip, would say look at that girl coming home by herself. My mother would talk to her but it did no good. And then one day, my sister wanted to pay board. She was 18. My mother said, "What do you mean board?" She said, "I give you so much and keep the rest." So my mother said, "Alright, do what you please." 7

In this instance the young woman labeled a "bad girl" by her patriarchal community actually achieves the independence she longs for by asserting herself and thus refusing to commit the womansin of being a "good girl."

Often, perpetually playing "good girl" so disturbs a child's sense of "reality" that she grows into a submissive adult, who then commits the sin of denial as well. More often than not the focus of her denial will be her own body. That is partly because the "world" a perpetual "good girl" inhabits cannot exist unless she denies elements too threatening for her to see. Her not seeing often includes body parts patriarchal thought calls "bad." Therefore, when she looks at herself she may see little more than a disembodied head. Mrs. X, a woman in her late seventies, tells how for years she would look in vain for arms, legs, or torso whenever she tried to picture herself.[8] "I would see none of them. Just a large head with rather solemn eyes." Denial of the body in various forms commonly characterizes female responses to the patriarchal world. As in the case of Mrs. X, it is primarily with her head that a woman brings "the world" into being. If she has been taught to repress her body awareness she cannot safely allow her senses to contribute to its creation. Nonetheless, it is hard to understand how a disembodied head could substitute for a full body. At age sixty-three Mrs. X was still the perpetual "good girl" denying her body. She recalls:

> One time, when I was five years old, my mother took me to eat lunch with a neighbor named Fefine. When we arrived, Fefine was nursing her baby. I had never seen anything like the mammoth, deeply veined breast which hung out of her blouse. I stared, fascinated, and could not eat my lunch.
> About that same time in my life, knowing nothing whatsoever about Freud, including the fact that there *was* such a man, I longed for a pair of boy's shorts, navy blue and white herringbone with a fly. It was then, too, that I yearned to send off for a Charles Atlas body-building kit. In my mind, if I obtained such a kit, the change from 98-pound weakling (I must have been all of 47 pounds at the time), would automatically eliminate any chance of breasts. I didn't know then that I was denying my body, hence my womanhood.

Sometimes denying her body does not suffice. A "good girl" may intensify this sin by not "being there" at all. The experience of Alice illustrates this sin. Alice tells of an incident which epitomizes her adolescent experience of her mother:

> I was in eighth grade. One day on the way home from school, Frank, a junior, asked me to go to the Friday night school dance. As soon as I got home I asked my mother if I could go. She was sitting at the kitchen table reading the paper. As I talked it was almost as if I were talking to myself. Oh, she was physically sitting in the room with me, and she wasn't reading while I spoke. Nor did she interrupt. But it was as if *she* weren't there: "Well, I don't know, we'll have to see. . . . Let's see what your father says." And when Dad came home it was more of the same from her: "Alice has something she wants to ask you, dear." Mother was still sitting, only now

she was in the living room, with a drink to keep Dad company. He was much more direct, asking questions, clearly not pleased, but *doing* something, *responding*. She never once said a word in favor of my going nor, for that matter, did she say much against it. Just, "Well, I don't know. . . ." [9]

"Not being there" is a device of powerless, ineffectual women who wish to remain the equivalent of "good girls" all their lives. They use it to avoid situations they feel inadequate to handle. Alice's mother presumably did not want to take a firm stand that might later be challenged by her commanding husband. Rather than risk being contradicted in front of her daughter, she unwittingly chose even greater humiliation by doing absolutely nothing. This is the behavior of the aging "good girl" who never dares to contradict Daddy.

Perhaps Alice's mother refused so often to "be there" that she lost sight of her complicity in maintaining the patriarchal status quo. But most women who collaborate with patriarchal oppression by playing "good girl" partially sense what they are doing. Yet once a woman recognizes her complicity in maintaining patriarchal reality in these ways, why does she frequently continue sinning this way? What makes her so often deny the evidence of her own senses and continue collaboratively creating a reality obviously inimical to her own well-being?

The most compelling answer is fear. This is fear so intrinsic to women's lives that many do not consciously notice it. It is simply there, all day, every day, at the bottom and around the edges of most women's experiences. It is a fear that "they" will "do something to me"—taunt me, hit me, stop me, rape me, maim me, kill me if I do not play their game by their rules. A woman may try not to think about it, but just reading a newspaper, even one so nonsensational as the *New York Times,* reminds her every day. Item: A woman new to the neighborhood wanders into a men-only bar in New Bedford, Massachusetts. The result? She is gang raped for several hours by some of the men; not one of the bystanders, among them the bartender, tries to help her. Item: A woman lost in Trenton, New Jersey, stops to ask directions. The result? Nine men rape her and steal the single dollar in her purse. Why are so many women afraid to drive after dark, to take long trips alone, to travel by themselves? The causes of their fear are not hard to discover. It is a fear that never leaves. A friend walks down Grove Street in Greenwich Village in broad daylight with people on both sides of the street. Approaching her is a young man in a suit, swinging a broom. As he draws even with her, he suddenly aims the broom at her vagina, "You've got a sweet ass, baby," he informs her.

Fear of men and of their anger also has economic causes. Given the dominant values of most patriarchal societies, economic fear probably has a greater impact on the daily lives of most women than does fear of physical or sexual abuse. For a woman whose husband is the major wage earner, acting as she sees fit may seem risky. At the purely pragmatic level, as many feminists insist, the middle-class married woman with young children is "just a man away from welfare." Increased numbers of working wives may have vitiated the impact of this ominous aphorism. Nonetheless, it threatens numerous middle-class women with undesirable lifestyle changes should they be deserted. In the absence of spousal support, how could they afford the house or apartment they currently inhabit?

But even if the actuality implied by this aphorism is mitigated for privileged women, it still embodies a very deep-seated fear of many women from all strata of Western culture. This is the fear contained in the term "bag lady fantasy." Barbara Lazear Ascher well describes this fantasy in the "Hers" column of the *New York Times* for 17 February l983. She spells out in full this terrible, chronic fear common to many women that one day everything material will be taken away from them. Even women professionals may harbor this fantasy, fearing they will find themselves unemployable and without funds. How easy to suddenly become *an ancient hag shuffling the streets in unlaced, warped men's shoes, legs full of circulation-created open sores, wearing an old gray coat over a hole-filled cardigan and unwashed washdress, with a knit hat pulled low on the head, and several oversized plastic shopping bags filling either hand.* This is a dread so deep that reason cannot banish it. Reassurances from husband, lover, or friend cannot stifle this fear which Ascher claims afflicts even women in professions as financially remunerative as law.

This dread is worth reflecting upon. Surely it revives in secular form the Christian fear of being cast down into hell. Bag-lady status is the hell of those individuals (there are bag men as well) who fail in our highly competitive, patriarchally oriented system. For a woman, any number of fears coalesce in the image of this city street phenomenon. First of all, the bag lady is usually physically repulsive, having no place but public restrooms to wash and change her clothes. Often she wears at one time every article of clothing she owns, her bags typically containing what middle-class persons consider junk: rags, scraps of paper, half-empty bottles of Coke, bits and pieces of candy and cake, discarded sandwiches. In her we rediscover the old witch of childhood nightmares. One cannot help but wonder, "Was she once pretty? Did she once love a man and he her?" She seems to symbolize what happens to "girls" who dare step out of line, refusing to play by patriarchal rules and remain "good."

Apart from these other fears—of patriarchal, physical, or sexual retribution, of economic deprivation—still another kind of fear haunts a woman contemplating the possibility of being in some other fashion: This fear is neither specific to women nor to outcast groups in general. It is the fear of disestablishing a pre-existing order. "The world" a woman sees all around herself, even though she may know better, seems always to have been the way it is now. And at least half, maybe even more, of what she takes to be herself seems just as fixed. To challenge such permanent-seeming structures would surely exceed her capabilities. Not only have women been taught that as women we must obey and acquiesce, we greatly fear what might happen if we disobey these injunctions, if we no longer lend our support to these structures. What would existence be like without them? If we were to demolish the patriarchal structures, what might replace them? Can many women even imagine the courage and the work it might take do so?

During this traditional time of testing, a first pregnancy, thoughts of the womansins that deflect us from the way to true gynocentric selfhood often obsess a woman. All these sins seem to add up now to tell her that women are merely hollow creatures tacked together with scraps of absorbed patriarchal "wisdom." But women want to become our own gynocentric selves instead. If women can create life *inside* ourselves, why can we not create life *for* ourselves as well? Learning how to do so is not easy. Before a woman can create a life that is genuinely her own, she must take this necessary first step of recognizing her womansins and then go and grow beyond them. She must now look more closely at what it is that leads her to these particular kinds of sins: She must understand the temptations that perpetually lure her to live a life dictated by others. These are the temptations of patriarchy.

CHAPTER 15.

Temptation

In his traditional quest, one common ordeal the hero must face is tempta-tion. Almost invariably this temptation is symbolized by a woman. Often, as Oedipus discovers, she is the "adultery-ridden, luxurious and incorrigi-ble mother."[1] In a patriarchal view of life, "the seeker of the life beyond life must press beyond [woman, the temptress], surpass the temptations of her call, and soar to the immaculate ether beyond."[2] Seldom is the hero to blame when he succumbs to temptation; rather, it is always some woman, whose powerful allure has dazzled him.

For a woman following the way of the mother, the temptation motif assumes very different form. For her neither man nor woman symbolizes evil temptation. Instead, her temptation lies embodied within an institu-tion. What she must learn to withstand if she is to succeed in the mother's way is the temptation of patriarchy. Such temptation is often as subtle in its allure as that attributed to the fabled female temptress of patriarchal lore. Not surprisingly, patriarchy tempts a woman where she is most vulnerable: her sense of self. If a woman looks closely at creation stories she realizes that women often appear there not as humans created by nature or deity, but as creatures derived from men. This realization forces her to look closely at herself. Is she nothing but "woman," an invention of man? Or does her identity transcend familiar definitions? What happens to a woman who so questions her familiar, patriarchally constructed identity that she ends up rejecting it?

A woman who rejects her womanhood is apt to turn to the only other model she likely knows: man. In doing so, surely, she can reject the patriarchal distortions that try to force every woman into some variant of a "good girl" or its unspeakable opposite. Here is the key to becoming a true self. Physically unable to become a man (until mid-twentieth century), she has settled instead for a reasonable facsimile: the role of pseudo-man. That she should choose this role is scarcely surprising. Her culture would denigrate her womanhood anyway if she happened to succeed in traditional male pursuits, as this amazing comment indicates: "The woman of genius does not exist but when she does she is a man."[3] Thus spoke an influential male art critic in 1912.

Pseudo-manhood exemplifies the extreme of male identification among women. Assuming this role is relatively common among contemporary Western women. Many, particularly those who came of age before the late 1960s, grew up identifying not with women, but with men. While being a pseudo-man clearly holds some advantages for women trying to succeed in the public world of patriarchal space, it may also grotesquely deform a woman's self-image. Throughout history adopting male dress is one method women have used to establish themselves in this role. George Sand is one whose subjective account of this pattern of behavior we have. In her day such a stratagem was often the only one open to a woman who longed for a lifestyle not approved for women. In her words:

> . . . I yearned to deprovincialize myself and became informed about the ideas and arts of my time . . . . I was well aware that it was impossible for a poor woman to indulge herself in these delights.[4]

Her mother suggested she adopt male dress. Sand describes the shapeless man's outercoat, pants, and vest she had made for herself:

> With a gray hat and a large woolen cravat, I was a perfect first-year student. I can't express the pleasure my boots gave me: I would gladly have slept with them, as my brother did in his young age, when he got his first pair. . . . It seemed to me that I could go round the world. And then, my clothes feared nothing. I ran out in every kind of weather, I came home at every sort of hour, I sat in the pit at the theater. No one paid attention to me. . . .[5]

If, like George Sand, a woman can successfully cross-dress, concern for behavior will quickly supplant considerations of dress. As a pseudo-man, a woman will learn what it means to create a superior-inferior I-It relationship. As a pseudo-man, she relates not from the familiar androcentrically imposed woman's perspective of the "it," but from that of the "superior" "I." No longer must she shrink to inferior object-status herself. Now she can reduce others instead, appropriating this patriarchal *modus operandi* as one of her own survival skills.

To operate this way, she must first separate herself from her context. She must learn to say, "*I* am not this; *I* am separate from it. *It* is an object." Implied in this stance is the belief that "not only am *I* alive, animate, and human, *I* count and *it* does not. *It* has no meaning other than to serve *my* needs." This is true no matter what the referent of her "it" happens to be.

If a pseudo-man chooses to dig up earth to make a housing development, that earth does not matter because "it" is neither living nor made in God's image (her pseudo-image): "It" is utterly unlike her. Neither does the air matter, for "it" neither lives nor has discernible form. Therefore if a pseudo-man wishes to erect factories whose smokestacks belch soot and noxious fumes, that is no matter. Likewise, if she chooses to pollute the streams.

The farther away "it" is from her on this scale of things based on closeness to the patriarchal biblical God's image, the more freely can she dissociate herself from it. But what does she do, as pseudo-man, when she encounters a woman? Surely this situation will create problems; likely it does not. Consider: the pseudo-man does not belong to the class, woman. The pseudo-man is different. She is special. She exists in a select group apart. She believes she is accepted as "one of the guys." Women just don't "know any better." *They* don't count.

What does count for the pseudo-man is "me." This "me" equals pseudo-white-male. If successful, that "me" replicates the image of man, sanctioned by Genesis to dominate all of nature. If a pseudo-male is not actually white she will probably compound her sin by denying the reality of her color along with that of her sex. Now that "she" is legitimated by the biblical tradition, she must at all costs keep that tradition viable. She cannot do so as a fundamentalist, because if she were literally to adhere to every word of both testaments she could not possibly be anything but a woman. But she can observe the secular counterpart of biblical fundamentalism. Then what she maintains is a structure of thinking that emerged gradually from the biblical tradition but whose content has now become desacralized. She no longer prays to or overtly worships any deity whatsoever. Nonetheless, she retains the I-centered structure of thinking which not only places humans at the center of existence, but males in particular, especially white ones. That means that she still copies the Hebraic God of creation who steps back from His creation and separates himself from it.

How very different is this god-creation relationship from that of the prepatriarchal Goddess traditions in which the roots of true gynocentric selfhood lie. In the Goddess traditions, every part of nature is suffused with deity. In those traditions, too, each individual "I" respects rather than dominates its natural context. In prepatriarchal systems of thought the "I" and its context mutually balance each other. Without a context, no "I" exists. Similarly, the natural context does not "exist" without the presence of deity. In this way of thinking, nonspirited matter is inconceivable. Matter "matters": It is not *just* rock, not *just* dust. By analogy, all matter holds within itself sacred presence just as a blessed Holy Communion wafer does. In such a system of thought, meaning, in the form of sacred presence, surrounds everyone and everything. One need not seek far away for it. Meaning does not reside way up off in the sky somewhere: it is right here and now.

But our inherited Judeo-Christian structures of thought forever alter the sacredness of nature. These structures of thought remove sacred presence from the "here and now" world of nature, which is believed to be inherently sinful, and relegate it to the most distant point imaginable—the sky above. Meaning is not here, not now. It is "there and then." God is there in the sky and we will not meet Him face to face until then, the hour of our death.

But patriarchal thought has devised a way to bring "there and then" into "here and now." Western patriarchal thought teaches that a male Savior god, once son of the revered Earth Mother, now the Christ, came down to earth. He made this descent to permit this transformation of "there and then" into "here and now." Some see Christ's coming as a historical, once-only occurrence; others, as a mythic event repeated, not simply commemorated, in every Holy Communion ritual. But either way His sacred presence defies the natural order of things; his presence is special—so special that his birth denigrates the natural birthing capacity of women, for his birth occurred *supernaturally*.

Influenced by that God-ordained, supernatural order of things, many women commit the grave sin of avoiding life. They sin this way because they grow up indoctrinated with the belief that "there and then" are better than "here and now." But "there and then" are always ineffable—we cannot quite specify what they are. By definition, they are not part of nature. That means that they are "beyond" our senses. We can name them, as indeed throughout history we have done, and we can try to imagine them. But in the naming patriarchy once again deludes women.

The name we learn to give "there and then" is "Heaven." But to tell what the "there and then" of Heaven are like, we discover that we must, paradoxically, resort to "here and now" words. That is because "here and now" experiences are the only ones available to us. In the absence of any better alternative, our language must therefore start with these words. Nonetheless, we generally treat the experiences these words bespeak as but pale imitations of the "there and then." We use them *by analogy*, any time we want to show what "there and then" are like.

This transfer of meaning from known experience to unknown requires the use of metaphor. Obviously metaphor is neither sinful nor unique to the patriarchal Judeo-Christian tradition. It characterizes human thinking in general. From a gynocentric perspective, however, received metaphor frequently leads one astray, out of the way, into sin. That happens because a patriarchal hierarchy of values almost inevitably accompanies metaphoric usage within existing cultures. These patriarchal value systems result in patterns and processes of lopsided reciprocity. They more frequently take value from the "here and now" world "below" and reassign it to the "there and then" world "up above" than they do the reverse. Thesepatriarchal transfers automatically rob nature of its meaning. Such robbery makes this particular system of thought sinful from a gynocentric perspective because the "here and now" world, though passing, is simultaneously ultimate. To displace this ultimacy by focusing only on the ephemeral quality of nature is not only dishonest, it also destroys divinity. And deicide, the destruction of divinity, in any thought structure, is highly sinful.

We can begin to understand the mechanism of this gynocentrically "sinful" metaphoric process by considering any concept central to it. Take the word "home." Unquestionably this word has powerful meanings in both gynocentric and patriarchal contexts. Yet "home" has traditionally been primarily a place of women and children, its qualities typically reflecting women far more than men. Furthermore, home is a place whose deep meaning arises out of our lived, "here and now " experiences of it. For both these reasons—its connection to women and its "here and now" quality—"home" is a word more fully realized in gynocentric than in patriarchal thought. Yet the way the underlying meaning of the word functions in patriarchal thought reflects exactly the kind of metaphoric transfer of meaning by which patriarchy robs women of our symbols and deepest significance.

Consider the way "home," as symbol, tacitly carries many cultural associations for what Henry James referred to as "the great good place," whatever and wherever that place may be for any individual. Typically, that "great good place" has been imagined in two distinct ways. Either it is a place or time long past, an imagined Golden Age, or it lies in the future, a utopia. Home, as both point of origin and place of return, is the underlying conception for both these notions. In the process of metaphoric shifting, qualities associated with "home" are lifted from their original context and shifted onto the remote "great good place" Western patriarchy most often names "Heaven." Thus "to go home" in an ultimate sense, is to reach Heaven.

The sinfulness of this metaphoric transfer of meaning is threefold. First, what is rightfully a "here and now" quality is lifted out of its original gynocentric context. In this case that context is the vehicle "home." From this immediate natural context, meaning is then abstracted and transferred onto a faraway, patriarchal tenor, "Heaven." In this way the present time and place are deprived of some of their inherent positive attributes. Second, to the extent that women create some of these prized positive attributes, we, too, like the "here and now" world of nature, are robbed of what is rightfully ours. Third, when women collaborate in this theft by employing terms like "heaven" this way, we are as guilty as any man of desacralizing our lived present in favor of some theoretical unlived future.

The principle involved in this transfer of meaning is precisely the same as that involved in the sin of exchanging womanhood for pseudo-manhood. In both instances a woman is assenting to patriarchal beliefs that male-centered values transcend her own gynocentric ones. In the one case she denigrates her natural condition, that of being a woman. Instead, she affects all the values of manhood she is capable of assuming. In the other case, she commits exactly the same sin, but more abstractly this time: She claims her own experience is not adequate to represent ultimacy. Only something far far away is sufficiently suitable, so she will lend to that far far away "place" the most valuable images of her own experience. Because that place must be better than anything a woman can possibly know, she will attach to it all the most positive values she knows. She will ignore the fact that such projection consequently robs her of what she could be valuing right now for its own sake.

Such temptations of patriarchy are difficult for many women to resist. The people women traditionally have seen "succeeding" have over-whelmingly been men. Like the nineteenth-century art critic, women cannot help but notice that this was traditionally true "even if those successful people were women." Sadly, many women must note that most of the women who have "made it" in patriarchal space, at least until recently, have adopted the ways, if not necessarily the dress, of men. How very tempting it is to follow them. Their example rivets many women. How can we possibly want to go on following the way of the mother? Unless, like Ulysses, we have tied ourselves to a mast and stopped the ears of those rowing the boat, we may simply founder here. A very large part of many women wants the rewards that attend a woman skillful enough to camouflage herself as a pseudo-man. Like the hero who often remains captive to the temptress for great spans of time before finally getting on with his quest, women may remain locked into this stage indefinitely, victims of the temptations of patriarchy. But any woman who values the goals implicit in the way of the mother must overcome this temptation and move on. The time has come for her to test her resolution for motherhood still more deeply: She must now confront head-on this tempting world of the fathers.

PART IV

The Fathers

CHAPTER 16.

Atonement with the Fathers

One of the toughest ordeals a woman faces along the way of the mother is uncovering her true selfhood. She can far more easily collude with or rebel against patriarchal culture to create a false self. She even has a range of patterns of collusion or rebellion to choose from. At one extreme, she can accept the patriarchal invention known as "good girl"; at the other, she can choose woman's own invention, pseudo-man. Quite apart from these opportunities to collude or rebel, temptation often leads a woman to sin against her authentically gynocentric selfhood in yet another way. This is the temptation to atone herself with the fathers. A major problem is that within the patriarchal heroic quest, of course, such atonement is vital to success.

Atonement, for the traditional hero, necessitates coming to terms with the patriarchal father god. When the hero does so, he understands that the god's terrifying aspect provides the necessary complement to his beneficent side. Mythologist Joseph Campbell speaks of atonement this way:

> The paradox of creation, the coming of the forms of time out of eternity, is the germinal secret of the father. It can never be quite explained. Therefore, in every system of theology there is an umbilical point, an Achilles tendon which the finger of mother life has touched, and where the possibility of perfect knowledge has been impaired. . . . The hero transcends life with its peculiar blind spot and for a moment rises to a glimpse of the source. He beholds the face of the father, understands—and the two are atoned.[1]

Campbell's words well illustrate the patriarchal assumption that creation is a *male* prerogative. Not only does the "Achilles tendon" of woman's touch mar the "perfection" of male creation, the "hero *transcends* life with its peculiar blind spot" (emphasis added). So representative of patriarchal thought are these words that they readily show why atonement with the father devastates a woman. Such atonement exactly reverses the process women need for our own inner development. In fact, the very system that expects and demands such atonement has placed women in the awkward situation of not being quite sure who or what we are.

Traditionally, for several thousand years throughout the world, women have filled a specific niche in the patriarchally defined natural order: deities at the top, followed by men, then women, animals, plants, and inanimate objects. (In some societies women actually rank below economically vital animals, such as cows or camels.) For a woman to atone herself with the major symbol of such a system, the most powerful male, is to assent to the very system that denies her selfhood or soul.

The reward typically promised women for atoning ourselves to such a system appears in the story of Cinderella. Although this tale has been analyzed repeatedly, apparently no one yet has noted that the manifest tale actually reverses the content of most traditional women's lives. According to this story, an unkempt, hardworking, abused, and impoverished girl is "rescued" from her misery by a "savior" hero. Not surprisingly she then lives happily ever after. That familiar tale and its many variants undeniably capture a common daydream. But what does the story mask? In "real life" young girls characteristically make themselves as attractive as possible, dress as well as their means permit, and attract as many "princes" as possible. By contrast, after marriage, many deteriorate. Their decline occurs variously through overwork, "letting themselves go," or abuse from their erstwhile "saviors." Somehow the popular Cinderella tale wherein drudge beomes beauty exactly reverses the actual pattern of many women's lives, particularly those who are forced to live as traditional full-time mothers and housewives.

Nonetheless, many variants of the Cinderella promise perniciously influence young women. Most often victimized by this false promise is the woman who unquestioningly atones herself to the dominant patriarchal system. Typically, such a woman is just as guilty of placing herself in a position of inferiority to men as are the men who subordinate her. Like her oppressors, she has thoroughly internalized the dominant value system: While she may welcome motherhood and accord it great importance, she nonetheless typically views heroes as larger or stronger figures. To the extent that she "worships" heroes, she compensatorily weakens mothers. As a mother, this means that she will unconsciously denigrate her own capabilities relative to those of "heroes." Such a woman may function as both culture-bringer and as savior to her children. Yet when it comes to enacting the savior hero aspect of the motherself role in her own behalf, she often fails miserably.

This failure runs a gamut. At one end it may be as simple as not being able to execute simple day-to-day procedures for her own benefit. Using a computer banking card, for example, may completely thwart her. More detrimental to her selfhood are failures of nerve involving hiding. If she telephones a dryer repairman, she may identify herself as Mrs. O'Brien rather than Karen O'Brien. Such behavior is not without reason. Her married name almost always receives more respect than her given name. The stranger at the other end of the line typically defers to the "Mrs." but not to the "Karen." "Mrs." automatically insures formality. If a woman identifies herself as "Karen O'Brien," the listener often brashly addresses her with the informal "Karen," in preference to the formal "Mrs." A woman's choosing to "cover" herself with her married name is therefore understandable.

But such "hiding" behavior can become more serious. What if a woman hides still further? Suppose her husband holds a high-status title like Judge or Doctor. Instead of telephoning as Karen O'Brien or Mrs. O'Brien, she may stretch her identity a bit to become "Dr. O'Brien's secretary." Now she can telephone the plumber and say, "I'm calling for Dr. Richard O'Brien. . . ."

This is a seemingly minor occurrence of atonement with the father. Yet several factors interconnect here to allow a woman to be "rescued" by her husband while simultaneously denying her own capabilities. First, by posing as her husband's secretary she is borrowing the power undeniably attached to his title. A woman married to such a man well knows the distinction nodding acquaintances make between the two of them. Whereas she is "Karen," her husband remains "Doc" or "Judge." She recognizes, too, small preferential courtesies frequently accorded "the Judge" and his wife which she, in her own person, never receives.

But if a woman posing as "Mrs. O'Brien" rather than "Karen O'Brien" is not fully herself, how much further does she disappear when "Dr. O'Brien's secretary" takes over? Certainly the meaning of this situation depends on the particular performer. If Karen Olson O'Brien knows that she is purposely playing a role to facilitate a trivial but annoying process, probably she does no harm to herself. She may even enjoy the humor of her little game. But if she is a shy, nonassertive individual who dreads openly stating her wants, she may further denigrate herself in pretending to be someone else. Instead of learning to confront the world in her own right, she repeatedly hides her own self while someone more powerful "saves" her. Enacted at the far end of the scale, this process of atonement with the patriarchal power structure becomes even more harmful to a woman's sense of self.

When a mother herself needs succor, she may succumb to the dominant cultural belief that *only* heroes save. In our own less-than-heroic era that belief has largely dwindled to a weak parody; nonetheless, it still exists, despite its often ridiculous attenuation. Take Iris, for example, a young mother who works as a hospital receptionist.[2] Having just pulled into her assigned parking space one morning, she opens her car door only to find she cannot get out; she has pulled to within three inches of the car on her left. She begins to perspire. How will she get out? On the other side she has about twenty inches, maybe twenty-four. Neither driver left her enough room, but mentally berating them will not help. She begins to think of Jared, one of the young doctors at work. Backing out, she pretends Jared is doing it for her. He would be so skillful that he would never dent the car to the left. She can see him backing up for her. He has the engine going; now he is slowly applying the gas, slowly, slowly inching out, keeping the car absolutely straight. By performing that little drama in her mind, Iris successfully executes her task. Having felt insufficient to handle it on her own, she invoked a savior, in the form of her "hero," Jared, to do it for her.

Obviously it was not Jared but Iris herself who performed this tricky maneuver. Does it really matter that she told herself he was doing it so that she could manage? Those who are primarily results-oriented, believing that the end justifies the means, may think not. But that attitude ignores both the procedure and its cumulative effects. Iris's method extracts a large price: She must relinquish her own strength, projecting it onto an imagined other, one who is not of her own "inferior" gender. By imagining Jared her savior she simultaneously reinforces her own sense of inadequacy and her belief in masculine superiority.

Furthermore, while her method "worked" in the immediate situation, chances are she will get herself into trouble if she relies on it in all instances. Her method replicates the cultural pattern of helpless maiden relying on strong man to save her. How easily this pattern turns into addictive hero worship, a condition sometimes referred to as being a love junkie. In this condition a woman (less commonly a man) needs love affairs or casual sex as an emotional crutch much as a drug addict needs heroin.

The process works like this. Iris has felt unfulfilled by her work lately. For the past seven years she has been a receptionist in the pediatric wing of a sizable metropolitan hospital. Although she likes the doctors and enjoys the patient contact, she never imagined spending her entire life this way. When she took the job her first year out of high school, she did not expect to be here more than a year, two at most. She will be thirty in April. Every time she begins thinking this way she becomes panicky. Sometimes her heart pounds so hard she fears a heart attack; other times she cannot sleep at night. It is when she is lying in bed, her arm and shoulder muscles so stiff they ache no matter how she settles herself, that she obsessively thinks about Jared. She closes her eyes and pictures the handsome young resident with his dark, nearly black, straight hair, his sideburns exceptionally full, throwing his head back in a hearty laugh. Just this afternoon—did she imagine it, or did he lean against her meaningfully when he reached around her for a patient chart? She can feel the pressure of his arm against her now, as she reconstructs the scene, with embellishing details: His arm begins to move, gently, gently, until the movement is unmistakable. Now it is just the two of them alone in the office, both detained after hours. As his arm moves so suggestively she is no longer sitting bent over the appointment book. She is standing, and as he . . . Her dream repeats itself endlessly with minute variations.

By no means does such hero worship characterize every woman atoned to patriarchal values. Unfortunately, however, it is common enough to warrant concern from a gynocentric perspective. Only those women who manage their roles without dependence on or even help from men totally escape the underlying hero-worshipping principle involved here. These include the minority of women who survive alone, perhaps as artists, independent entrepreneurs, or farmers, and those who manage with help only from other women. Such women would respond far differently from Iris to the predicament she found herself in.

Iris could repark her car very differently, preserving and enhancing, rather than denying her own gynocentric capacities. This method reflects a different vision of salvation and self. At the moment Iris realizes her predicament and feels panicky, she can connect to a helping image other than that of her heroized Jared. This is the mother image that she, as a daughter, automatically carries within herself and that,because Iris is herself a mother, she actually embodies. By invoking the mother image she can treat herself with the care, warmth, love, and kindness she recalls or idealizes from her own mother or that she would provide for her own child. How, for example, would she comfort her own crying child (assuming she is not an abusive or incompetent mother)? She would, of course, hold it close, perhaps walking it back and forth in a rocking fashion. While Iris cannot precisely hold herself, she *can* hold her own hand, exerting a steadying pressure on it. And she can talk to herself, either out loud or in her mind. She can tell herself to be calm, reminding herself that trying as it is, this annoying situation is not life-threatening. Once she has calmed down, she can then encourage herself. Again, this is what she would do for a child fearful of extricating itself from an unpleasant situation. Ideally, she need not be quite so literal in mothering herself. Perhaps just meditating quietly for a moment on her inner image of the mother will suffice. Now she should be able to repark her car more satisfactorily.

On the surface, invoking the power of the mother appears identical to invoking that of the hero. In fact, however, the difference between the two is profound. To fantasize about and invoke the presence of the male savior hero is to lose power, not gain it. Such invocation actually leads a woman to give away her own attributes to someone whose extreme "difference" she presumes is so great that she cannot identify with him. By contrast, to invoke the mother, the one who is like herself, is just the opposite. To do so is to reclaim power rightfully belonging to women.

The psychological metaphors of projection and introjection name these opposed experiences of invoking the hero, on the one hand, and invoking one's own motherself, on the other. Both phenomena naturally occur in everyday experience. Only when carried to extremes, as in the case of Iris's daydream about Jared, does either become harmful. The way we understand both depends on what our conception of "reality" is. In extremely general terms, we can conceive of "reality" in two ways. We may assume that whatever is "out there," external to us, gains its particularity from the way we perceive it. In that case external reality is entirely subjective. It can be likened to a giant Rorschach test: It is an ink blot open to individual constructions.

On the other hand, we may view "external reality" as objectively "out there," apart from any perceiver. Given this understanding of "reality," the word "projection" applies only to situations in which a person is obviously taking his own qualities and attributing them to someone else. Thus, if Fred, who is known for lifting minor items such as pens and paper clips, accuses his innocent secretary of stealing office supplies, Fred is obviously projecting onto his subordinate an undesirable trait of his own.

Introjection works just the opposite way. If a man is a slow-speaking, deliberate individual who ponders carefully before making any decision, his daughter may also speak deliberately, considering all angles of a situation before speaking. Unconsciously, she has taken into herself, or introjected, these characteristics of her father, making them her own. In that area at least, she has internalized her father.

Not only familial values, but cultural ones as well, are passed on by introjection. Introjection on this scale helps account for the fact that many women are as patriarchal in their thinking as most men are. In a culture that values men and debases women it is nearly impossible for a woman to avoid introjecting some of those negative attributions. Conversely, it is easy for her to project onto men the positive values her culture teaches her to find in them. For Iris, the situation is something like this. Without necessarily being conscious of it, she has absorbed her culture's belief that she, as a young woman, is weak and without much worth apart from bodily attributes. Since she is relatively pretty and amply bosomed, her value in this respect is quite high. Furthermore, until this year she has been "young." Now, with her thirtieth birthday approaching, that advantage is slipping away. Accepting as a given her culture's valuation of herself as a sex object, she has learned her lesson well: She grooms herself carefully, dresses well, and comes on to men. Her value resides not in her own self-estimate but in the attentions men grant her. As long as they keep noticing her, her value holds. Once they stop, it plummets. Hence she is as much at the mercy of male "investors" in her worth as any market commodity is.

In this externalized value system, "power" resides in the investors, not in the "investee," a woman herself. Thus, whenever she experiences her own personal insecurities she logically looks for rescue from the accepted source of power, a man. If she cannot move her car, then she can "borrow" strength by invoking her "savior." In more serious need, when personal anxieties overwhelm her, she can also find temporary succor by invoking him. His presence, however, merely masks her underlying problems. Thinking of him so diverts attention from her worries that she no longer attends to them. As long as her infatuation lasts, she is freed from doubts. But if she actualizes her fantasy, once the immediate delight of the initial romance diminishes, her still unresolved life problems intrude again. Now she must either recognize the impossibility that a male hero can solve them for her or, failing such recognition, break off and begin her entire escapist procedure anew.

But if she invokes the Mother instead, what happens? Here, the figure she invokes is defined neither as "other" nor as different. Hence, the mode of relationship will be entirely dissimilar. In this instance, Iris is invoking a figure whose sexual identity reinforces—rather than subverts or seduces—her own. Here is one of her own kind, someone she can actually identify with. In fact, she can actually become, even *is* this figure. And this is the essential difference. She and the mother image she invokes are sufficiently alike that she is less likely to feel helpless, more likely to realize her *own* strength by invoking Her. Nonetheless, some problems exist with this kind of invocation as well. For a woman who can see her own mother only through the male-conditioned eyes that still dominate our culture, this image may not work. If she envisions mothers in general as weak, ineffectual, exploited creatures, such invocation cannot be expected to strengthen her. But if she herself has reached the stage where *she* has functioned as a mother, she surely knows the power involved in that role.

But for most patriarchally acculturated women the father's power is so constantly reinforced, often at the expense of the mother's, that patriarchal identification retains its hold. Even women aware of this situation find atonement with the Father necessary: "Success" in the world of patriarchal structures demands acceptance of and obedience to the demands of the Father. Atonement with the Father seems integral to the life of any woman who intends to "succeed"—whether vocationally or amorously. Unlike her masculine counterpart, a woman cannot afford rebellious separation from the patriarchal status quo. But instead of carrying her closer to herself and her womanhood, atonement to patriarchy alienates her further from both, either turning her into the creature known as "good girl," invented by man and his patriarchal mirror in the sky, or, in the case of her hero-identifying sister, a kind of pseudo-man. What women need is anything but rituals of atonement to a father God. Far more appropriate are rituals of estrangement from the Father God. Such rituals decreate, rather than perpetuate, patriarchal structures.

If she does not ritually estrange herself from patriarchy, a woman risks losing her way along the often perilous path of the mother. If that happens, instead of experiencing motherself positively, she may fall into one of two familiar patriarchal traps. On the one hand, she may lose *all* sense of self, being swallowed up by the Mother Goddess archetype, which seems to be what *every* good mother "should" be. On the other, she may so fear that possibility that she herself, in reaction to patriarchal admonitions about the kind of mother she should be, becomes the swallower. In that case what she swallows is the growing selfhood of her child. For any woman attempting to create for herself the motherselfhood essential for following the way of the mother, some measure of the decreative estrangement from patriarchy, no matter how painful the process, is therefore essential.

CHAPTER 17.

Estrangement from the Fathers

Women's need for estrangement from the fathers significantly differentiates the gynocentric way of the mother from the traditional patriarchal quest of the hero. Only one of the hero's goals is atonement with the Father, but atonement with the fathers is expected of women from infancy on. Consequently, if women are to achieve our own way of the mother, we must work very hard to estrange ourselves from the fathers in all their many guises. The atonement the hero must work *for,* women must work *against.*

Women's estrangement from the fathers is not impossible; nonetheless, within patriarchy it is extremely difficult. Because estrangement so totally vitiates the atonement with the fathers essential in patriarchy, it constitutes a patriarchally heinous sin. To realize how patriarchally "sinful" estrangement is, consider these parts of the Nicene Creed:

> I believe in one God, the Father Almighty, Maker of heaven and earth, and of all things visible and invisible. . . .[1]

And this general Thanksgiving from the Episcopal service:

> Almighty God, Father of all mercies, we, thine unworthy servants, do give thee most humble and hearty thanks for all thy goodness and loving kindness to us, and to all men. . . . We bless thee for our creation, preservation, and all the blessings of this life. . . . And, we beseech thee, give us that due sense of all thy mercies, that our hearts may be unfeignedly thankful; and that we show forth thy praise, not only with our lips, but in our lives, by giving up our selves to thy service, and by walking before thee in holiness and righteousness all our days. . . .[2]

Anyone who has grown up with these words or their counterparts from other traditions cannot help but tremble at the thought of disobeying the patriarchal Father God. Even listening to the inner voice of the Mother Goddess creates fear, especially when she offers the contrary advice, "Go and separate yourself from the Father who demands your perpetual atonement to Him and His world."

What distinguishes a woman who practices atonement to the fathers from one who knowingly estranges herself from them? Unlike the woman who estranges herself from the Father, the woman who practices lifelong atonement is a dutiful daughter. Caroline A., born in 1904, is a perfect example.[3] Outwardly Caroline appears to have been very much her own person. She earned a doctorate and became well recognized as a botanical taxonomist. She never married, but unlike her own two maiden aunts, Caroline *wanted* to marry. Hers was not chosen renunciation: It was bad luck combined with paternal decree. Bad luck intervened when her first beau died of what was then called consumption. Paternal decree forbade it when the last names of her second and third beaux did not accord with his notions of WASP propriety. Other factors enlarge the story of Caroline's lifelong atonement with the fathers. When her mother grew incapacitated late in life, Caroline took leave from her position to care for her at home. This staying home stretched out for ten years, necessitating that Caroline give up her career for that time. It was not that her mother lingered so many years. After her death, Caroline's father needed her; after his death, the remaining aunt, Mary, required care. That such devotion was taken for granted by the family is apparent from this excerpt from a relative's letter: "I heard from Kate that Caroline has given up her job in Boston to come home and care for Ruth [Caroline's mother] as is of course her duty."[4]

In marked contrast to Caroline's lifelong atonement to the fathers is the overt estrangement of Joan. Joan's father has been an alcoholic ever since Joan can remember.[5] In spite of his drinking, as a child she loved him very much. He often verbally abused her mother, but never Joan. As he aged he became more and more bitter about his life, blaming everyone but himself for his failures. When Joan's mother was dying he became particularly difficult. Joan arrived home, after having not visited for two years, to find a strange, stooping figure, more gorilla-like than human, inching toward the screen door in answer to her knock. This muttering creature wiping a torn dish towel at his fingers, she realized, was her father. Finally arrived at the door, he offered no greeting, but immediately launched into complaint: He could not remove the smell of onions from his hands.

From the doorway, Joan spotted dozens of empty whiskey bottles beneath the dining table. Following her father into the living room she sat on one of two fading couches, carefully avoiding the uncased bedpillow at one end, ringed as it was with circles of sweat. Totally unable to speak, she sat watching as her father consumed a brimming double-sized coffee cup of whiskey, neat. The horror of that weekend Joan abridges, except for its conclusion: "When I got into my rented car to leave, my father clung to my arm, which was resting in the open front window. He begged me not to go: 'You've got to help me. Just give me $50.00. That's all I ask, Joan, just give your poor old Pappy $50.00. That's all I ask you.'"

Ever since Joan can remember, her father has so consistently borrowed from family members, that he not only wiped out his own legacy from his father before his father died, he also dipped heavily into that of his too-forgiving sister. "The hardest thing I ever did in my entire life," Joan says, "was to say, 'No, Daddy,' when he tried to tap me. I told him, 'I'm not going to give you $50.00. I'm going to leave now and if you don't let go of the car window I'm afraid you're going to get hurt.'" Then she drove off.

It has not been easy for Joan, but she has maintained her refusal despite repeated demands from her father. She has said no in a situation almost impossible to say no in. That gives her strength to refuse the impossible demands of other patriarchs as well. Such legitimate nay-saying is what the painful circumstance of estrangement from the Fathers is all about.

Probably the most common, and the most dangerous, form of estrangement from the fathers a woman has to deal with is "unlicensed" sexual activity. From an official patriarchal perspective, of course, "unlicensed" sexual activity on the part of a woman is always sinful; by definition, it represents disobedience. Both "disobedience" and being "unlicensed," as all women know from the example of Eve, are women's most egregious sins against patriarchal authority. Unlicensed sexual activity also severely challenges male sexuality by making paternity difficult, if not impossible, to determine. On the other hand, sexual "sin" sufficiently entices men that masculine attitudes often waver on this point, underneath their public severity. Historically women who flouted monogamous sexuality in cultures demanding it were publicly shunned and excoriated; privately, however, many men gravitated toward them for their own personal pleasure. Now that more permissive attitudes dominate many circles of Western culture, this ambiguity is often reversed: Many males publicly praise sexual liberation, while feeling privately threatened if "their own" women wish to practice it.

For a woman, however, the ambiguity of sexual activity is different. While sexual activity estranges her from the fathers, it may or may not help her to enter her own gynocentric space. It depends what sexual activity means for her. On the one hand, historically, risk of public censure has been a high price for a woman to pay. On the other, private approbation by admirers has often seemingly lessened that toll. The issue of whether "unlicensed" sexual behavior constitutes patriarchal entrapment, patriarchal estrangement, or gynocentric creation hinges on how a woman uses it. Such activity may place her more deeply within patriarchal structures; it may also express her own deepest needs and desires *in spite of* patriarchy. The difference between these two ends is enormous.

The case of Clea well illustrates this point. Clea is a woman who seems unable to exist without constant masculine attention.[6] Now thirty-five, she has thrived on masculine interest since about age twelve, when she first began to date. As she puts it, she does not "feel alive" unless she is with a man. She spends a great deal of her time shopping for clothes, fixing her hair, applying cosmetics, and painting her nails. Always she has an eye out to what some Jason, Richard, or Lawrence thinks. She is constantly in love, though seldom for long. Her early marriage, which resulted in one child, ended after six years. Even during her marriage she was frequently unfaithful, and now she admits to multiple adulteries.

Judged by conventional morality (which, despite a brief permissive streak in the sixties and seventies, is now once again patriarchally restrictive in most contemporary Western cultures), Clea's behavior is wrong. Yet it is also "wrong" from a gynocentric perspective. Being Clea means living in relation to an adoring man or men. When she must spend a night alone, which despite her sexual proclivities she frequently does, she feels nonexistent. This is how she describes it: "I'm in the house with Lawrence, or Jason, or Richard. So long as one of them is here with me I feel 'safe.' His presence legitimates me. But once morning comes, particularly if he leaves before I do, I'm on my own. That's a very different feeling, hard to describe. It's as if all the life animating the house a moment ago has suddenly died. Things go cold and dark; warmth and light disappear with the man. And I'm left all alone. Only I'm not really there anymore. It's like what I always imagined as a child would happen when the lights were turned out in a room; all the contents simply disappear. Only if you turned the light back on would they reappear. I'm like that. Without the man, I seem to disappear, too." Possibly because she feels nonexistent outside the presence of an attractive man, Clea accomplishes relatively little of what she is always intending to do. To be sure, she lives the semi-chaotic life of a perpetual graduate student who never quite manages to finish any course on time. But her entire raison d'être is to entice men. As she herself puts it, "she" does not exist apart from a man.

By contrast Jane has been married to Arnold for at least thirty years, maybe longer.[7] Everyone sees this marriage as "good," and it is. Except for one thing. Arnold is impotent. "I love him," Jane says. "And I try to be faithful. Impotence doesn't have to stop all sexual activity you know. But

. . ." Jane has struggled for years, trying to decide what is right. "I can't just leave him. Besides, I don't want to. But I can't tell him either. It would kill him. He's very traditional. And very sensitive about his condition. I suffer for it, terribly. But there's something in me that can't be confined. I go for a while and I think with relief, well, that's no longer part of my life. And then something happens. I feel a need inside me to express a part of my being that can't ever come into existence with Arnie. I don't know what to say about it. It troubles me."

Traditional patriarchal morality would indiscriminately lump Jane and Clea together. Actually, their behaviors distinctly differ. Clea tries to live out an almost stereotypic masculine dream of the attractive available woman; Jane represents a very different struggle indeed. She alternates between two different worlds. Most of the time she makes her peace with the patriarchal world view of her husband. Now and again, however, a deep inner need drives Jane to actualize parts of herself that otherwise remain unrealized. Then she violates the patriarchal world, temporarily estranging herself from it. But in so doing, she saves a bit of herself at least for the moment.

Jane's is the dilemma of all oppressed peoples: how to actualize herself when she feels she has no other world to live in. And that is an issue which all too many radical thinkers overlook, whether they are feminists, Marxists, or nihilists. Unless a woman is so revolutionary that she wants physically to destroy everything in the existing world, how does she find alternative structures? Where does she go? For a woman like Jane, destroying the present world of her marriage would necessitate destroying many things she values, including the husband she loves. To destroy that world would be to destroy a part of herself, just as to maintain it prevents part of herself from coming into being. "Sometimes I despair at my hypocrisy," she says, "But walking out is not the answer. He needs me and I need him. Furthermore, I'm not cut out to live a countercultural lifestyle. Or to be poor. . . ." Jane must be in her mid-fifties now, and although she is well-educated, she has never had a paying job and would presumably have great difficulty finding one. To say that Jane "should" leave, as some radical feminists would do, is to consign her to a life as confining, in a different way, as the one she lives now.

A vivid example of Jane's probable fate were she to leave is Rachel. At slightly past fifty, Rachel walked out on Harold after thirty years of mostly unhappy marriage.[8] With much trouble, she managed to find a low-paying job editing for a legal textbook company. Her colleagues are all young enough to be her children, the work is excruciatingly boring, and the only apartment she could find within her price range has cardboard walls. Her sole happiness is Jack, the still-married man for whom she left Harold. Meanwhile, Harold threatens everything he legally can to deny her any assets in the divorce. "If I had known," she says, "just how awful this kind of life would be, I don't think I would have done it." Jack, it turns out, is married to a believing Roman Catholic and has nine children of varying ages, some of whom he still must support.

These women—Clea, Jane, and Rachel—all defy patriarchy's traditional sexual taboos. Yet each sees a man or men as her means of "salvation." Typically such women find their "salvation" more victimizing and more patriarchal than the original trap from which it was designed to spring them. Even for someone like Jane, "unlicensed" sexual activity is an extremely dangerous path to estrangement from the fathers, for in choosing it she risks losing so much of herself that she could well end up like Rachel. Yet the vision of man, not woman, as savior, is one that has dominated patriarchal thinking from the start. The behavior of these women and women like them simply varies the familiar feminine theme of escaping home through marriage.

In both home and marriage, a woman finds herself within a confining patriarchal circle, one controlled and dominated by her father in her early years, by her husband later on in life. But it does not occur to her to conceptualize her situation this way. If it did she would realize how foolish she is to think one man provides rescue from the other, both being cut from the same patriarchal mold. In both instances the pattern is familiar: A woman exists right now in this fallen, sinful, unjust world. But "out there" is another to which she aspires. In it she will be treated differently. There she will be appreciated for who and what she really is. She will be "saved." And the one who will save her is John, or Charlie, or Dave, whose realm it is. How very like the Kingdom of God it is—that faraway place to which she will be whisked by Jesus, the male Savior hero *par excellence*.

Estranging themselves from unquestioning acceptance of such beliefs is essential for all women searching for their own genuine selfhood. Yet this process of estrangement so consumes many women that they never progress beyond this stage. Instead of seeing estrangement as the first of many necessary steps, they accept a tenuous balance between estrangement and atonement. On the one hand, they adore men and think they cannot live without them. On the other, they refuse wholly to accept male definitions. Often they use men sexually to rebel against them. Such women fail to realize that their own selfhood does not come into being this way. A necessary next step leads women beyond the tentativeness of estrangement to outright decreation of patriarchy.

CHAPTER 18.

Apotheosis: Decreation of Patriarchy

One of the high points of the quest of the hero is his apotheosis. Apotheosis refers to the "divine state to which the human hero attains who has gone beyond the last terrors of ignorance."[1] When this takes place, the hero and his mirror image projected into the sky, the Father God, become as one. For a male hero this pattern is typically envisioned as *elevation* to the level of the Father God. This is the ultimate accolade a patriarchal system of values can confer on anyone. As such, it is necessarily the nadir within the complementary gynocentric pattern of the way of the mother. Apotheosis is therefore not only to be avoided by the mother, but the entire system which produces the concept must be reconsidered, posssibly even destroyed.

This is a point well known to the few women in every era who have bravely defied the norms of their cultures. It is only since the mid-sixties, however, that large numbers of women have begun this necessary tearing apart of the patriarchal structures we have all been acculturated to call "reality." One of the first and most effective tools women have consciously used for this purpose is consciousness raising.

Consciousness raising cannot be separated from the origins of the second wave of feminism. In contrast to the "first wave," usually dated from the 1848 Seneca Falls Convention, the second grew out of radical women's disillusionment with the radical left in the 1960s. One of the first to try to raise women's consciousnesses was a young black woman, Ruby Doris Smith Robinson. In 1964 she wrote a paper on women's position in SNCC (Student Non-violent Coordinating Committee), of which she was a founding member. At the time she was merely laughed at and the issue was ignored. But the next year two white women long active in SNCC and other civil rights organizations wrote an article for *Studies on the Left* (long since defunct), on the position of movement women. Shortly thereafter, various women began forming caucuses within their movement organizations, and by 1966 some demanded a plan for women's liberation within the SDS (Students for a Democratic Society) resolution for that year. Despite male hostility and ridicule, such caucuses continued to form. Eventually they broke off to become much-needed independent groups devoted to women's liberation.[2]

At the same time, but independent of the Left movement, Betty Friedan helped found NOW (National Organization for Women) in 1966. In contrast to the radical politics of the women's groups, which emerged out of the Left, NOW is reformist and predominantly middle-class. Not only does it allow men to join, it works within the system. Thus the orientations of the two wings of what is broadly called the Women's Liberation Movement diverge widely. But common to both wings is the very important strategy now known as consciousness raising.

Consciousness raising requires a small, continuous group in which each member testifies about her own experiences. To facilitate this procedure and prevent the more articulate women from dominating a group, members typically speak in turn, often in answer to specific questions related to individual expansion of consciousness. Discussion of various ways women avoid awareness of their oppression is often another focus of discussion. A very important element of consciousness raising is searching for ways to overcome repression. To this end each woman analyzes her own responses to change. For instance, fear that past behaviors such as marrying inappropriate men or bearing unwanted children have negated a woman's life might focus a discussion. Using material generated by these different foci, groups would then try to develop feminist theory. Each member of a group would eventually lead a new group, so that consciousness raising could reach more and more women.

Such groups enlightened large numbers of women about the nature and extent of their oppression. Subsequent political and social action designed to change the patriarchal status quo often resulted. Consciousness raising remains a valuable tool of women seeking to decrease patriarchy.

Next to consciousness raising, probably the most widely disseminated process for decreating patriarchy has been educational reform. Once critical numbers of women recognized women's non-status within patriarchy they quickly realized that simply being *aware* of shared experiences, anger, hurt, and deprivation was not enough. Changes were needed. And one of these changes must be educational. It was time for women not only to learn about ourselves but to learn about so-called "reality" in ways that were not patriarchally skewed. One of the first official steps to remedy this deficiency was the appointment in 1969 of the Modern Language Association Commission on the Status of Women in the Profession. The Modern Language Association, the professional organization of college and university teachers of English and foreign languages, numbers about 30,000 members, of whom one-third are women. The aim of this commission has been twofold. First, it is designed to help women teaching modern languages, including English, at the college level; second, it is needed to disseminate information about ideas, courses, and scholarship pertaining to women. In its latter capacity, the commission has sponsored a forum and a series of workshops on women writers, feminist critics, textbooks, teaching Women's Studies, and related issues at annual meetings of the Modern Language Association.

Also crucial in disseminating information about this challenge to patriarchy is *The Women's Studies Quarterly* which first appeared in 1972 in the form of the *Women's Studies Newsletter*. What began as four pages has now grown to forty-eight, which report on programs from preschool to graduate school, from prisons to women's centers. In 1977 the National Women's Studies Association was formed, and now regional and campus-based newsletters on Women's Studies complement the larger national journal.

The creation of Women's Studies as a legitimate scholarly field has helped women enormously. College-level courses have helped focus the psychological discoveries of consciousness raising along intellectual lines, giving large numbers of women access to formerly unavailable factual material about women's lives. Much of this material refutes "facts" long promulgated and accepted by patriarchal ideologies.

An early challenge to these "facts" comes from the so-called matriarchal hypothesis. J. J. Bachofen, a nineteenth-century scholar, originated this so-called matriarchal hypothesis with his study, *Das Mutterrecht (Mother Right)*, published in 1861. Bachofen asserts that "mother right" grew out of the biological connection of mother and child. He claims that matriarchy, the rule of mothers in both family and society, arose from women's dissatisfaction with unregulated, promiscuous sexuality. Out of the matriarchal family individual marriage eventually evolved. With marriage came the transmission of property and names through the woman— that is, matrilineally. According to Bachofen, civil rule by women, which he calls "gynocracy," ensued. He places the mystery of women's ability to give birth at the heart of this gynocracy. This mystery gives Mother Right the sacred quality found in various prepatriarchal religions devoted to worship of the Great Mother Goddess. Bachofen deduces that "matriarchy is not confined to any particular people, but marks a cultural stage. . . . that was overlaid or totally destroyed by the later development of the ancient world."[3]

Other males who have significantly espoused this position are Robert Briffault *(The Mothers)* and Robert Graves *(The White Goddess)*. Some representative feminists who have taken it up are Elizabeth Gould Davis *(The First Sex)* and Charlene Spretnak *(The Politics of Women's Spirituality* and implicitly in *Lost Goddesses of Ancient Greece)*, and Merlin Stone *(When God Was a Woman)*.

Unfortunately, hard evidence to support this matriarchal hypothesis is lacking. At the time Bachofen wrote, armchair anthropology was the fashion, and he based his theory almost entirely on myths, language, customs, place names, and works of ancient writers such as Herodotus, Hesiod, Pindar, Ovid, Virgil, Strabo, Horace, and Homer. Once field-work became the norm in anthropology, the nineteenth-century belief that all cultures went through the stages of sexual promiscuity, matriarchy, and patriarchy was found to be overly simplistic.

Another major problem in Bachofen's work is his confusion of the two terms "matriarchy" and "matriliny." To date, matriarchy—rule by women—has not been found in any culture at any time. By contrast, matriliny, which refers to descent reckoned through the female rather than the male line, has characterized many cultures worldwide. In a matrilineal society, a woman's children use her name and inherit her wealth, and if she is royal, her son or sons-in-law inherit the throne. Her brother, rather than her husband, wields power in the family. It is he, rather than her husband, who functions in the role we are conditioned to think of as "father." But the power is still wielded by a *man*.

Despite scholarly rebuttals of the matriarchal hypothesis, many women continue to espouse it. The important issue for these women is not the scientific proof of matriarchal civilizations. Rather, it is *belief* that they once existed. In any culture a major task is constructing an identity, both for individuals and the community as a whole. For that purpose a past history is essential. To answer the question "Where am I going," one must first be able to answer the prior question, "Where have I come from?" The matriarchal hypothesis provides a mythically powerful answer for women.

Like the matriarchal hypothesis, the study of women's history, some-times referred to as "herstory," also helps to decreate patriarchy. Women's history has grown dramatically over the past two decades. Apart from isolated exceptions such as Mary Beard's *Woman as a Force in History*, women's history originally dealt mainly with women's social reform efforts on behalf of such varied causes as abolition; elimination of prostitution;

prison reform; temperance; humane treatment of American Indians; improved care of the insane, handicapped, and ill; and women's suffrage. In contrast to the hundreds of American men whose names schoolchildren memorized, the women mentioned in textbooks typically numbered fewer than a dozen: Elizabeth Cady Stanton, Harriet Beecher Stowe, Lucretia Mott, Amelia Bloomer, Susan B. Anthony, Catherine Beecher—these names exemplify the token women average American schoolchildren learned about in American history classes before the 1970s.

Several factors combined to bring women's history into being. One was the resurgent feminism sparked by peace, civil rights, and New Left women, on the one hand, and the publication in 1963, of Betty Friedan's landmark book, *The Feminine Mystique,* on the other. Another influential factor, extrinsic to feminism, derives from changes within the field of history. Intense philosophic self-questioning impelled historians to question what can and cannot properly be considered the domain of history. This questioning shifted emphasis away from almost exclusive preoccupation with the doings of presidents, legislators, and generals. Traditional "outer history" slowly began sharing space with "inner history," the thoughts and everyday lives of "ordinary people" as recorded in private journals. Consequently, women, along with other formerly ignored groups such as workers, peasants, servants, and slaves, suddenly acquired a place of our own in history.

The patriarchally decreative aspects of this shift in women's historic displacement involve two broad categories. In part, women were newly discovered to have played a much larger role than had hitherto been acknowledged in traditional "outer" history. Thus, such women as Elizabeth Blackwell, the first American woman to become a physician, suddenly seemed to emerge from nowhere into general awareness. But the numbers of such women, while impressive, are nonetheless limited for all the well-known social, economic, legal, and cultural reasons women are still struggling to surmount. Of potentially even greater significance, for two reasons, is the inclusion in history of women who were not "extraordinary," whose lives did not resemble those of men. These are unknown women, their names still largely unfamiliar, whose letters and diaries have recently been studied by scholars. The entry of these women into the academic study of history holds far greater potential for decreating patriarchy than does that of the exceptional tokens like Blackwell. This is so partly for the obvious reason that there are far more "ordinary" women; hence by sheer numbers alone they are formidable. More important, however, than their numbers is their very "ordinariness." The "exceptional" woman who entered history did so precisely because she *was* an exception—that is, she was different from most women. And that difference from other women, which allowed her historic status, invariably meant she had a likeness to men. She was judged by the standards of male behavior, and if she measured up, she entered history. By contrast, "ordinary" women are "ordinary" because their lives generally resemble those of the vast majority of women.

Like the matriarchal hypothesis, women's history poses certain dangers to women as well as to men. These dangers need to be examined because they partly explain the reluctance of many women to become liberated. There is good reason why some women feel as threatened as most men do by women's history. For women and men alike, what is "decreated" by women's history is a certain structure of "reality." And like it or not, this "reality" has been as "real" in many respects for most women as for most men. To alter it is therefore to destroy a large part of any individual woman, for part of any woman has necessarily been patriarchally constructed. To experience such destruction of one's sense of reality is extraordinarily painful. Often the easier course is to ignore the new truth and cling to the old fiction.

Undertaking such revision of the past, even if it is not one's own, personal past, is akin to embarking on a shamanic initiation flight. Typically during initiation, a shamanic candidate enters a trance state in which he experiences his own death followed by rebirth. Often he subjectively experiences the tearing apart of his body to such an extent that his bones seem to be severed from his flesh. Following this dreadful dismemberment, he is re-membered, returning to "this world" as a truly new person.

For a woman to suffer dismemberment of her assumed past is to undergo something of the shamanic ordeal. Just as in the shaman's case, re-memberment cannot be taken for granted; it may or may not succeed. A woman may indeed "return" feeling renewed. It is also possible, however, that she will simply feel cut off from everything familiar. In that case, instead of joyously embracing her "new" heritage, she may end up doubting she has any heritage at all. This possibility raises a significant issue: Is some sense of a past, no matter how negative, preferable to a sense that all pastness is both fictive and unfixed?

This question is a variant of one raised by the movie *Zelig*, in which Woody Allen plays the part of a man with so little sense of self that he is nicknamed "Chameleon Man." Amazingly, this man displays the characteristics of whatever person he is with. Thus he may be obese, black, fluent in French, artistically gifted, as the case may be, depending upon the personality of his companion. No stable core-identity holds this Woody Allen character together. In much the same way, a contemporary woman's sense of identity may grow terrifyingly fluid if she grows up believing in a patriarchal vision of women as nonpersons and then discovers, sometime in adulthood, that the "facts" she memorized in school are not valid.

In no way is this caveat meant to suggest that the study of women's history is a negative development. Rather, it is intended to help explain the otherwise puzzling phenomenon of women who refuse to leave the patriarchal edifice despite all the humiliation, pain, and deprivation associated with clinging to it. To feel certain that a place, no matter how "low," exists for her, traumatizes a woman far less than the fluidity of an altered self-image. Nor is it only women who have lived out traditional housewife-mother roles whose "selfhood" is necessarily most endangered by incursions from women's history. Token women are equally threatened, albeit in different ways. A woman who "made it" in the man's world of business, law, or medicine at a time when few women even entered it often cannot bear to reassess her status: Discovering that she is not the unique exception she has always thought she was severely disorients her. To maintain her accustomed self-image, old-fashioned, male-centered history must remain.

The responses of these women—the almost extinct "traditional housewife" and the "token woman"—to women's history are both patriarchal. Women who came of age believing in the standard patriarchal hierarchy of men "on top," women "on the bottom," know that being on the bottom necessarily means "not being as good as" those on top. Circular logic informs this way of thinking. The token woman using this logic will think: "Women belong on the bottom; I am not on the bottom; therefore I am not a woman." By contrast, a housewife accepting this pattern will think: "Women *belong* on 'the bottom'; I am a woman; therefore, *I* belong on the bottom. To be anywhere else, even to aspire to it, violates the natural order of things; therefore I will not consider it."

By this same logic, the housewife-mother role must necessarily be "on the bottom," for by definition, in patriarchal cultures, both are indissolubly connected to women: Woman equals housewife-mother; housewife-mother equals woman. A woman who has lived out much of her life adhering to this pattern resists suddenly being told that, contrary to everything she has ever been taught, relatively large numbers of women before her have engaged in roles other than those "ordained by God." Such realization devastates her. To require such a woman to accept an altered view of history is to demand that she see herself anew. Like the shamanic initiate she must "die" and allow "someone else," someone other than the self she has always thought she was, to take her place. Is she willing to do this? Why should "she" die? Why should she re-evaluate herself? It is one thing to be "low" if all or almost all others of her kind are similarly placed. But if not. . . . No, it is easier to ignore women's history or, if forced to acknowledge the existence of such a thing, to laugh at it. Her husband and his cronies laugh about it—why shouldn't she?

But apart from the threats women's history may pose to the psyches of both women and men, there is a larger decreative issue to consider. If the lives of "ordinary" women can now be seen to hold historic interest, that means either patriarchal norms have been drastically altered or women's experiences have been. The private space of woman's domestic sphere is no longer historically insignificant. The traditional patriarchal insistence on hierarchical distinctions between men's and women's places and spaces has therefore been somewhat leveled. The question that must be addressed in this situation, however, is just what happens to those formerly ordinary or private lives that are now historicized. Unquestionably patriarchal prestige suffers as a result. Is it necessarily the case that women benefit correspondingly? To women who envision feminism as integration into the patriarchal mainstream, this form of patriarchal de-creation represents an advance. But for those who opt for entirely a-patriarchal forms and valuations, inclusion in patriarchal history can be construed as yet another instance of cooptation. Instead, such women might demand a whole new category, for which as yet no name exists, except perhaps in the minds of some visionary women who may even at this moment be creating appropriate new classifications for women's experience without reference to patriarchy's construct, history.

In this connection, efforts by some feminist scholars to reclaim language which is rightfully women's are particularly relevant. One excellent source is *The Woman's Encyclopedia of Myths and Secrets,* edited by Barbara G. Walker. An example of the kind of linguistic reclamation this work accomplishes occurs under the word "cunt." In contrast to the highly pejorative, vulgar meaning "cunt" has when applied to a woman within patriarchal society, Walker claims it actually derives from the Oriental Great Goddess Cunti, the Yoni of the Universe. She lists various cognates including "kin," which "meant not only matrilineal blood relations but also a cleft or crevice, the Goddess's genital opening."[4] Quickly apparent from the rather lengthy entry for this word is the way our underlying patriarchal world view creates woman-denigrating definitions. It also shapes interpretations of woman-connected words. Conversely, in this woman-celebrating context, the other definitions arrayed under the listing for "cunt" surprise the reader less than this startlingly positive meaning of the word in its primary sense. Outside of patriarchy a cunt is *not* something to hide or be ashamed of: It is an opening long considered sacred.

Seeing in print this extended definition legitimates for a woman her own, previously hidden, inner knowledge that this is so.

Another example of genderized semantics, applied this time to a man rather than a woman, occurs with the word "cuckold." Much as "cunt" devalues a woman in a patriarchal context, "cuckold" denigrates a man. Yet within a prepatriarchal context, where the religious focus of attention was the Goddess, the concept of a "cuckold" was not derisive. The horns implied by the word are those of the horned god, the consort of the Goddess who was ritually sacrificed only to be reborn again. Within the context in which that ritual occurred, the sacrifice was appropriate—it was not cause for shame.

Other significant examples of feminist linguistic change occur in the writing of feminist writer Susan Griffin. In her collection of poetry (which is also history, philosophy, and science), *Woman and Nature: The Roaring inside Her,* Griffin replaces familiar androcentric labels such as "Renaissance" with others more appropriate to women's lives: "Andromeda," to signify the age in which woman loses her name; "Lepus," to name the years she might have had had she not been raising children.[5]

Another contemporary feminist writer deeply concerned with linguistic change is Monique Wittig. Being French, she must deal with the problem of gender with each word she uses. Consequently, the linguistic challenge is more overt for her: " 'I' [*Je*] as a generic feminine subject can *only* enter by force into a language which is foreign to it, for all that is human (masculine) is foreign to it, the human not being feminine grammatically speaking but he [*il*] or they [*ils*]. . . . The 'I' [*Je*] who writes is alien to her own writing at every word because this 'I' [*Je*] uses a language alien to her; this 'I' [*Je*] cannot be *un ecrivain*."[6] Wittig's response to this problem is to change the genders of symbolic persons. Thus, for example, she speaks of "Patroclea," the "tendon of Achillea," and "Christa the much-crucified."[7]

Some writers concern themselves less with language per se than with content as a catalyst for decreating patriarchy. Erica Jong, for example, created a furor in 1973 with *Fear of Flying* because it was reputedly the first pornographic, as opposed to merely erotic, novel detailing a woman's fantasies, actually written by a woman. That is, it was intended to arouse its readers, not merely enlighten them. It seems odd, scarcely more than a decade later, to think that previously, received patriarchal wisdom held that women didn't fantasize pornographically.

Visionary writers like Joanna Russ and Ursula K. Le Guin who imagine single-sex or sexually changed societies also help decrease patriarchy through content subversive to the presumed order of things. And a popular writer like Jean Auel in *The Clan of the Cave Bear* helps decreate patriarchy by depicting a woman who is truly a hero and not a heroine. The protagonist Ayla, an orphaned Cro-Magnon woman adopted in infancy by a Neanderthal tribe, is both taller and smarter than even the wisest members of her adoptive tribe. An outsider in all senses, she is well-suited to function in the traditional heroic mode of culture-bringer to her tribe. In all ways Ayla belies patriarchal stereotypes of woman as the weaker sex. She thereby helps decreate a favorite tenet of patriarchy, if not in her adoptive tribe, at least in the minds of her readers.

Also deeply threatening to the structures of patriarchal thought are all avowedly lesbian writings: Radclyffe Hall's *Well of Loneliness,* Anaïs Nin's *Diaries,* Jane Rule's "romances," Rita Mae Brown's *Rubyfruit Jungle*. In these and similar works, as also in most writings by contemporary black women writers, women create and live in worlds where men either do not figure or become irrelevant to the women's survival. Alice Walker's *The Color Purple,* Toni Morrison's *Sula,* and Ntozake Shange's *For Colored Girls* all represent such women's strength in black women's writing.

Often decreation of patriarchy assumes a highly visual form as in the works of some contemporary women artists. Perhaps no American artist quite so blatantly decreates patriarchy as Louise Bourgeois, who was born in France in 1911. From the early seventies on, her work has challenged masculinist assumptions. For example, her 1970 work, *Black March,* consists of twenty smooth black marble objects which can only be called phalli, attached to a rough, pumicelike base. Still more overt is her 1974 seven-foot construction, *The Destruction of the Father,* in latex and stone. From the top of a cavelike setting she suspends numerous large spheroid objects which strikingly resemble enormous breasts. Beneath them lies a roughly oblong base from which protrude numerous spheres and eggs. To one side of this base lie objects resembling body parts, specifically buttocks with attached legs. The effect of the whole is both eerie and fascinating.[8] The darkness of the interior implies a mysterious cave. The distorted female icons, together with the body parts so suggestive of sacrifice, produce an impression of darkly negative female power. This is the power associated with the Mother Goddess in her destructive aspect. Work of this magnitude, employing this sort of imagery, undeniably decreates patriarchy.

Another contemporary artist whose work just as strongly demolishes patriarchy is Mary Kelly, who was born in 1941 and works in Britain. In 1975 she worked on an exhibition called *Women and Work,* which highlighted reproduction as the central cause of division of labor in the home. Out of this exhibition developed her *Post Partum Document* of 1976. In this work she even more radically challenges patriarchy by uniting "the public and the private, the domestic and professional, whose categorical separation has structurally defined what is and what is not called art."[9] Here Kelly uses such items as a series of diary-recorded conversations written at weekly intervals, notes recording her child's development, and objects, such as diapers, emblematic of the mother-child relationship. Specifically marking her challenge to patriarchy is her refusal to show the mother, a refusal which automatically precludes the patriarchal tendency to objectify women. Still more radical is the way she challenges the patriarchal assumption that a mother instinctively knows what to do. By juxtaposing her close documentation of such mother-child circumstances as the child's early bowel habits with medical feeding charts, she forces the viewer to see the contrast between the mother's subjective responses and the ideology of patriarchal assumptions about motherhood.

The work of Canadian-born (November 15, 1923) artist Miriam Schapiro provides yet another example of the way some contemporary women are working to decreate patriarchy. In 1970 she and Judy Chicago taught in the newly founded Feminist Art Program at the California Institute of the Arts in Valencia. The result was *Womanhouse*, a feminist environment collaboratively created by them and their twenty-one women students. Out of a Hollywood house slated for demolition, the group produced a celebration of traditional women's arts and crafts. Not only was this a house and not a museum, the art within it openly defied patriarchal aesthetic canons. It denied the accepted division between Low and High art, between "craft" and "art." This same leveling of traditionally accepted (patriarchal) definitions of art occurs throughout Schapiro's post-1970 work, in which she repeatedly draws both themes and techniques from women's, not men's, traditions. In her celebrated *Anatomy of a Kimono*, 1976, a series of ten panels totaling 50 feet in length, she creates several monumental kimonos and details of them out of fabric and acrylic on canvas. Her own words well express the "patriarchally decreative" aspects of this work:

> . . . I chose the kimono as a ceremonial robe for the new woman. I wanted her to be dressed with the power of her own office, her inner strength. . . . Then there is the question of *territory*.
>
> We know about all the women that Jansen [male art historian] forgot—that they painted small still lives or portraits, sometimes miniatures. The artist-makers did lap work—and all of this, not to take up space. Women must not make waves, must not be immodest, must not challenge habits which are men's habits.
>
> So I thought that . . . I would do a larger painting to announce the comfort that a woman has with "territory."[10]

Besides kimonos, Schapiro also enlarges hearts, dollhouses, and fans, each enlarged far beyond ordinary size to make "large" statements with and about women's icons.

Various kinds of woman-centered rituals are yet another means by which some women are working to decreate patriarchy. These regularly occur both inside and outside patriarchal institutions. In a Christian context, some of the most active women are those belonging to the Roman Catholic Church. Possibly this is because both it and the Eastern Orthodox Rite constitute the most overtly oppressive branches of Christianity, neither allowing women to perform priestly functions. Among Roman Catholic nuns unauthorized ritual consumption of bread increasingly takes place in women-only settings. That means that one or more nuns officiates. Such forbidden celebrations unquestionably decreate patriarchy in one of its strongest, most deeply entrenched religious forms.[11]

Lay Roman Catholic women, too, often develop women-centered rituals by which they try to decreate the patriarchal stranglehold of the Church.[12] Whether by their rituals they actually decreate so thoroughly patriarchal an institution is not always clear. Typically their attempts occur at Church- or women-related conferences. A good example of the ambiguous nature of this kind of ritual occurred at a conference called Women-Church Speaks, held in Chicago in 1983. Attending were twelve hundred women from six national organizations such as the Women for Ordination group. The conference theme was story. Three women—one black, one Hispanic, and one white—told their stories of being Roman Catholic women, emphasizing their growth as women, either despite the Church or because of it, as the case might be. Following their presentations, each of the other women in the room, seated at tables of ten, shared a portion of her own story with her tablemates. Their common focus was, How do you survive as a woman within a Roman Catholic context? Anger, disillusionment, struggle, and, above all, loneliness as women in a man's church repeatedly surfaced as themes from these shared tellings.

Each table held a dish of water and a shell filled with nard, an expensive perfumed ointment made from an East Indian plant. After the storytelling, the women joined in reading Mark 14:1-9, the section of the Gospel which tells of Jesus and the woman from Bethany who anoints him with costly nard. For so doing, she is reproached by some of Jesus' companions. They reason that she might better have sold the ointment, giving the money to the poor. But Jesus rebukes them, saying, "For you always have the poor with you, and wherever you will, you can do good to them; but you will not always have me." Jesus ends this passage saying,

"And truly, I say to you, wherever the gospel is preached in the whole world, what she has done will be told in memory of her." As the gospel reading occurred, participants at some tables began to wash each other's hands with the water. What happened in the conference to this point had all been planned. How individual tables chose to use their water and nard was up to them. At one table, a particularly moving ritual developed spontaneously. As participant Nancy Murray from Syracuse, New York, tells it, "I took some nard and rubbed it on the face of the woman next to me. As I did I said to her, 'You are forgiven, forgive yourself.'" Murray tells of the deep feelings which arose as first one woman then another repeated her words and actions until each woman at the table was anointed and forgiven. Murray, who has subsequently repeated the ritual at women's retreats, says, "Something happens in this ritual. It is so powerful in and of itself that two women left the circle at one retreat and couldn't even do it. It provides a way of reclaiming the work women do, which is forgiveness work, and lifts us up as Roman Catholic women to a real sacramental level." Ambiguity is nonetheless generated by this ritual because of the particular text chosen. For women who cannot readily accept the male-savior Jesus, it is difficult to value the challenge of women ritually forgiving each other. Just how fully decreative such a ritual is depends on the perspective of the individual woman. One who feels Christianity is too inherently patriarchal to be redeemed is unlikely to find this ritual convincing.

In Judaism, a similar ambiguity arises. The difficulties for women in this tradition may be even more immense than they are in Christianity. As Cynthia Ozick writes in her Talmudic essay, "Notes toward finding the right question," to be both woman and Jew is a contradiction. According to Jewish law, "women *qua* women are seen as a subdivision of humanity, not as the main class, itself. . . . the male is the norm and the female a class apart."[13] Nonetheless, many women choose to retain both their Jewishness and their feminism. One is the writer E. M. Broner who, along with Naomi Nimrod, has created a women's Passover ceremony. Instead of the male-oriented questions of the traditional ritual, they substitute four directed specifically to women: " 'Why is the Haggadah [rabbinical explanatory material] different from traditional Haggadoth?' 'Because this Haggadah deals with the exodus of women.'. . . 'Why have our mothers on this night been bitter?' 'Because they did the preparation but not the ritual. They did the serving but not the conducting. They read of their fathers but not of their mothers.' . . . 'Why on this night do we recline?' 'We recline on this night for the unhurried telling of the legacy of Miriam.'"[14] Everything that follows in this ritual names and celebrates women. So successful has it been that numerous Jewish groups and even some Christians concerned with new rituals for women have performed it.[15]

Some women, eschewing all patriarchal rites but seeking to belong to some established tradition, look to ancient prepatriarchal practices of witchcraft. Within such practices, rituals abound. An example is a self-blessing ritual described by Zsuzsanna E. Budapest, founder of the Sisterhood of the Wicca and the Susan B. Anthony Coven #1. This ritual is intended to honor a woman's own divinity.

The practitioner begins by bathing to purify herself. Then she takes from her altar or a specially prepared shelf, candles and incense, salt, wine, and water. The salt represents wisdom; water, the life force, or Aphrodite; and the wine, ecstasy. First she pours the salt on the floor and steps on it. Now she is standing on her wisdom. Next, she lights her candles and says, "Blessed be, Thou creature of fire." Then she lights her incense and dips her fingers into the mixture of wine and water, touching them to her forehead and saying, "Bless me, mother, for I am your child." She repeats the dipping and touching until she has appropriately blessed all the parts of her body. At the end she again stands on the salt, feeling her power flow through herself. When she snuffs out her candles she thanks the spirits to conclude the ceremony.[16]

Many women's rituals are not so specifically tied to past traditions. Some women prefer, instead, to create their own rituals out of their present circumstances. One such group of women lives near Wolf Creek, Oregon. Each year they perform a ritual for the Autumn Equinox to which each woman brings an object representing a recent accomplishment. The women gather in a circle, their representative objects placed in front of them next to a harvest symbol such as a fruit, seed, or cone. Joining hands, they chant in unison each woman's name followed by the months of the year from the Winter Solstice to the Autumn Equinox. In the next stage of the ceremony each woman in turn holds up her article and tells what she has learned from it. Each then picks up her harvest object and inwardly meditates on the process of growth from seed to plant to flower and back to seed. Again each woman speaks, telling now of her accomplishment in terms of growth. Those who feel thankful express thanks in whatever way suits them. The ceremony closes with the women forming a tight circle to chant a paean to harvest time.[17]

Some of the most compelling rituals created by women focus on birthing. The writer E. M. Broner tells of participating in such a ritual. The home delivery included women friends of the mother-to-be, several children, and the father-to-be. As the father massaged her back during her labor, the mother called to the baby, "Come down, baby." And as she labored she crooned the baby into birth. After delivering, the mother was not confined to her bed as though she had been ill. Instead, after showering, she joined the others to celebrate. Shared listening to the tape of the mother calling her baby into life climaxed a time of quiet talk and champagne drinking.[18]

Nelle Morton, late Associate Professor at Drew Theological School, describes another home birthing in which ritual played a big part. All who participated in it had at one time lived in the same house; consequently, they considered themselves one family. All wished to honor the arrival of a new member. About twenty-five attended, including two children. As the mother-to-be labored, one of the men breathed with her during her contractions. Some of the women massaged her and talked with her. At the end everyone pushed with her. When the baby cried, they all cried, hugged, and kissed. A large dinner culminated the occasion. [19]

And some women are helping their daughters to celebrate menarche just as women customarily did when humans still lived in tribes. Writer Judy Grahn tells of plans for such an occasion to which each woman was to bring a present. "What sort of present?" Grahn asks the girl's mother. "Just bring whatever you would have wanted to receive on this occasion in your own life."[20]

In all these ways—through new academic disciplines, language, art-forms, and rituals, women have learned to undo the patriarchal structures we were taught to believe in. As women use various mediums to decreate patriarchy, we also learn to use them to create visions of our own. While rage at the historical injustice of patriarchy holds some women at this decreative stage, women who want to fully actualize their gynocentric selfhood by completing the way of the mother must move on. It is not enough to estrange ourselves from the fathers. Nor is it sufficient to decreate their realm. We must eventually come to terms with a realm of our own instead. To do so we must find a way to meet the Mother Goddess who represents this realm so we may atone ourselves with Her.

PART V

Atonement with the Goddess

CHAPTER 19.

The Meeting with the Goddess

Meeting the Mother Goddess represents a crucial juncture in the hero's mythic quest: Symbolically, within a patriarchal context, She represents his opposite—the unknown aspects of his own deepest self. For a woman following the way of the mother, meeting the Mother Goddess is just as important. But for her the Goddess is not opposite; She is like.

Patriarchal thinking always portrays this meeting with the Goddess from the hero's point of view. For him, the significant woman he encounters on his journey *incarnates* the Goddess. Joy characterizes his meeting, which traditionally culminates in a *hieros gamos,* a mystical marriage in which the hero-soul unites "with the Queen Goddess of the World."[1] So central to mythic thinking is this great marriage that it is found worldwide. Just as death conventionally culminates a tragedy, marriage traditionally climaxes a comedy. Originally sacred, this marriage ushers in a new reign in which the favored couple symbolizes renewal of life through the promise, implicit in their union, of children to come.

Necessarily the specifics of this meeting with the Goddess will vary for any woman, just as they do for any hero. For either sex, meeting the Goddess comprises one of life's transcendent moments, which no one is privileged to experience often. Such moments exist outside the ordinary time frame surrounding them.

How much more complex this transcendent meeting with the Goddess is for a woman than for a man! Although patriarchal myths make any woman a potential incarnation of the Goddess, they tell nothing of a woman's *own* meeting with Her. The complexity of this problem immediately becomes apparent as a woman puzzles out not just how to meet the Goddess but even how to recognize Her. In myth and fairy tale She is frequently disguised. Often She resembles an ancient, hideous hag. A true hero, in contrast to an impostor or failure, characteristically acknowledges this hag, despite her hideousness. Consequently, he earns a very special boon: She now transforms herself into a lovely woman and becomes his bride.

At first sight, the Goddess appears no lovelier to a woman than she does to a questing male. After all, like male heroes, women have been acculturated to see beauty only as our patriarchal culture defines it. For that reason, years may pass before we ever suspect Her presence. Furthermore, this apparent "hideousness" of the Goddess is not fixed in any specific form. It varies. This fluidity of the Goddess further compounds the difficulty of recognizing Her. I myself have experienced this problem. Twice the Goddess revealed Herself to me before I was ready to meet Her. The first time I was in graduate school. During one particularly intense afternoon of study at home, I lay down to rest. Once on the bed, with the shades pulled down, I felt my eyes open wide. Lying there, I "saw" before me, in a kind of waking dream, a gaping hole embedded in stone. Four incised sets of parallel triple lines fixed the rock in place. As in any dream, I immediately "recognized" this completely alien image: It was a "jaw of death." My task was to enter it. But the thought so terrified me that I refused. Sweat dampened my hands and forehead. My fear intensified. Dropping all pretense of nap or study, I rushed to the safety of preparing dinner. Given my reaction of extreme fear, no meeting with the Goddess could possibly take place on that occasion.

Never have I forgotten this incident. Only in hindsight did I realize that this "jaw of death" was the Goddess in one of Her many "hideous" forms. A subsequent encounter revealed Her in yet another "hideous" disguise.

This encounter happened nearly ten years later. A colleague drove me to an out-of-town women's workshop on guided imagery. Toward the close of the first session we were instructed to lie on the floor for forty-five minutes listening to a tape of Handel's *Water Music*. With eyes closed, we were to follow silently whatever images the music produced, for the full time. In less than five minutes, I encountered absolute nothingness: I died. As in my earlier experience with the "jaw of death," I could feel my heart palpitating, my hands sweating coldly. Again I resisted, forcing my eyes open. Once again I had refused to meet the Goddess in Her terrible phase. I was still not prepared either to understand or withstand Her power.

Barriers other than fear also hinder recognition of the Goddess. Rendering Her invisible are various patriarchal structures such as language, categorization, symbolization, and valorization. Women quickly discover how strongly these factors intervene in our seeing when we explore the question, Who or what is it that we will meet with when we encounter "the Goddess"? On one level this question resembles the more familiar "Who or What is God?" To a degree, both are unanswerable. The referent of "Goddess" is ultimately as ineffable as that of "God." What can be talked about, however, are the differences commonly attached to the two different concepts which make it so difficult for a woman in an androcentric culture to recognize the Goddess, whereas she can recognize God by means of the symbols, such as the Lord's Prayer or the cross of Christianity, her particular tradition teaches her to use.

Theoretically, as theologians both past and present have pointed out, "God" is a non-gender-specific term. "He" is either androgynous or beyond sexuality. To think of Him as "He" is therefore inappropriate. However, such theorizing ignores the way human beings actually do think. To say that "He" does not mean an idealized heavenly version of a flesh-and-blood male, is to disregard the spontaneous images triggered in most people's minds by the word. This theological argument focuses on the way some theologians believe the word "God" *should* work. It merely varies an equally common argument that generic "man" does not exclude "women." Both arguments bypass the *actual* working of the human mind in favor of reasoning about how words like "God" and "man" are theoretically *intended* to work.

For most people, the word "God" does conjure up images of an aged male patriarch. The "Goddess," by contrast, automatically connotes very different images. For some, she may be a partially draped, voluptuous female, with or without child. For others, "She" may be less specifically anthropomorphic but nonetheless associatively connected with women or women's attributes. My own experience of the jaw of death falls in this category: In my waking dream I was "asked" by an unseen speaker to enter the jaw, to be reborn. Such "asking" suggests the presence of deity. My second encounter, though even less anthropomorphic, nonetheless immediately suggested my earlier experience. I therefore recognized "Her" presence in this occurrence, despite the fact that once again I refused to stay and actually meet with Her. But had I not been trained by my studies to work with symbols from many traditions, I would have been unlikely to recognize Her at all in either instance. I was fortunate, but many women may wander into Her presence without ever knowing they have done so because Her symbols are not part of androcentric symbol systems.

Apart from the intertwined problems of recognizing and visualizing the Goddess, another difficulty inhibits women from readily meeting with Her. This is the problem of faith, a condition which can neither be willed nor reasoned into being. One either has it or not. It is significant for meeting with the Goddess because it is through faith alone that most people encounter deity. In extreme need, to what or whom does a woman pray? Only at this moment of invoking and naming does the conflict between the two very different contexts of patriarchal and gynocentric faith structures become fully apparent.

In childhood, a woman might have prayed daily to God. Perhaps what she said was just a rote, "Now I lay me down to sleep" or a hastily recited Lord's Prayer. At certain times it might have been an impassioned pleading of her own invention. As she grew to adulthood she might have felt less comfortable with either kind of prayer. Adolescent loss of faith might eventually have inhibited all petition. Slowly, however, she might have resumed occasional prayer, now perhaps with heightened self-consciousness. Initially, self-consciousness might reflect previous loss of faith. Logically, how could she pray to a God she did not believe in? Suppose that later still she develops a feminist spirituality. Then she would feel doubly uncomfortable: Who or what does she now name by the word "God"?

This latter problem haunts many women deeply. Different *naming* can determine very different events. In her very deepest need a woman may automatically cry out to God. What does she experience when she invokes that name? This is a crucial issue. In my own case, though I do not exactly "see" anything in my mind's eye when I say "God," I nonetheless "know" that with that word I experience the male father God I was taught to believe in as a child. "He" is there. If I switch and say "Goddess" or "Mother," then something else occurs. Sadly, the switch automatically triggers an intellectual rather than a feeling mode of relationship. And that makes what I am doing no longer prayer. Consequently, trying to meet meaningfully with the Goddess, even though I can now recognize Her, is nearly impossible for me.

Like many contemporary women, I am trapped. Two different worlds of discourse grab me simultaneously. In the Goddess world I have not yet learned to pray, although I am entirely comfortable thinking in it. But patriarchal visions so shaped my earliest experiences of religion that I have not yet learned how to pray genuinely outside my original, necessarily patriarchal, religious context. At the same time, though I can occasionally still pray in the God world, my mistrust of partriarchy immediately counteracts that mode of prayer as well. I am therefore left with no world in which I can honestly pray.

I am of two minds about this dilemma. On the one hand, I find the underlying vision of deity as exclusively male extremely harmful. If the greatest value a woman can imagine is inextricably linked with maleness, then maleness remains enshrined as better, stronger, higher. Maleness appears more important in all respects. On the other hand, I cannot genuinely pray in a context which does not allow me to "meet" with deity. For the moment, I am stuck. I am ill at ease in the old, familiar patriarchal context because of its exclusive language and imagery. I am equally uncomfortable in the new, gynocentric structure. In it I cannot yet sufficiently establish contact with the Goddess to make my prayers authentic.

It is not that I feel the Goddess does not exist. Rather She has been so veiled through layers of patriarchal filters that she has long been reduced in size to a she who "fits" the categories of patriarchal thought. A novel which beautifully illustrates this kind of reduction is C. S. Lewis's *Till We Have Faces,* a retelling of the myth of Psyche.[2] Instead of presenting the story from the perspective of the beautiful Psyche, Lewis tells it from the viewpoint of Orual, one of her two sisters. Orual grows up aware that she herself is so terrible to look at that she will never have suitors. She therefore goes through life veiled. Only after living out her role in the Psyche story and ruling long and ably as a powerful, well-loved queen does she realize that she herself has now become Psyche. But simultaneously She is also Ungit, the terrible goddess of her people. Here the reader sees that the Goddess, in this particular incarnation, is initially unrecognized and unrecognizable even to herself. By her own estimation, internalized from the patriarchal culture in which she lives, Orual-Psyche-Ungit is "ugly." So ugly is she, in fact, that she feels compelled to live out her entire life veiled.

The problems women encounter because of this belief concerning the ugliness or terribleness of the Goddess cannot be overstressed. Because of this belief, women not only fail to recognize the Goddess, we also fail to recognize important aspects in ourselves as well. This belief in the ugliness of the Goddess reflects a patriarchally imposed belief system commonly accepted by many Western women that we ourselves are ugly. How strongly our Western culture inculcates women as a class with the belief that our natural bodies are somehow lacking. Unless a woman happens to be one of the exceptions (another kind of token woman), with measurements appropriate to selection as Miss America, she is unlikely to think differently. Two books of the 1980s which probe this issue are Susie Orbach's *Fat Is a Feminist Issue* and Kim Chernin's *The Obsession: Reflections on the Tyranny of Slenderness.* As their titles indicate, both connect "acceptable" images of women as slender beings to attitudes common to women as well as men, for both sexes alike live in a patriarchal culture. Chernin recounts an early fantasy in which she would envision her body transformed from its "state of imperfection to a consummate loveliness, the flesh trimmed away, stomach flat, thighs like those of the adolescent runner on the back slopes of the fire trail, a boy of fifteen or sixteen, running along there one evening. . . ."[3] She is far into adulthood before she connects this imagined transformation to "a bitter contempt for the feminine nature of my own body. The sense of fullness and swelling, of curves and softness, the awareness of plenitude and abundance, which filled me with disgust and alarm, were actually the qualities of a woman's body."[4] Chernin's insight underscores a self-loathing common to many women based on deep hatred of the sex to which we belong. Given such self-loathing, is it any wonder that many women find meeting with the Goddess, in whose image we are created, difficult?

Like the black child who chooses white dolls and identifies with them rather than black ones, the woman who internalizes masculine standards of bodily acceptability will often attempt to remake her image, rather than accept one patterned on the image of the Goddess. Furthermore, this kind of deep disgust of adult women's natural bodies internalized by many young women in contemporary Western cultures does not stop at body shape. It often extends to body secretions and odors as well, particularly in the United States, where body odors are not tolerated the way they are in many other parts of the world. It was long considered improper for women to sweat visibly. In fact, in "polite" society women, renamed "ladies," did not sweat: they perspired. Only women and men sweated. Until physical fitness became so chic, women in movies or on television were never shown with telltale underarm rings. Even more than underarm wetness and odors, fear of vaginal smells particularly occasions discomfort for women in patriarchal Western cultures. A case in point is the writer Lillian Hellman. Hellman reportedly suffered a lifelong fear of her presumed vaginal odors due to comments her first lover made to her.

Internalizing such feelings, as the case of Hellman suggests, incalculably harms a woman in two ways. Personally, it makes her uncomfortable with herself, leading to severe self-doubts. Often, fear of smelling bad (in either sex) signals severe neurosis, even psychosis. Such fear in a woman certainly suggests alienation from her woman's body. Apart from this personal harm, fear of odors can damage a woman in another way as well. In the case of a woman who has internalized the notion that *all* women smell bad, negative effects extend to women as a class. Not only does such a woman fear her own body; she also fears and suspects those of other women. Such fear makes it almost impossible to imagine a symbol of ultimacy in womanform. How could such a being as a Goddess possibly exist?

Such dissociation from women's body shape and body odors does not characterize all patriarchal cultures, nor does it characterize all women and men in cultures that do espouse svelteness and deodorized bodies. But certainly the prominent exposure given to weight loss and various deodorants in the United States indicates the importance of both to large numbers of contemporary America's population. Furthermore, it is primarily women who attend weight loss clinics, as it is primarily women who are ostracized for smelling bad.

In terms of the Mother Goddess, such negative attitudes toward women's natural bodily attributes automatically preclude the ability to envision Her in all Her radiance. Instead, what a woman will see is the "loathly lady" of myth and fairy tale. Rather than Her full majesty, we will see only the outer "covering," which is all patriarchally acculturated eyes are normally capable of seeing.

But just what is so loathsome about this figure? And what occasions the belief that woman, the creature made in Her image, is also naturally loathsome? This problem is partly aesthetic, encompassing notions of beauty and ugliness in general. But ordinarily whenever aesthetic judgments are made, knowing critics take care to judge in terms of the particular category to which a given object belongs. A poem is not judged by the same criteria as a novel; a sculpture by those of a painting; nor twentieth-century American art by those of fourteenth-century Italian. When it comes to aesthetic standards for judging women, however, increasingly in the United States, the standard of bodily beauty has worked against the natural appearance of most adult women. To say that the underlying model has lately been the preadolescent body as Chernin claims[5] is not precisely accurate, given the mammary obsession of American men, but certainly the leanness and also the muscularity now so ubiquitously prized are both more natural to men than women. It is only fair to say, however, that body shape has lately become as great a concern to many men as to women, particularly gay men, so that it is more a *body* issue per se than one of women's bodies in contrast to men's. To the extent that patriarchy devalues nature and sets up in its place *control* of nature, then it scarcely matters whether its "victims" are the bodies of women or the bodies of men. Nonetheless, historically within patriarchal thought, woman has been associated with the body in contrast to man who has been connected to mind and/or soul. Consequently, at the symbolic level, this recent interest of men in body shape may not perceptibly alter androcentric constructions of woman. Furthermore, as the bodies of both sexes increasingly become arenas in which individuals seek to impose their will, the patriarchal mind-body split is more drastically enacted than ever before. Now parts are lopped off in reduction surgery designed to make large, flabby breasts small and taut, or as one medical student once flippantly put it on a patient's chart: "Has super droopers, wants pippy pointeroos."[6] Or flabby thighs and buttocks are lifted and tightened to make "youthful," tight derrieres. And so on throughout all the offensive body parts. No wonder it is difficult to envision the Goddess!

This body hatred, whether on the part of women or men, carries with it a direct rejection of the Mother Goddess. It is She, after all, incarnated in the form of one's own particular mother, whose body a woman first encounters. As Dorothy Dinnerstein points out in *The Mermaid and the Minotaur,* it is the mother rather than the father who traditionally first comes in contact with an infant's body.[7] Uterine existence, nursing, diaper changing, feeding—these are functions primarily performed by the mother or a female surrogate. Not only will the body of this maternal figure automatically influence her children; so will the attitudes she holds toward bodies and bodily functions. Daughters in particular, because they characteristically identify more closely with the mother than do sons, are prone to "catch" both her body image and her feelings. If the maternal figure finds changing diapers repulsive, chances are her daughters will "inherit" a similar disgust, perhaps also extending it to the processes of urination and defecation. Consequently, a view of the Goddess as loathly is likely to originate in infancy.

In addition to any bodily inhibitions the mother herself passes on, the sight of her body may also affect her children. Even if the mother is modest, her children will now and then glimpse her nude. Perhaps the mother's flesh excites them, leading daughters as well as sons to fantasize about her erotically. But perhaps, sensing an even greater prohibition against such eroticism for them than for their brothers, her daughters will repress their attraction and feel shame instead. As writer Edna O'Brien says, "If you want to know what I regard as the principal crux of female despair, it is this: in the Greek myth of Oedipus and in Freud's exploration of it, the son's desire for his mother is admitted; the infant daughter also desires its mother but it is unthinkable, either in myth, in fantasy or in fact, that that desire can be consummated."[8]

Or children of either sex may, for whatever reasons, find their mother's body loathsome. Some daughters, even at very young ages, will unconsciously judge their mother's slightly round and sagging flesh against the Western cultural ideal of firm smoothness. If the mother's breasts are pendulous, her stomach protuberant, her veins varicose, her daughters may shrink from the sight of her body. Perhaps that sight may even freeze them, making them want to dissociate themselves completely from the maternal body. How could they ever have been *inside* it? The idea is repulsive. How readily they imagine slime surrounding them *in utero.*

Were their fetal selves anything more than bowel movements waiting to be expelled? In this fashion not only do perfectly natural body functions become disgusting, the self-image of the child does so, too. Sufficiently intense disgust with either or both may cause a woman to dissociate herself as completely as possible from her body functions. Anything at all connected with body may become literally unspeakable. Carried to extremes, such repugnance creates the euphemisms of the Victorian era. Even the "limbs" of tables had to be covered in polite society during this time when patriarchal values were clearly in the ascendant and authentically gynocentric ones nearly invisible.

Even if a woman's daughters do not experience disgust and loathing to a high degree, different possible effects can occur. A daughter may deny her natural body, coercing it into a form she finds more acceptable than that of her mother. Or she may repress awareness of her body as much as she can, becoming a relatively asexual or frigid adult. On the other hand, she may feel attracted to this "disgusting body" which pulls as much as it repels her. In that case the very "nastiness" she feels may become eroticized, making her long secretly for precisely what she abhors—the body of the mother. In her case, meeting with the Goddess therefore assumes a forbidden dimension, not unlike that patriarchal thought attributes to it when it renames Goddess worship witchcraft.

The significant factor, in terms of coming to atonement with the Mother Goddess, is a daughter's ability to re-see the seemingly "loathsome" mother and Mother Goddess. An excellent example of such re-seeing occurs in Anne Tyler's novel *Earthly Possessions*. Charlotte, the thirtyish, married protagonist, says very early in telling her story:

> My mother was a fat lady. . . Notice that I mention her fatness first. You couldn't overlook fatness like my mother's. It defined her, it radiated out from her, it filled any room she walked into. She was a mushroom-shaped woman with wispy blond hair you could see through, a pink face, and no neck; just a jaw sloping wider and wider till it turned into shoulders. All year round she wore sleeveless flowered shifts—a mistake.[9]

But when her mother is dying, Charlotte comes to terms with this woman from whose loathsome fat flesh she has always before felt alienated:

> Then I had my mother to myself. For I couldn't let loose of her yet. . . .
> "Mama," I said, "look." I turned on the reading lamp at the head of her bed. She flinched and closed her eyes. I held the photograph in front of her face. "Look, Mama. . . . Who is this a picture of? . . ."
> "Oh, me," she said. . . . I took the picture away and stared at it. . . .
> For now I saw that of course it was Mama. Obviously it was. And here I'd

> found so much in that little girl's eyes, imagined such a connection between us! . . . I returned to her, avoiding tubes and cords, careful not to jar her, and more gently than I'd ever done anything in my life, I laid my cheek against my mother's.[10]

For Charlotte, the loathsome mother and the previously unknown but idealized child of the photograph have now merged. This new oneness of the "terrible mother" and the beautiful child with whom she identified symbolizes Charlotte's hard-won meeting with her mother.

As long as women's natural bodies remain purely loathsome, few women can truly "see" their mothers, themselves, or other women, apart from the few beautiful exceptions. In such patriarchally infected circumstances the image of the Mother Goddess is hardly going to be visible. If, on the other hand, women's bodies are simultaneously loathsome and erotically compelling to women, the Goddess may be partially seen, but connected variously in women's experience to such conditions as lesbianism, nymphomania, forbiddenness, and "dirtiness," depending how they react to Her.

Only if women learn to see the natural beauty of women's natural bodies will we see the Goddess in all Her radiance. That is because the Mother Goddess simultaneously includes both good and evil, beauty and ugliness, nurture and destructiveness. What She represents is truly gynocentric thinking, a phenomenon very different from its patriarchal counterpart. In contrast to patriarchal thinking which splits wholes apart, gynocentric thinking is inclusive. It does not split opposites; instead it makes them coincide. One of the best examples of this inclusiveness is the Hindu goddess known variously as Parvati, Uma, and Durga. As Parvati, She is the beautiful young wife of Siva who often converses with him on topics ranging from love to metaphysics. As Uma, She seeks to attract Siva by harsh ascetic practices. As Durga, She is a bloodthirsty devouring goddess with ten arms, each holding a weapon.

Less all-encompassing but still representative of incorporated opposites is the ancient Sumerian goddess known by various names. As Inanna, She is the beloved goddess of the living; as Ereshkigal, She is the dreadful queen of the dead. Such goddess figures, who contain within themselves qualities patriarchal thinking consistently divides into separate deities, are sources of deep mystery and revelation.

In keeping with this holistic nature of the Goddess, a decisive step for a woman meeting Her is learning not to reject the natural female body. If a woman can achieve this step, she must then take the next one: She must actively accept the female body as well. This acceptance may occur in several ways. For some women it involves ritual. Such is the case for

Marian, a young anorexia victim who finally overcomes her obsession with skeletal thinness by baking a cake in the shape of a woman:

> . . . Marian, as she begins to chew and swallow, is symbolically reclaiming her hunger and her right to hunger. By eating up this cake fetish of a woman's body she assimilates for the first time her own body and its feelings. It is re-enactment of the ritual feast, in which the eating of an animal's flesh, or a piece of cake shaped like a breast, signifies the coming together of human and divine, individual with collective, tribal ancestor with member of the tribe, human community with nature, or a woman with her own body and feelings.[11]

Or a woman seeking to accept the natural body in order to meet with the Goddess may experience a sudden "seeing" in which the accustomed patriarchal filters fall away and she sees anew. Such was the case for me on a trip to Vienna in the summer of 1983. There, repeatedly, I saw middle-aged and elderly women wearing a kind of dress seldom seen in the United States since the late 1940s or early '50s. Not a housedress because made of "good" material, nonetheless it resembles one. It is somewhat square of cut, with cap sleeves, in a multicolored print. Such a dress immediately says "middle-aged" or "old." It also reveals the flabby undersides of arms. What I once would have ignored or found ugly and somewhat horrifying unexpectedly appeared very different. A true reversal of my habitual seeing took place. Now these homely women with their fleshy arms assumed beauty in my eyes. I saw the Goddess shining forth from within them. And for once I did not shrink back from Her. Instead of something to be avoided, these women's sagging folds of flesh signaled the changes in skin elasticity that occur in any woman who lives long enough. These sagging folds of flesh simultaneously signify her survival and symbolize her approaching death. In that moment, the previously hideous skin folds revealed far more: Looking at them, I understood deeply the fear of death so strongly infusing patriarchy. This insight granted by my meeting with the Goddess was truly revelatory, especially here in this city of Freud, who postulated that "the aim of all life is death."[12]

Yet this connection of life and death posited by Freud and made visible in these aging arms is not so simple. Freud also goes on to say that "the organism wishes to die only in its own fashion."[13] Against this hypothesized "death instinct," Freud posited the intuitively more acceptable "life" or "pleasure" principle connected with reproduction and sexuality. In that single, infinitely extended instant in Vienna, I understood the intensity of patriarchal aversion to aging women's flesh: All too vividly it connotes the end for which we are all destined. Paradoxically, the "heroic" bloodshed of war avoids that end because it allows the "hero" to control his fate by choosing a time earlier than that likely in the natural course of events. As soldier hero, *he* wills to either battle death or die; by contrast, as old man he must inevitably succumb to the Goddess.

Yes, I realized, Nature, the Goddess, symbolizes what Freud called Ananke, Necessity: She, the source of our being, is also our end. We cannot avoid Her. "She" is that over which the biblical God gave "man" dominion. But ultimately She has dominion over us.

In my long-delayed meeting with the Goddess there in Vienna, I realized that I was in a very different realm from the one in which I was raised and ordinarily reside. Consequently, my perceptions had to shift, too. I could not simply apply patriarchal constructions to such a meeting. But dropping these constructions is not easy. As a result, I found myself inadvertently shifting back and forth rather dizzyingly between a patriarchal and a gynocentric evaluation of what was happening. Whenever I slipped back into the more familiar patriarchal context, I saw only flabby arms and tackily dressed, hideous aging women. But as long as I remained in the context of the Mother Goddess, I saw their inherent beauty.

In those exhilarating moments, I finally met the Mother Goddess fully for the first time after years of perpetually denying Her. Such meeting is essential for any woman attempting to atone herself with the Mother Goddess. Only after it has occurred can the next stage of atonement take place: the mystical marriage with the Goddess.

CHAPTER 20.

The Mystical Marriage

From a patriarchal perspective a woman's atonement with the Mother does not so much resemble the hero's atonement with the Father as it does his mystical marriage with the Goddess. This mystical marriage typically occurs about midway on his quest. For a woman, just as for a hero, this meeting represents "the crisis . . . at the central point of the cosmos . . . or within the darkness of the deepest chamber of the heart."[1] In a woman's case the crisis occasioned by this meeting is her acceptance of the fact that she and the Mother are one—that she *is* the Mother. Inevitably, this crisis is one of the most crucial along the way of the mother. Unless a woman can successfully negotiate it, she will find further progress difficult.

Women who either miss or refuse the symbolic meanings of the way of the mother never experience this mystical marriage. For some women, this stage along the way of the mother is so difficult that *not* experiencing it almost feels positive rather than negative. That is largely because surprisingly few culturally acceptable models for this mystical marriage exist in contemporary Western cultures. The nineteenth century is far more replete with viable examples than our own. An excellent essay on "The Female World of Love and Ritual," by Carroll Smith-Rosenberg well establishes this point.[2] Drawing from a variety of sources, but particularly from collections of letters and personal diaries, she describes a rich world of female love as the norm for nineteenth-century American women. At its core is a mother-daughter bond which remained close throughout the lives of both women. Sisters, cousins, aunts, and school friends were all "loved" as well, with a devotion few women nowadays seem to share with each other much past grammar school.

Just how to categorize these close female friendships is a bit of a puzzle. To quote from just one of Smith-Rosesnberg's examples: "I laid with my dear R[ebecca] and a glorious good talk we had until about 4 [a.m.]—O how hard I do *love* her. . . ."[3] A late twentieth-century mind is likely to categorize this as lesbian behavior. Yet as Smith-Rosenberg's essay indicates, such readiness to see what we now label "pathology" is to oversimplify and stigmatize a commonly accepted love whose hallmark was ambiguity, not clear-cut simplicity. Although repeated references such as this one to lying in bed with a beloved friend or wildly embracing or even kissing her are common, these sensual expressions of deep feeling are not necessarily, nor perhaps even likely, genitalized. What these passionate female friendships reflected was "a female world in which hostility and criticism of other women were discouraged . . . a milieu in which women could develop a sense of inner security and self-esteem."[4] As such they enact the underlying meaning of the mystical marriage with the Goddess—the love a woman bears toward both herself and her own kind. If she cannot love other women, how can she love herself? Conversely, if she cannot love herself, how can she love other women?

By contrast with such open caring for other women, the feelings of most women for each other in contemporary Western cultures are remote indeed. Relatively few women are encouraged to develop such close ties with their female relatives and friends, many of whom are perceived as rivals for available males. Hence they often become hated enemies instead of loved friends. Rather than learning to love other women, we more typically learn to fear and distrust each other. Instead of mirroring ourselves positively, other women therefore more often reflect what is least desirable in ourselves. As a result, what we uncover in each other is anything but the fullness of the Goddess.

Where, then, are our contemporary models? At the risk of offending some readers, it is helpful to look for them among that group of women commonly referred to as "women who love women." These women provide a helpful model because they try to act toward themselves and other women according to woman-centered rather than patriarchal dictates. Therefore, their attitudes toward women tend to be somewhat less patriarchally contaminated than those of heterosexual women. Nonetheless, because this is a touchy subject, some readers may prefer to skip the remainder of this chapter. It should be clearly understood by all readers, however, that the essential issue here is not a woman's sexual preference. Rather, it is her acceptance and caring for those like herself. As with any group dominated by another, the tendency is to identify with the oppressor, seeing in him images of value. By contrast, those of the oppressed group, including oneself as a member of that group, are typically despised. Overcoming such self-hatred and denigration is the essence of the mystical marriage.

As we will see in the next chapter, some women participate in this mystical marriage through childbirth and transformation into motherselfhood. But women who love women actualize the mystical marriage more literally. These are women who love other women. Like the body and its functions, the idea of women loving women disgusts many women. Patriarchal thinking combines with heterosexual attitudes to create this disgust which traps some women into believing this is indeed "the love that dare not speak its name." In fact, the very word for this love of women for each other, "lesbianism," repels many people. But women who react so strongly against women loving women might consider what qualities so contaminate this love in their eyes.

A woman reluctant to examine lesbianism dispassionately might momentarily set aside the word "lesbian." Surely she can think of women friends toward whom she feels deep affection, even love. "But," she may say, "the love I feel for my women friends is not sexual. I 'love' them the way I love my sister. I even think of them as family." That kind of response is common from heterosexual women. Given a strict division of sexuality into hetero- and homosexual, it is logical.

Part of the problem is the division itself. One of the categories of thought central to patriarchy is the "norm" of "heterosexuality." Since the nineteenth century Western cultures have generally stigmatized individuals who exhibit traits deviating from the "natural" behaviors of heterosexuality. Such people are classified as homosexual or, more recently, gay. Before the nineteenth century, however, no such category existed, despite the fact that sexual relations between members of the same sex have been documented from at least the time of the ancient Greeks. What changed in the nineteenth century is the way these behaviors were interpreted. In ancient Greece older men customarily took young men as lovers, usually schooling and sometimes even adopting them. These older men were also married, however. Furthermore, once a favored youth reached his maturity, all sexual relations between the two were expected to cease. Two adult males engaging in sexual relations were ridiculed. As might be expected from the relative paucity of historical information on women, far less is known about lesbian relationships. Sappho, from the island of Lesbos, which gives lesbianism its name, is our major source from the ancient world. Little of her work is extant, however, because her books were all burned in the early Christian era. Only fragments quoted in other classical works still exist.

Nonetheless, despite the relative scarcity of details about women, homosexual *behaviors* in both sexes are known to have existed from antiquity in most cultures. What is different about post-nineteenth century homosexuality is the idea that one can *be* something called a homosexual: That is a relatively recent phenomenon. As John D'Emilio points out in

Sexual Politics, Sexual Communities, defining an individual according to sexual preferences and behaviors simply did not occur before the nineteenth century in Western culture.[5] Unquestionably, persons who engaged in same-sex erotic behaviors were often censured. This was particularly true within a Judeo-Christian context. But it was their *behaviors* that were condemned, not their entire selfhood. As human beings they were not cast aside into a totally separate, stigmatized category of existence with its own special name. Once they altered the culturally offensive behaviors, they were no longer ostracized.

Attitudes of this sort which contribute to the *stigma* attached to lesbianism matter greatly, especially for women trying to meet with the Mother Goddess. Within our heterosexually dominated culture, women generally react to the very idea of women loving women along a scale. Some adopt the predominant heterosexist pattern. These women automatically stigmatize women loving women—lesbianism—as something entirely outside themselves. These are often women who learned early that canceling an engagement with a woman, even just hours before the projected meeting time, was entirely acceptable behavior if a male had called for a date. For these women, men are so much more "important" than women, that women scarcely count. Only a constant stream of beaux can persuade such women that they, unlike their less attractive sisters, are "important," too. Other women feel irresistibly drawn to women as erotic objects, hence, in fact, manifest what is generally referred to as lesbian behavior. Between these two extremes fall women who do not feel erotically attracted to other women but who are not threatened by those who are. Among heterosexual women, it is this group who may learn to love women without feeling compelled to eroticize their love or to literalize the metaphor of the mystical marriage. For them, as for most nineteenth-century women, close female friendships throughout life seem perfectly natural. To sometimes prefer the company of these close friends in preference to that of men who are not friends does not appear strange.

Broadly speaking, women erotically drawn to women have two choices: If they so choose, they can embrace what the dominant culture characterizes as a stigmatic existence in which they perpetually enact a scapegoat role. Alternatively, women who love women can learn to see beyond heterosexist and patriarchal structures to nonheterosexist, gynocentric ones. Such seeing can help all women to reconceptualize lesbianism, thereby lessening its stigma. In so doing, women must automatically think deeply about what it means to be a woman, hence drawing closer to the Goddess.

This range of women's responses to the idea of women loving women may seem irrelevant for the vast majority of women who are heterosexual. Actually, however, it is extremely important because it parallels the range of women's attitudes toward other women in general. Therefore it is a critical aspect of understanding the mystical marriage with the Goddess. A woman who dislikes women may denigrate women as a class. Similarly, a woman who dislikes lesbians may stigmatize lesbians. Or, feeling stigmatized by her own womanhood, she may internalize her negative feelings instead. Rather than criticizing other women, she may defensively act out the stigma of womanhood in her own life. To do so, she may present herself in any one of numerous patriarchal stereotypes from "clinging vine" to "castrating bitch." Similarly, a woman drawn to a lesbian lifestyle may stigmatize that lifestyle, even though it is her own, just as the surrounding patriarchal culture does. In a variant form of stigmatization, she may act out a negative stereotype of that role. She may become "butch," acting and dressing in as masculine a fashion as she can.

Instead of projecting or internalizing negative responses to either womanhood or lesbianism or both, a few women learn to see beyond patriarchal cultural norms to envision nonreactive ways of being women. A heterosexual woman wishing to assert herself may appropriate the patriarchally opprobrious "bitch," turning it into a word she pridefully applies to herself. After all, she may reason, "bitch" is really just a label for a woman who gets ahead on her own terms without deferring to men or allowing them to confine her. Some radical lesbians similarly turn patriarchal stereotypes back upon themselves by using patriarchally derisive terms such as "dyke" with pride. As one contemporary lesbian puts it, "we've even taken back our names—they used to put . . . women down as 'dykes,' because we didn't fit society's mold. Well, to me and to a lot of other women, a dyke is a self-identified self-defining woman without limit . . . I'm a dyke and I'm damned proud of it."[6] This ability to claim a seemingly negative self-image with pride rather than shame is highly relevant to all women trying to achieve the difficult mystical marriage with the Goddess; it is not just a lesbian issue.

While concern about women loving women may appear overly hypothetical for thousands of women with no personal interest in erotic relationships with other women, nonetheless, a woman's underlying attitude toward such eroticism matters greatly. In *The Hite Report,* Shere Hite indicates its importance for all women when she says:

> Any woman who feels actual horror or revulsion at the thought of kissing or embracing or having physical relations with another woman should reexamine her feelings and attitudes not only about other women, but also about *herself.* A positive attitude toward our bodies and toward touching

ourselves and toward any physical contact that might naturally develop with another woman is essential to self-love and accepting our own bodies as good and beautiful.7

As Hite's words suggest, inability to accept the female body, whether one's own or another's, greatly handicaps a woman trying to develop the gynocentric selfhood derived from following the way of the mother. Carried to extremes, hatred of women's bodies can lead a woman to reject bodies in general. Even so innocuous a bodily function as another person's eating may revolt her. Sounds of chewing and swallowing may make her cringe, as many people commonly do when fingernails scrape against a blackboard. Unable to stop her anger and revulsion, she may be over-whelmed by negative feelings conventionally associated with bodies: their uncontrollable noises, their interior sliminess, their odors. Innumerable repulsive qualities may converge in her mind whenever she hears the smacks and slurps of food being chewed and swallowed.

Often such noisome qualities characterize patriarchal visions of Hell. In Hans Christian Andersen's fairy tale "The Girl Who Trod on a Loaf," for instance, they contribute significantly to hellishness. The story centers on a small girl so proud that she turns a perfectly good loaf of bread into a stepping stone rather than dirty her shoes. In consequence, she falls into the underworld realm of the Marsh Wife:

> . . . no one can stand being there long. A scavenger's cart is sweet com-pared to the Marsh Wife's brewery. The smell from the barrels is enough to make people faint, and the barrels are so close together that no one can pass between them, but wherever there is a little chink it is filled up with noisome toads and slimy snakes. Little Inger fell among all this horrid living filth.8

In Dante's *Inferno*, too, confinement to a circle of loathsomeness is common, as in Canto VI:

> Large hail, and turbid water, and snow, pour down through the darksome air; the ground, on which it falls, emits a putrid smell.9

And in Canto VII, noxious effluvia surround the souls of the angry:

> Thus, between the dry bank and the putrid fen, we compassed a large arc of that loathly slough, with eyes turned towards those that swallow of its filth; we came to the foot of a tower at last.10

Most religious traditions symbolize sin by interconnected concepts of impurity, defilement, and pollution. Within the predominant patriarchal religious traditions of Western culture—Judaism, Christianity, Islam—an individual wishing to atone himself with the Father God must first ritually cleanse himself. The Confession and Penance preceding Holy Communion in Roman Catholic ritual well illustrate this act. In Christianity, the symbol of ultimacy, God the Father, is pure; humans, by reason of our creatureliness, are not. To meet with God, humans must remedy this deficiency insofar as possible. This approach to deity, so deeply engrained in our culture as to seem "natural," differs totally from the approach necessary for atonement with the Mother Goddess.

Unlike the wholly good Father God, the Mother Goddess encompasses both good and evil. Whereas He stands against evil, typically represented as Satan, She incorporates it. Unlike Him, She is not one half of a dualism. Nor does she symbolize only the fertility and nurturance typically associated with mothers. Instead, she simultaneously includes death and decay, characteristics patriarchal thinking places in opposition to the nurturant qualities it prefers to separate out. As if to counteract Her holistic nature, patriarchal thinking repeatedly splits Her into parts even smaller than the halves of a dualism. The Greco-Roman pantheon well illustrates this tendency. There, many of Her qualities have been separated out to form individually distinct goddesses. Her rationality is personified as Athena, Her amorousness and beauty as Aphrodite, and so forth. But originally these, and many other traits, all belonged to the one Goddess. Because She is simultaneously good and evil, loving and hateful, peaceful and destructive, beautiful and ugly, embodied and spiritual, and so on, through all the so-called "pairs of opposites," a woman must *not* purify herself in preparation for the mystical marriage. To do so is to totally miss Her, to destroy any possible chance of the revelation this "marriage" will bring.

Yet somewhat surprisingly, to *refrain* from self-purification in preparation for this marriage is no easier than to engage in it. Consider first the nature of purification for ritual atonement with the patriarchal God. A penitent churchgoer may find herself sitting, purified and waiting for Communion, only to be overcome by all the "bad" words she knows: "fuck," "shit," "goddamn." There they all are. Her face flushes, her heart palpitates, her hands sweat and grow cold at the same time. What should she do?

A woman who has felt purity elude her in this way may suppose it easy to approach deity unpurified. But when she tries to present her natural, unpurified self to the Goddess she discovers just how difficult this task is, too. Instead of banishing all her "impure" thoughts, she must now avoid passing judgment. But suppose she sees the sagging flesh of an approaching woman. How does she respond? Does she immediately blot this woman from awareness? Does she think to herself, "What a slob. She should take care of herself." If she hears somebody chewing, do feelings of fierce rage and disgust choke her? Does changing a Kotex leave her feeling "unclean"? These and countless similar situations may force a woman into the learned responses of patriarchal culture. No matter that it was her mother, rather than her father, who overtly taught her to distinguish "clean" from "unclean"; inevitably mothers, too, are imbued with culturally shared patriarchal values. Therefore, only a rare woman does not constantly "purify" herself by thinking in certain patriarchally prescribed ways. When she does constantly purify herself, a woman automatically precludes the chance for enacting the mystical marriage with the Goddess.

For this "marriage" to occur, women must develop greater awareness of possibilities. Rather than immediately filtering everything that happens to us, we need to develop sufficient openness for raw experience itself to reach us without patriarchal constructions informing it first. Instead of immediately judging every situation (as in thinking, "the body and all its manifestations are 'bad'; women loving women are 'bad'"), we need to consider alternative responses. We can begin by examining a variety of patriarchally clouded issues. How do we feel about the exchanges of lovemaking? A heterosexual woman willingly exchanges saliva when she kisses a man she loves. Looking at the matter objectively, why feel disgust at the same exchange with a woman, just because she *is* a woman? An important distinction here is whether a woman rejects the idea from honest lack of physical attraction to another woman or whether she feels *disgust*. This difference is important. Regardless of an individual's own orientation, the difference between neutrality and disgust focuses a major issue of the overall theme of atonement to the Mother Goddess.

Logically lesbian women should find atonement with the Mother Goddess comparatively easy. Yet this is not always so. Not all forms of lesbianism readily yield such atonement. For some women, it is being *stigmatized* rather than love of same sex that is the primary attraction. That condition differs considerably from positively accepting women as lovers. Consider this description of a first visit to a lesbian bar:

> Images rise up . . . of sexual depravity and pseudomen, images of people "sick" and different from her, images that have hidden in the shadows of her reflections on her own sexual identity. And there is fear, also, of taking the first step through a door that might affirm what she has often tried to deny about herself: that she is a lesbian.[11]

If this young woman were to find images of "sickness" more attractive than women, then deviance, not love of women would be her primary concern. In that case her quest would focus less on meeting the Goddess than on rebelling against the Father. Her attention would remain at an earlier stage of the way of the mother and rebellion against patriarchal structures would essentially define her selfhood. Deviance from patriarchal norms counts more in this version of lesbianism than adherence to gyno-centric modes. Hence truly meeting the Goddess, much less mystically marrying Her, rarely occurs for this kind of woman. For her, lesbianism is actually the negative condition that patriarchal and heterosexist thinking assumes it to be.

Very different from the woman attracted to lesbianism for its stig-matic appeal is the ideological lesbian. This woman carries the logic of rebellion against patriarchal thinking to its obvious conclusion: "If men as a class oppress women-as-a-class, then how can I as a woman, possibly love a man? To love a man is obviously to betray my own kind. Therefore, logic demands that I love only women."

Superficially this argument makes good political sense. Undeniably if all women accepted it, they would severely challenge patriarchy. But such a challenge resembles that posed by the existence of nuclear arms. To act upon the challenge, in either situation, would be to invite annihilation. Total rejection of men by all women would literalize the metaphoric war between the sexes. Imagine what would happen if the majority of women were actually to stop loving men on a permanent basis. The anger of men at such behavior would likely produce harsh retaliation. A holocaust of women might ensue. In that event, instead of mystically marrying the Goddess, women would be guilty of allowing Her to be killed.

But spurious logic is not the only flaw in purely ideological les-bianism. Ideological lesbianism represents a reactive rather than a proac-tive stance. The thinking behind it divides rather than includes. Such thinking can therefore only partially reflect the Mother Goddess. In Her place, the patriarchally created goddess Athena, warlike and male-created, is apt to appear. This is so because purely ideological lesbianism merely reverses patriarchy. Patriarchal civilizations apparently developed defen-sively against women's mysterious powers to create life out of our own bodies. Purely ideological lesbianism merely reverses and extends this logic: "If you have all the power and you will not share it but use it to oppress me, I will refrain from loving you. Furthermore, I will withdraw from your culture and exist separately within one of my own." Lesbianism chosen for its ideological meaning, like lesbianism chosen for its stigma, displays divisiveness as its dominant theme. And divisiveness is a major principle of patriarchy. Consequently, the woman who chooses lesbian withdrawal as the answer to patriarchy is less truly free of the thinking she so longs to overcome than her rhetoric suggests. She inverts patriarchy, reflecting it from a patriarchally indoctrinated woman's point of view. This is not the same as seeing gynocentrically.

The lesbian woman more apt to meet the Mother Goddess contrasts sharply with both her stigma-loving and her ideological sisters. This woman simply loves women for their own sake. For her the stigma of lesbianism is painful, not attractive, and ideology is not the primary factor in her life, although she may be ideological as well. Central for her is love of women, not hatred of men. (She might even be bisexual.) Her primary motivation is a positive feeling for others of her kind, rather than a negative reaction against those unlike herself. Can such a woman, still largely castigated for her behavior, her affectional preference, her very self, love freely? To the extent that she can, she represents one of the major images of a woman able to meet with the Mother Goddess. That is because once this woman has learned to accept herself, she sees that women are not inferior, smelly, dependent, silly—all the countless negatives we have all been taught we are by patriarchal culture. Monique Wittig, throughout her book *The Lesbian Body*, writes of such acceptance of the beloved woman's body. Here is a representative excerpt:

> THE UREA THE MILK THE
> ALBUMEN THE OXYGEN THE
> FLATULENCE THE POUCHES . . . .[12]

In so writing, Wittig sees beauty and strengths of many different descriptions. If more heterosexual women could learn to see women through Wittig's eyes, more of us would recognize the power and loveliness the Mother Goddess stands ready to reveal to all of us. When we can see Her in this way, we mystically "marry" Her, that is, we become one with Her by accepting Her qualities as our own. When that happens we are atoned with Her. Literal enactment is not the point. A particular way of seeing women is. It is not uncommon for Christian mystics to describe union with Jesus or God in erotic terms. Such language is equally appropriate to describe what some women experience in their relationship to the Goddess.

CHAPTER 21.

The Mysteries of the Goddess

If apotheosis, both literally and metaphorically, constitutes the high point of the hero's quest, participation in the mysteries of the Goddess forms the metaphoric counterpart for a woman. Through such participation a woman achieves the fullest possible atonement with the Goddess, in which she is truly one with Her. In so doing, a woman also transcends the ordinary limits of mundane existence as she plays her role in the ancient drama of renewing life. It is this drama, ritually enacted in prehistory, which constitutes the deepest mysteries of the Neolithic Great Mother Goddess.

Cults devoted to such ritual worship of this Great Mother Goddess flourished in Eurasia, particularly in the Mediterrannean lands, during the Neolithic and Chalcolithic eras (c.6500-3500 B.C.E.).[1] The Goddess is a multifaceted image of deity who governs both the fertility and the decay of nature. In Her latter capacity She is known as the Terrible Mother. The rites sacred to Her, regardless by which of her many names She is called, typically play variations on the interconnected themes of death and fertility. Consequently, the death and rebirth of vegetation are perpetual mysteries to be celebrated. Probably the best known of these ancient mysteries sacred to Her are those connected to the Greek goddess Demeter, although similar mysteries are known to have attended Her worship elsewhere under different names.[2] These are the famous Eleusinian Mysteries. Based on the story of Demeter and her daughter, Persephone, sometimes referred to simply as Kore, maiden, these rites were celebrated for some two thousand years before Christianity replaced them. A major source of knowledge about this famous mother-daughter story (summarized in chapter 12) is the Homeric Hymn to Demeter.

Chief of the Greek festivals associated with this ancient story is the Thesmophoria, celebrated only by women. Because such great secrecy surrounded all these rites, details are sketchy. Typically the Thesmophoria took place about the beginning of October and lasted for three days (except in Attica where other festivals attached to it stretched it to five). The first day was called Anodos, ascent, or Kathodos, descent. Reasons for this naming are purely conjectural. Scholars generally believe that both names refer to a rite involving pigs, animals sacred to the Great Mother Goddess in her many forms. Prior to the festival, pigs were thrown into a pit until they rotted. Their remains were later brought up by women called Anthetriai, "drawers up." These remains, together with certain ritual fertility objects such as pine cones and dough figures of serpents and men, were then placed on an altar. After the ritual the rotted pigs are thought to have been thrown back down into the chasm. Hence the ascent and descent.

The second day was the Nesteia, which signifies fasting. At this time the women fasted while sitting on the ground, both acts being magical rites connected to agriculture. The final day, *Kalligeneia*, means "the fair birth."

Another of Demeter's festivals is the Haloa, a word derived from ἅλως, threshing floor. This one is a harvest festival in which the first fruits were carried from Athens to a threshing floor in Eleusis. There a priestess presided over the sacrifice, for men were forbidden to perform that function. A major component of this festival was the initiation of women by a woman. Accompanying obscene gestures and phallic emblems emphasized its fertility aspects.

In the spring Demeter was honored by the festival of the corn beginning to sprout, the Chloeia, named after Chloe, the Green Demeter, goddess of growing vegetation. In the Chloeia, the young men, known as Ephebes, marched to Eleusis for "the holy things." Presumably these were small figures of the Goddesses, which they brought back to the Eleusinion in Athens. On the 16th of the month, those receiving instruction in the mysteries, the catechumens, assembled before the hierophant. Following his address, they marched to the sea to be purified. Besides sea water, sprinkled pigs' blood, a substance commonly used for catharsis, may also have been used in this ceremony. Upon their return, they offered some sort of sacrifice. On the 19th of the month a great procession took place with many stops at shrines along the way from Athens to Eleusis. At Eleusis a mystic ceremony involving two levels of celebration was held. Only those who had previously passed the first level were admitted to the full ceremony. The actual ritual is not fully known. Its focus was a dromenon, or acting out, of a holy pageant in which sacred objects were revealed. A cut cornstalk is believed to have been central to this revelation, for corn commonly symbolizes new life.

Whatever the precise nature of these mysteries of Demeter involved, most scholars see in them a strong link to agrarian rituals of planting and harvest. Their major agricultural themes of burial in the dark ground followed by subsequent regeneration become in this context the descent and "rebirth" of the lost daughter. Hence Demeter's story imitates the mystery of plant fertility. Conversely, the mystery of plant life springing up from the buried seed suggests a possible "rebirth" after death for humans. This is the rebirth which the Persephone myth acts out.

Few contemporary Western women can experience firsthand the aspect of the Mysteries which so strongly intertwines the fertility of the soil with that of woman. Almost none of us still lives a sufficiently agrarian life to do so. Most women now grow up in suburbs or cities without ever smelling the good rich smell of newly plowed earth or pushing seeds into soil unbounded by red clay pots. For such women the deep human connections to the soil assumed in agricultural societies often appear remote. What *is* still available to urban Western women, however, is this same profound mystery as the act of giving birth reveals it.

Yet the familiar patriarchal process of demonization intervenes here, to alter this most sacred of the mysteries of the Goddess into something quite alien. In Western thought this demonization automatically appears in the biblical connection of childbirth with sin rather than joy and renewal. Such reconstruction of women's natural experience of the sacred mystery of the Goddess is directly traceable to the Old Testament account of Yahweh chastising Eve for her part in the fall from Eden:

> To the woman he said, "I will greatly multiply your pain in childbearing; in pain you shall bring forth children. Yet your desire shall be for your husband, and he shall rule over you." (Gen. 3:16)

So strongly has this negative view of childbirth as pain and the wages of sin conditioned patriarchal Western consciousness that women as commonly espouse it as men. Consider, for example, how the protagonist of the novel *Dad* reflects on his aged mother's views. She is reacting to her granddaughter's casual mention of natural childbirth:

> Marty mentions how she wants to have the baby by natural birth, mentions *Birth Without Violence*. Mother's convinced it's all nonsense and dangerous.
>
> "You'll see, Martha. When you start having hard labor pains, you'll want a shot. I can *tell* you."

Marty's taking it easily. She doesn't know, but she's mucking in one of Mom's favorite martyrdom areas. Nobody, but nobody, should have a baby without fear, pain and violence. It's what verifies a woman.[3]

Yet what patriarchal authority so thoroughly demeans that it becomes "fear, pain and violence," or out-and-out sin, is actually one of the most deeply religious experiences a woman can have. Through the natural processes of childbirth women inherently possess means for experiencing the mysteries associated with ancient earth mother goddesses such as Demeter. Like the "dead" seed of grain buried for a season in the ground, the human seed planted in the woman's body also forms new life. Rather than cause for guilt, this is reason for joyous wonder. Emergence of life from the womb—whether that of woman or earth—incorporates the essence of women's mysteries.

The term "women's mysteries" is sufficiently familiar that it has been used as a book title (*Women's Mysteries*, by M. Esther Harding).[4] Yet for the most part, conceptualizing women's childbearing capability as a sacred mystery is highly unusual in patriarchal cultures. As a means of denigrating our natural capabilities, ignoring the name "mystery" is less overt than renaming them as sin but just as powerful in its effect. Nonetheless, ignoring the name means denying women the fact that childbirth really means participating in the mysteries of the Goddess. Actually, industrialized cultures pay scant attention to these mysteries either as mysteries or as sources of revelation. Instead, they have allowed these once sacred mysteries to dwindle to events mainly taken for granted in our technologized society. Therefore, we repeatedly forget how miraculous the gift of life really is. Just how taken for granted birth generally is becomes especially evident when it is looked at within the world of art.

Although the works of artists are typically considered major sources of revelation, artist Judy Chicago is so far almost unique in the West in depicting the mystery of childbirth. Her gigantic needlework, *Birth Project,* completed in 1984, consists of a series of childbirth images executed on a hundred or so pieces of canvas and fabric. Women from around the United States worked Chicago's painted designs in various mediums, including batik, beadwork, appliqué, crochet, embroidery, needlepoint, and quilting. The work came about partly because of Chicago's discovery, actually incorrect, that Western art included no images of women giving birth![5] Yet the few exceptions such as Chagall and Kahlo who prove her wrong scarcely vitiate the point that artistic depiction of this greatest of the mysteries of the Goddess has been extremely rare.

Nor is childbirth the only women's mystery largely ignored as a source of art or revelation in the West. Most of the natural functions of women—menarche, menstruation, pregnancy, lactation, and menopause—have similarly been ignored. Thus menarche, which most tribal cultures consider a deeply religious event deserving special initiation ceremonies, is treated clinically in the industrial West. Here menarche, far from being a mystery, is a "stage of development." Consequently, it is often experienced more as a disease read about in a plain-wrapped booklet than as a deeply meaningful event in a woman's life. While some young women do greet it with joy, many more are embarrassed, frightened, or even ashamed. Ancient connections tying menstrual blood, as the presumed source of life, to sacrality remain deeply hidden from consciousness in a culture which finds sanitary napkins embarrassing.

Similarly, pregnancy and menopause have both been primarily understood in twentieth-century industrialized Western cultures as conditions more akin to, sometimes even identical with, illness than as occasions worthy of ritual celebration. In traditional cultures, for example, a postmenopausal woman, now relieved of her dangerous powers for creating life, enters a new stage of life. Having moved through her maiden and mother stages, she is now in her crone phase. As crone, she is typically revered as a Wise Woman. By contrast, "crones" in our culture more often bleach their hair blonde and move to Florida, hoping to catch an eligible widower.

The association of childbirth with illness is of far more recent origin than its connection with sin. It dates from the time in the nineteenth century when midwifery largely gave way to obstetrics. In our largely desacralized culture associations of birth with illness may devastate more women than do those connected with sin. Whereas few but fundamentalist believers are likely to feel "sinful" about their birth-related functions today, many women do feel "sick," rather than "sacred" when they "suffer" from them. If nothing else, just the fact that most births take place in hospitals attended by physicians makes the idea of sickness more prominent by far than that of sacredness.

This insidious illness model of childbirth was particularly strong in the United States from the end of World War II until approximately the mid-seventies, when a strong backlash developed against medicalization of this great mystery. More and more women are now demanding control over their own bodies. Especially important in this movement for autonomy is women's demand to experience the act of giving birth for ourselves, rather than being anaesthetized into total amnesia. When the birth takes place "behind the mother's back" so to speak, she not only has no control over it, she is deprived of the truly gynocentric revelation this mystery of the Goddess can reveal.

The depth of a woman's loss of deep meaning through medicalization of childbirth is dramatically apparent in the context of a hospital delivery typical in the United States of the 1940s, '50s, and '60s. At that time the young mother would arrive at the hospital emergency ward only to be plunked immediately into a wheelchair. Her bag of waters might already have broken, her pains might be less than two minutes apart, her cervix might be dilated to seven. Nonetheless, she or her spouse must stop to fill out the admitting form. Then she would be propelled down long corridors, in and out of elevators, bumped over thresholds. At last she would reach a prep room where she must change to a graceless hospital gown. At this point her greatest humiliation would occur: A nurse's aid would shave her pubic hair, leaving her pale and hairless as a chihuahua. Now she would be strapped onto a delivery table and wheeled into a labor room, there to be left alone with but intermittent monitoring by a nurse. Only if she were at risk would she be attended constantly:

> She said that the hospital was filled with noise. That women were moved from bed to bed. From room to room. That the lights were too bright. The chrome too shiny. That the place reeked with antiseptic. She said in this atmosphere, what she had seen before, what she had felt before attending a birth, this ghostlike presence, was not there. But she said despite all this activity, the woman lay alone. She lay alone in labor. And no one looked into her eyes. No one responded to the questioning of her murmurs.[6]

This lonely, frightening experience far more resembles a tribal initiate's ordeal alone in the woods than it does the woman-attended, home-based event that preindustrial childbirth was. In a labor room of this sort a woman often had to endure by herself hours and hours of painful contractions. To ease the pain she would usually be given little or no medication because most effective painkillers inhibit dilation. Nor in that era would she have been taught breathing techniques for counteracting pain. In the absence of caring others, placed in a context predominantly associated with illness, it is no wonder that a woman experiencing medicalized childbirth typically was deprived of participating in the sacred mystery of the Goddess.

Not only was a woman in that era denied a positive experience of childbirth, negative qualities were actually added onto it. From rooms around her she could hear screams from other women. Sometimes those screams of strangers would be harder to bear than her own pain. Did their cries mean her pain would grow worse? Would she humiliate herself by also shrieking that way? The attitude of Mira, the protagonist of Marilyn French's *The Women's Room,* well illustrates this fear. Overhearing another woman's screams, Mira vows: "She would not utter a sound. She would be good. No matter how bad the pain got, she would show them that a woman could have courage. . . . Suddenly Mrs. Martinelli shrieked again. A nurse came in, sighing angrily under her breath. She did not speak; Mrs. Martinelli was simply screaming now." [7]

By the time a woman was finally wheeled across into the terrifying green-walled, shiny steel-appurtenanced delivery room, she would be only too happy to have a mask clapped to her face or a needle jabbed into her spine. Anything, anything, just to end this ordeal. Thoughts of the baby might long since have dissipated. In their stead would be burning desire to expel the wretched encumbrance from her body, to end this pain. She would be so tired, so tired. . . . Waagh! Waagh! Waagh! She would blink her eyes and realize she had a baby of her own!

But what was it she had missed in this experience? Just how does the medical model of birth deprive a woman? For one thing, it deprives her of a certain kind of self-understanding. In our prevailing symbol systems in the West, men have traditionally been placed in the slot of "knower," women in that of "known." Men have symbolically come to "know" the unknown aspects of life, including their own "unknown" portions of self, through knowing women. That is because women, historically, have symbolized "otherness"—everything that is not "same," hence the hidden, inferior portions of life, of men themselves. But this symbolic relationship has not been reciprocal. Men have not functioned as corresponding symbols of otherness for women. Consequently, women have not interpreted unknown parts of ourselves through our experiences of men. Rather, men have interpreted our unknownness to us. Historically we have therefore learned who and what we are presumed to be, not through our immediate experiences of ourselves nor through our experiences of men, but through what men tell us about ourselves. Even the most sacred mystery of the Goddess, the act of giving birth, an event no man has ever yet experienced, has been defined for us. In Western cultures childbirth is the painful wages of our original sin; alternatively, it is an event painful by nature which can only be ameliorated by patriarchally approved medical techniques. For women to experience ourselves as ourselves within childbirth, we must, at a minimum, be fully awake.

Being absent from her own childbearing because of anaesthesia also deprives a woman of genuine counterparts to the male's initiation rite and to his atonement with the Father, which in her case becomes atonement with the Mother. Various ritual preparations such as baby showers still exist as attenuated, desacralized relics of ceremonies once designed to help a woman prepare for the transition of self occasioned by childbirth. But not even a full-blown ceremony can ever be so fully initiatory as the actual process of giving birth itself. To deny a woman this major life experience is to cheat her out of knowledge rightfully hers, the knowledge naturally imparted by this great mystery of the Goddess.

Part of this sacred experience of childbirth involves the mythic motif of being swallowed and expelled. This is part of the larger hero-versus-monster pattern, which is too familiar to need elaboration—that is, as it is usually presented. But its very familiarity is the problem. Rarely does anyone think to turn the pattern around to observe it from the perspective of the monster/mother. Like the far side of the moon, this side is always mysteriously hidden from us. What, then, is it like?

Seen from the monster/mother's perspective the encounter with the hero superficially appears much as it does for him. He must fight to be born; she must battle to give birth. But despite its apparent sameness, this situation of giving birth is actually strange for most women because our connections to the Goddess and what She stands for—immediate gyno-centric experience—have long ago been severed by patriarchal interven-tion.

At the time of labor, as a woman's contractions unbearably intensify, the original pain, possibly unendurable for hours, even days, paradoxically turns nearly pleasurable. Now the pains change shape. Heretofore they have continuously expanded. They have carried her farther and farther outward until she feels as large as the universe. Now they reach an outer limit. Miraculously, at that point she feels herself pop, like Alice, into the circles of pain which she herself with her fearful stretching has created. While this strange inversion takes place, her now-bounded expansion outward continues. Yet simultaneously she also contracts to a point of intense hardness. It is as if everything in her were simultaneously infinitely expansive and infinitesimally dense. In this moment of contraries she experiences herself as being born, even as she herself bears a child of her own.

During this instant, in which the laboring woman and the Mother Goddess are fully one, the great mystery that a woman discovers is that birth is simultaneously death. In the words of an Italian peasant the experience is like this: "Every time one of my babies was about to be born I'd think to myself, You're going to die! This time, you're going to die! Then it'd come out. Somehow—I don't know how to explain it—but somehow it was like I had been born again." [8]

For all its ineffability, this sacred mystery of giving birth has a "shape." It is a shape composed largely of waves. These waves, which have formed a woman's contractions throughout labor, form a kind of double spiral, labyrinth, or, as Anaïs Nin describes it, a tunnel: "There is blood in my eyes. A tunnel. I push into this tunnel, I bite my lips and push. There is a fire and flesh ripping and no air. Out of the tunnel! All my blood is spilling out. Push! Push! Push! It is coming! It is coming! I feel the slipperiness, the sudden deliverance, the weight is gone."[9] This pattern is simultaneously both expansive and contractive. From an external perspective, the pattern points to birth from one direction, to death, from the other. From the internal perspective of the birthing woman, however, both birth and death are occurring at the same time.

Mythically the associations attached to this tunnel-labyrinth-spiral image strongly indicate that both sexes early connected it to the two limits of human existence, birth and death. Commonly, spiral and labyrinthine images decorate tombs, simultaneously reflecting passage into death and transformation into new life, a belief common to cultures everywhere. According to anthropologist John Layard:

> . . . labyrinth ritual and belief always has to do with death and re-birth relating either to a life after death or to the mysteries of initiation; . . . the presiding personage, either mythical or actual, is always a woman; . . . the labyrinth itself is walked through, or the labyrinth design walked over, by men.[10]

Archaeologist Marija Gimbutas further underscores the mythic importance of the spiral when she asserts that "the snake and its abstracted derivative, the spiral, are the dominant motifs of the art of Old Europe." [11] This is art produced from approximately 6500-3500 B.C.E. in the pre-Indo-European Goddess-worshipping culture of an area of Europe extending roughly from the western Ukraine to the Adriatic part of the Mediterranean and up to the Baltic. The famous Cretan labyrinth widely known from the perspective of the hero, Theseus, "must have been a symbol of the abode or 'palace' of the 'mistress of the Labyrinth,'"[12] according to one of the Linear B tablets from Knossos. Reference to this famous labyrinth as a death-rebirth motif occurs in Book Six of Virgil's *Aeneid*. Seeking to visit his father Anchises in Hades, Aeneas first visits the female sibyl who guards the entrance, near which is painted a representation of the Cretan labyrinth.[13] Sometimes the labyrinth loses its circularity and becomes rectilinear instead. But its essential pathlike aspect nonetheless remains clear.

On Celtic stone crosses the labyrinth image also frequently symbolizes rebirth, as is the case in over-door and floor designs found in many Gothic churches. In England the motif occurs in mazes through which village children run, and in Scotland and northern England women draw "tangled thread" images, a variant of this image, on their thresholds to prevent evil influences.

Besides these material examples, anthropologists have uncovered instances of labyrinth rituals from around the world. Not only were they a strong component of Hellenistic and Roman dances and games; they also continued into this century on the far side of the globe in Malekula, an island midway between the Solomons and Fiji in the South Pacific. There when a man died, a labyrinth design was drawn and presided over by a female Guardian Ghost who sat beside a cave. Before the dead man could be reborn into his new life after death, he had to walk through the labyrinth.[14] How similar this passage is to that of the birth canal through which an infant must pass into life. In the birth passage the infant remains passive throughout the first stage of labor. During this time the contractions of the mother's uterus do not disturb the baby, which remains as it has throughout the nine months, safely protected within.

But during the period known as transition, between the first and second stages of labor, when the cervix dilates the last three centimeters out of the ten of total dilation the contractions grow in frequency and length. This stage affects the baby and marks the time at which a woman is most likely to become frightened. This is clearly the point of no return. The baby *must* come out now. Postponement to some other time is no longer possible. Now begins the final stage when the mother feels an uncontrollable urge to bear down, the muscles of her vagina combining with her uterine contractions to help propel the baby through the birth canal. Much as the dead men must pass through the ritual labyrinth in Malekula, so must the baby now pass through the birth canal.

In literature, probably no account so ably portrays this interconnectd reversibility of birth and death symbolized by spiral and labyrinth as Tolstoy's famous story, "The Death of Ivan Ilych":

> Till about three in the morning he was in a state of stupefied misery. It seemed to him that he and his pain were being thrust into a narrow, deep black sack, but though they were pushed further and further in they could not be pushed to the bottom. And this, terrible enough itself, was accompanied by suffering. He was frightened yet wanted to fall through the sack; he struggled but yet co-operated. And suddenly he broke through, fell, and regained consciousness.[15]

As in a lengthy birth, Ivan Ilych's full entry into the sack does not take place immediately. He must first endure an ordeal of self-questioning and physical pain which eventuates in a mystical experience:

And suddenly it grew clear to him that what had been oppressing him and would not leave him was all dropping away at once from two sides, from ten sides, and from all sides . . . . He sought his former accustomed fear of death and did not find it . . . . In place of death there was light.

"So that's what it is!" he suddenly exclaimed aloud. "What joy!"

To him all this happened in a single instant, and the meaning of that instant did not change.[16]

As does the center of a spiral, the sack functions here as the threshold between two worlds in this highly descriptive reversal of the birth process. In contrast to an individual's birth, here the protagonist moves into, rather than out of, a small enclosure. In so doing, he approaches what, in a spiral, would be the smallest point, rather than the largest extension. Instead of expulsion out of the confines of the womb, Ivan experiences propulsion into its equivalent, the space of "a narrow, deep black sack."

Various responses are possible to such revelation, whether it is that given here to Ivan as he lies dying, or that granted a woman giving birth. One can, of course, pooh pooh all such revelation as mystical nonsense; a physician can even prevent its occurrence through anaesthetizing a birthing woman or a dying Ivan out of all awareness of its existence. In that case no awareness at all of the mystery of the Goddess occurs. But one can also accept such revelation, conceptualizing it as a natural, awe-inspiring phenomenon which simultaneously balances and either foreshadows or recapitulates its counter mystery—death or birth, as the case may be. When this happens in the case of a woman giving birth, it means a woman can experience the deep meaning of what she is doing. To say that a woman has experienced childbirth on her own terms as the deeply meaningful event it is, is to say that she has participated in the sacred mystery of the Goddess.

If one does conceptualize childbirth this way as the ancient mystery of the Goddess, what exactly does this mean? Surely it takes no great astuteness to see that giving birth for the first time does indeed provide women with a natural rite of passage from one state of being to the next. But in addition, each time childbirth occurs, it is a process of nature in which women are "graced" with the same knowledge which male initiates of rebirth ceremonies must struggle by means of artificially created rituals to attain. In childbirth, revelation occurs unasked: It is right *there*, inherent in the process itself. And through this kind of revelation the recipient learns, if only momentarily, the kinds of secrets that male initiation rites in tribal cultures have typically celebrated: Ultimately birth and death are one and the same; ultimately "everything is all right." Paradoxically, this second secret a woman learns, is repeated by almost every mother whether or not she recognizes it as such: "Everything is all right," she will say to her hurting child. The meaning of this "secret" which sounds so banal outside its revelatory context is that birth and death, birthing and birth, entropy and collapse, all finally coalesce: They all mean the same thing.

While such knowledge will not comfort those looking for personal salvation, it restates the knowledge of the *tao* or the vision of Arjuna in the *Bhagavad Gita*. As one example of traditional wisdom, it falls into the category of knowledge that, if heeded, can provide Robert Frost's "momentary stay against confusion." Knowing experientially this ultimate pattern of death and rebirth is saving knowledge so elementary that it is almost impossible to interpret further. As with Arjuna's vision, such revelation does not help a woman to comprehend the great "why's" of history: Why war? Why the Nazi Holocaust? Why the fission and fusion bombs? What such revelation does provide, however, is a rudder. It reveals clearly an underlying sense of order, which in a world of the Uncertainty Principle and absurdist drama is not to be discounted. Such revelation can, therefore, provide salvation in this way: It can alleviate the sense of existential panic which in a postmodern context may well be the counterpart of damnation. For in its equivalence of three major mysteries—birth, birthing, and death—it reveals symmetry, an order which at the time of revelation fully satisfies.

Almost paradoxically, such revelation also provides a kind of salvation which might almost be called "personal," were such a term not inappropriate to the real meaning of this mystery of the Goddess. In giving birth a woman incarnates the Mother Goddess. During delivery her body is undeniably the conduit of new life. Less generally recognized is the fact that her body at that time is also a natural passage for revelation. With the dilation of her uterus and vagina her entire body image metamorphoses. No longer is she primarily the solid she ordinarily feels herself to be. Now she approximates waves of motion surrounding an expanding void. This sensation is far removed from the body sense to which she is habituated. For the woman who attunes herself to it, this dispersed body connects her to realms of being beyond the ordinary human norm. Much as the stars are widely scattered across the void of the heavens, she experiences herself now as infinitely stretched. Her habitual sense of being a single unit of a certain weight and density has disintegrated. In addition, a certain accustomed balance between the solidity of bone and flesh and the interiority of empty space has now strangely altered. Paramount now is a sense of bodily stretching out, out, beyond the limits of possible selfhood. This unfamiliar body distension correlates physically to romantic longings to merge with the Infinite. These lines from Tennyson's "Ulysses" well illustrate this romantic tendency:

> And this gray spirit yearning in desire
> To follow knowledge like a sinking star,
> Beyond the utmost bound of human thought.[17]

Through her body's movement of outward expansion and inward contraction, a woman giving birth touches the two infinities: the infinitely large and the infinitely small. In so doing she unquestionably transcends the bounds of selfhood as it is customarily experienced in the West. At such a moment she subjectively knows the coincidence of opposites that T. S. Eliot describes in the "Little Gidding" section of his "Four Quartets," when he says "the fire and the rose are one."[18]

A woman able to retain the certitude of this moment, ideally perhaps to pass it on to her children, actualizes in her personal life part of the largely ineffable meaning of the deep mystery of the Mother Goddess.

PART VI

The Return

CHAPTER 22.

Perils: Dead Babies, Infanticide, and Postpartum Depression

Following her intense experience of the mystery of childbirth, it is inevitable that returning to "this world" should often desperately challenge a woman. Not only has a woman who has successfully negotiated her way through this great mystery of the Goddess repeated that mystery by producing new life. If she has been especially fortunate, she will have received the additional boon of unexpected revelation through her experience as well. Returning safely with either or both of these boons as severely tests her capabilities as achieving them in the first place did.

In a traditional story of a hero, attaining one or more boons is the ostensible point of the entire quest which engages him. Typically, he either seeks or is given some sort of magical object whose proper use accords him supernatural power. In fairy tales this boon may be a bottle with a genie in it, boots enabling him to cover seven leagues at one step, a cap which renders him invisible; in myths it may be a holy grail or some secret bit of knowledge.

But the quest for a boon forms but half the hero's story. Once he has successfully completed the quest, boon in hand, he must make his way home. Often, however, some power stronger than his own prevents him from successfully bringing back his precious gift. Such last-minute disruption of the heroic venture particularly characterizes mythic quests for the plant of immortality. The quest of the Assyro-Babylonian hero, Gilgamesh, is illustrative. Terrified by the death of his friend Enkidu, Gilgamesh braves the perils of the underworld in search of immortality. There he is granted knowledge of a wonderful secret: The plant of immortality may be found at the bottom of the ocean. After successfully plucking the magical boon, Gilgamesh sets off for home. En route, however, he unthinkingly sets down the plant that he may refresh himself in a fountain of fresh water. As he does so, a snake, lured by the smell of the plant, makes off with it. Thus, Gilgamesh loses the precious boon he had obtained at such peril, just as he is to return safely home with it.

In similar fashion, a woman with one of her precious, hard-won boons in hand, may find returning with it as difficult as journeying for it in the first place. She may, for example, reach full term, only to lose her baby during, or shortly after, childbirth. Gail Godwin's short story "Dream Children" vividly depicts the pain of this common loss of a boon:

> *The worst thing, such an awful thing to happen to a young woman* . . . She was having this natural childbirth, you see, her husband in the delivery room with her, and the pains were coming a half-minute apart, and the doctor had just said, "This is going to be a breeze, Mrs. McNair," and they never knew exactly what went wrong, but all of a sudden the pains stopped and they had to go in after the baby without even time to give her a saddle block or any sort of anesthetic. . . . They must have practically had to tear it out of her . . . the husband fainted. The baby was born dead, and they gave her a heavy sedative to put her out all night.[1]

Often it is not nature, however, but cultural mores which determine whether a mother will be permitted to keep the primary boon of her journey, her baby. Infanticide often destroys what she has just struggled so hard to deliver. Thus, in many cultures live birth itself is not the determinative factor for bringing new life into the world. Rather, as in ancient Greece, some form of *levanna*, "raising up the child," is typically practiced. Until the father lifts the newborn up, the child is not officially "born," or accepted into the life of the family. No matter how much the mother may have struggled to bear it, the decision whether or not this boon should be brought safely into "this" world is commonly out of her hands, as he ritually rebirths her child into patriarchal culture.

In other cases, the ability to return safely with the boon is not up to others but rests solely with the woman herself. Just as some women refuse the call to the way of the mother in the first place, some mothers refuse to return from the realm of the Goddess they have been privileged momentarily to enter, preferring to remain there indefinitely with the newly earned gift of revelation. Such a choice of two worlds faced Gautama, the Buddha, after he achieved Enlightenment under the Bo Tree: Should he forsake the world of humanity or should he return to it, bearing his boon of Enlightenment to the unenlightened? This same theme occurs in more secular fashion in Tennyson's "The Lotos-Eaters," a poem based on one of the obstacles from which the hero, Ulysses, must protect his men. Eating of this island's enchanted food produces seeming enlightenment. Now all worldly effort appears meaningless. As a result of this "boon," Ulysses says to his men:

> Let us swear an oath, and keep it with an equal
> mind,
> In the hollow Lotus-land to live and lie reclined
> On the hills like Gods together, careless of
> mankind.[2]

In marked contrast to the Buddha, in this Tennysonian version of the Ulysses story, the hero and his men refuse the journey home.

The same decision faces a woman who has just given birth. World-wide, it is well recognized that the days and weeks immediately following childbirth dangerously threaten a new mother's well-being. Christian prac-tice, for example, in earlier periods incorporates deep-rooted folk beliefs regarding the peril of the first days following childbirth. During this time, while a woman must remain unchurched because she is ritually impure, she must not leave the house, lest she incur bad luck. Following the churching ceremony, which takes place on the fortieth day in accordance with the presentation of Mary and the child Jesus in the temple, a woman is safe. Conversely, the community is now safe from her ritually defiling powers. Therefore, she may now rejoin the community at large without contaminating them with the mysterious birth-related powers patriarchal thought consistently demonizes. But prior to the time of her churching she and her baby are felt to be at severe risk of being snatched off to fairyland. Victims so abducted will never more be the same, either because they are forced to remain in fairyland forever or because some attendant evil changes their status.

This folk belief, which occurs worldwide in countless variants, is but another way of speaking of the tremendous change childbirth effects in a woman. For a new mother the actual birthing may be so transcendent an experience that returning to "this world" no longer interests her. Even if she does not experience birth ecstatically, having looked forward so long to having her baby, the reality of caring for it may seem anticlimactic. Or perhaps the baby itself was not her goal; maybe she simply dreamed of being slim again. No matter whether her expectations and experience are sublime or ridiculous, they may inhibit her return. Clinically, such refusal of a new mother to return is known as postpartum blues. In mild form, postpartum blues are common. Typically, a new mother feels depressed for a time. She is let down; she cries easily; life is just not worth living.

After a week or so, however, she normally "returns"; life once more engages her.

But occasionally a woman is so overcome by despair that instead of returning she remains in her own little world, psychologically and emotionally separate from her family. Sometimes she may need prolonged care, even institutionalization. Charlotte Perkins Gilman describes this state in her short story "The Yellow Wallpaper" (1891). In keeping with the attitudes of the day, the nameless protagonist, recovering from childbirth, is "advised" by her physician-husband: She must have absolute rest and isolation. Neither prescription helps; in fact, both exacerbate the condition they are designed to cure. As the story progresses, the woman grows more and more crazed. She believes that she must free a woman trapped behind the wallpaper of her room who ceaselessly crawls about like a baby. To this end, the protagonist peels off all the wallpaper in the nursery to which her husband has confined her. By story's end, now identifying completely with her papered-over alter ego, she informs her husband, " 'I've got out at last, . . . And I've pulled off most of the paper, so you can't put me back!' " [3] Rather than functioning as the mother she physically is, the protagonist acts out the part of the baby, crawling endlessly across the nursery floor in imitation of the "other self" she identifies with from behind the wallpaper. How clearly her action says it is the child-hero whose role she prefers to that of the Mother Goddess!

Such postpartum "madness" reflects an inability on the part of the new mother to return safely with her boons. While the story of "The Yellow Wallpaper" does not indicate if this woman was safely "delivered" of the boon of her baby, in many cases a woman delivers without harm but cannot manage the overwhelming gift of revelation she may have been graced enough to receive. Such a magnificent gift makes "this world" seem strangely lacking in contrast to the glorious one in which the Goddess reigns. Therefore, the new mother may simply choose to remain there. On the other hand, she may find that the third of her three boons, that of motherselfhood, is simply too unwieldy a gift for her to manage in the world as she has always known it. Whatever the reason, in any particular case, the return journey for a woman following the deeply sacred experience of childbirth is full of peril. Safe return can never be taken for granted.

CHAPTER 23.

Repudiation

Successful childbirth grants a woman a child. To even say so seems absurd: Everyone knows it. What everyone does not know, however, is that childbirth may sometimes grant a woman yet another boon as well— unexpected revelation from the Mother Goddess. But, as in traditional fairy tales, the boons bestowed on a woman traveling the way of the mother are often triple. The third of the three possible boons she may acquire through giving birth is new selfhood. No matter who or what else a woman thinks she is, once she gives birth she stands on the brink of new selfhood: the motherself. After she gives birth herself, "Mother" is no longer her own mother—someone else—but she, herself. This transition is monumental. Even in contemporary Western cultures which often dis-value motherhood, such transformation deeply affects a woman.

In some respects, this transformation may be the most special of the three boons a woman earns by following the way of the mother. Yet like the other two boons with which it is associated, the baby and revelation, motherselfhood is not always an easy gift for a woman to bring safely back to "this world." It, too, is a gift a woman frequently finds perilous. Her failure to bring motherselfhood back with her, however, usually differs from her inability safely to bring back either her baby or the revelation granted her by the Goddess. With those two boons, loss is ordinarily involuntary. By contrast, the third boon is more commonly one the mother actively repudiates.

In this case, although the woman may safely return without losing her baby or suffering prolonged postpartum blues, she may do so at the expense of her own experience. When she returns in this fashion, she typically repudiates some aspect of the *meaning* inherent in the birth process. After all, just because a woman actually gives birth does not mean she becomes a mother in the full sense of the word any more than a man undergoing an initiation rite necessarily experiences the rebirth believed to constitute the essence of the ritual. In both cases a deep inner self-transformation must take place if the external process is to succeed.

The woman who gives birth and then immediately relinquishes the boon of her baby by placing it for adoption is not, except on the most superficial level, doing the same thing as the woman who is eager to love and raise a child she has just borne. That in no way means that the one woman fails or is "bad"; it simply means that each woman is enacting a different stage of the way of the mother. One is refusing to transform herself fully into a mother at this time. Yet in choosing childbirth followed by adoption rather than abortion, she has taken a step closer to motherhood. She has taken the path just so far, and then chosen to let someone else complete it instead. Hers is an honest admission that this is not an appropriate time in her life for her to become a mother self.

Some women, however, choose to bear, then keep, a child, but yet refuse the gift of motherselfhood in other, more subtle ways. An early stage of the return journey at which such refusal often surfaces is nursing. To understand the significance of nursing for the mother's way, it helps to examine it first through the eyes of the hero. One of the most valuable of all the boons a hero may bring back from his quest to another world is the so-called "endless vessel" of fairy tale. From it the owner may drink or eat his fill by giving the proper command. Scholar Jessie Weston persuasively argues that this object becomes the Holy Grail in Christian tradition. It may actually be a vessel, as in the ancient Greek story of "Baucis and Philemon," or an object such as the magic tablecloth in the Grimm's fairy tale of "The Stick, the Table, and the Ass," which, once spread, produces limitless quantities of food. Or it may be the biblical Land of Milk and Honey where manna falls from the sky. Whatever its form, the magical, endless vessel is typically nonhuman, being either a coveted inanimate object or a longed-for utopian place. But its prototype is anything but inanimate or utopian: It is the lactating mother whose breast is always there for the hero in his role as her demanding child. A natural extension of this role of woman as endless vessel to the home she often symbolizes appears in Anne Tyler's *Celestial Navigation,* as the protagonist envisions his wife and her provisions:

> The basement walls were lined with case lots of Mary's household goods. There was an entire cabinet of sneakers, waiting to be grown into. Another of toilet paper. A barrel of detergent big enough to hold two children. Was this necessary? He felt that she was pointing something out to him: her role as supplier, feeder, caretaker. "See how I give? And how I keep on giving—these are my reserves. I will always have more, you don't even have to ask. I will be waiting with a new shirt for you the minute the elbows wear through in the old one."[1]

To *be* this endlessly nourishing, fulfilling object is not at all the same as questing for or possessing it. *Being* it is as messy as possessing it is magical. Even before her baby is born a woman's breasts enlarge. Occasionally she experiences the peculiar sensation of liquid unexpectedly trickling from her nipples. This is colostrum, a substance full of antibodies necessary to protect the baby during its first year of life. Immediately after birth the infant receives only this colostrum as it suckles. Several days must elapse before a mother's milk comes in. A woman immediately knows when that happens, because the resultant, painful engorgement of her breasts is unmistakable. At first she finds the baby's suckling nearly unbearable. Not only does unwonted fullness make her breasts tender, the repeated tugging of the baby on her teats often causes painful cracks. Eventually familiarity with nursing and toughening of skin help neutralize this pain.

As all-nourishing object, a woman must accustom herself not just to thin trickles of colostrum but also to copious amounts of milk spurting from her nipples at odd times. This embarrassing situation is one over which she has no control. The cries of any baby, not just her own, readily start her milk flowing. Even thinking of her baby makes milk come, particularly before her flow is regulated. Mornings she awakens with her breasts distressingly full. At times the smell of her milk slightly sickens her, making her feel unclean. Even when she showers, the spurting continues, stimulated by the flow of warm water. For all these reasons she may experience herself as nothing but an object, a body entirely subject to the cries of her child.

Furthermore, neither her sleep nor her own nourishment are entirely her own now. No matter whether she feeds on demand or on schedule, she still *hears* the baby when it cries in the middle of the night. And if she is nursing no one else can perform this task for her. If she feeds on schedule, she lies there in an uncomfortable pool of her own milk, which no protective, plastic-lined nursing brassiere can hold in forever. Falling back to sleep in that condition is nearly impossible. She might just as well nurse on demand and accomplish something in being awakened.

A similar situation controls her diet. As when she was pregnant she must consider carefully what she eats. If she consumes too few calories she deprives her child of sufficient milk. She must also limit or eliminate some of the indulgences she likes best: alcohol, coffee, and overly rich foods. Smoking and many medications are also taboo; these substances may contaminate her milk. Whether she likes it or not she herself must drink milk and stoke her body with vitamin-rich foods. These necessary controls of her behavior may cause her to experience herself only as an object to this demanding new force in her life. If these negative feelings of being nothing but an object subsume the countering feelings of pleasure she feels while nursing, she will not experience the final transformation into the binary-unity of mother and child. In that case she will have failed to bring back safely to "this world" the important boon of full motherselfhood.

By contrast, if the mother and her baby can successfully establish a rhythm, the situation in which she is object to her own child changes. As she cradles the baby in her arm holding it close to her stomach, the child sucking nourishment from her, she experiences her now physically separate baby as once again one with her. It no longer occurs to her always to think first of something called "my" needs. When the baby cries she automatically responds: Its cries become almost part of her. This is true whether she breast or bottle feeds. Once fears and anxieties rarely awakened her in the night; now her ear is always attuned, listening for any sound from her baby. Slowly, the baby's needs become *her* needs. This subtle transformation changes the mother's individual self into the binary-unity of mother and child—the motherself. When this important transformation occurs, she successfully returns to this world with her important boon of motherselfhood.

But very often, instead of following the pattern in which the Goddess is lover to her child, a woman follows its demonic inversion. Now each half of this important mother-child relationship functions as antagonist to the other. This situation in which the two perpetually battle each other begins when a woman refuses this reunification with her baby after it has been born out of her. In so doing, she appears to be rejecting her baby. However, this is not necessarily the case. Instead, she may very well be rejecting the particular kind of selfhood which motherhood implies, clinging instead to the more familiar pattern represented by the hero. In this regard, it is helpful to recall just what that pattern means for her.

In contemporary Western cultures formal education prepares women and men alike for potential hero status, which is another way of saying it prepares them for manhood. While manhood or hero status may appear to suit career women as well as it does most men, it unquestionably hinders women from functioning as motherselves. Manhood equals unitary selfhood rather than the binary-unitary selfhood authentic to the mother-child relationship. Therefore, it is definitionally an impossible state of being for a mother to assume in relating to her new baby.

Part of what happens when a woman refuses motherselfhood is that she continues the familiar task-orientation she once learned in school. Instead of teaching her baby to perform tasks for itself, she may prolong her infant's dependency by performing them herself. Rather than weaning her baby toward the end of the first year, she may continue nursing for several years. When she discovers how messy he is when he tries to feed himself, she may continue feeding him instead.

By contrast, behavior simultaneously appropriate to the needs of the infant and to the motherself encourages both the infant's independence from her and that of the mother from it. Gradually, a mother comfortable with her motherself abandons more and more of her caretaking role. She allows her child to assume control for himself until he cuts and eats his own food, ties his own shoelaces, selects and puts on his own clothes, and so on. But the extremely goal-oriented mother, modeling her self-image on that of the hero, may find it easier and more rewarding to perform these tasks herself. This way she enjoys a sense of personal accomplishment which must otherwise remain vicarious.

Unless a woman learns to interact with her child in the relational mode inherent in the motherself pattern, she risks great danger. Carried to an extreme, the heroself image allows a mother to fall into the negative pattern of becoming a monster-mother. When she tries to do too much for her child, that is exactly how she appears from the child-hero's perspective. Conversely, she also risks just the opposite problem. If she finds herself falling into the opposite pattern in which she allows the child to do whatever he wants, she may lose all selfhood completely. When that happens, the situation between mother and child is no happier: Now she has become a mere object to his desires. Instead of maintaining any core identity of her own, "she" has essentially disappeared, leaving only an automaton in her place. What she most badly needs in either of these situations is the precious gift of motherselfhood in which she and the child interact as two parts of a larger unit.

Despite the luxury childbirth grants a woman of obtaining three such precious boons as a child, revelation, and motherselfhood, these gifts are earned at great peril. Even if a woman finds she can handle them, she may not want to. Then again, if she does want to, she may discover that others are envious of her for possessing them. Can it be that these very boons which allow a woman to complete her perilous way of the mother also create the problems that cause hostility between the sexes?

An evaluation of the boons the Goddess bestows from Her realm, as well as the mysteries associated with Her, suggests that this may be the case. Certainly great heed must be paid to what both boon and mystery mean within a patriarchal as well as a gynocentric context. Otherwise, these boons and mysteries of motherhood may ultimately be misused for negative ends. If that happens, the very existence of the way of the mother is seriously threatened.

Conclusion: Theft of Women's Mysteries and Boons

> "Birth! Birth! Birth!" Luciente seemed to sing in her ear. "That's all you can dream about! Our dignity comes from work. Everyone raises the kids, haven't you noticed? Romance, sex, birth, children—that's what you fasten on. Yet that isn't women's business anymore. It's everybody's."
>
> —MARGE PIERCY,
> *Woman on the Edge of Time*

In the Grimm's fairy tale known as "The Water of Life," three brothers in turn quest for the magical water, the boon needed to rejuvenate their dying father, the king. In typical fairy-tale fashion, the youngest brother obtains the boon and brings it back from the courtyard of the enchanted castle where it lies. On his return, he searches out his two brothers that they may return safely with him. But they, jealous of his success, "waited till he was asleep, and then they emptied the Water of Life from his goblet. . . . Then the two went to the youngest brother and mocked him, saying, 'It was you who found the Water of Life. You had all the trouble, while we have the reward. You should have been wiser and kept your eyes open.'"[1]

As with this fairy-tale theft of the water of life, throughout the history of patriarchy men have been attempting to steal from women various boons and mysteries connected with the way of the mother. Of all these mysteries and boons—pregnancy, childbearing, lactation, menstruation, revelation, motherselfhood, and children—it is particularly the ability to give birth which has attracted men from prehistoric times on. Theft of this women's mystery, which assumes many forms, symbolizes the long-standing problem that lies at the heart of patriarchal oppression of women: womb envy. This idea that men secretly wish to give birth, hence suffer from womb envy, is by no means new. It has received attention in the writings of various thinkers such as Bruno Bettelheim, Joseph Campbell, Ashley Montagu, and numerous anthropologists.

In some cultures, often but not exclusively tribal societies, womb envy takes the form of couvade, a condition in which a husband experiences various symptoms of pregnancy. He may demand the attentions of his female counterpart, taking to his bed and choosing his foods idiosyncratically. Classical writers such as Apollonius Rhodius, Diodorus, and Strabo document this custom in parts of the ancient classical world, especially among the Gascons, the Spanish Basques, and the Corsicans. Womb envy has also been reported from China, India, Africa, the Americas, and the Russian Baltic provinces. A contemporary literary manifestation of this often disguised male desire to create life directly occurs in Gail Godwin's *A Mother and Two Daughters:*

> Once while they were lying together, he shocked her by saying he wished he could have a baby. On guard, Lydia had instinctively pulled the sheet up to her chin and said that, though she adored her sons, she didn't think she wanted to have any more babies. "No, I didn't mean that," he said dreamily. "I just meant I wished *I* could have one. Just one little baby that would come out of me and be all mine."[2]

In discussing such womb envy, Ashley Montagu, in his book *The Natural Superiority of Women,* argues that men, out of their jealousy of women's abilities for pregnancy, birth, and nursing, have devalued these capabilities and turned them into handicapping conditions.[3] In so doing, men have necessarily denied women the inherent beauty and significance of our own gynocentric mysteries.

Besides devaluing women's mysteries as part of their sly fox-and-grapes attempt to steal them, men have also tried more overtly to appropriate them for themselves. Although this idea of men "stealing" the ability to give birth, with all its related bloody characteristics, may seem far-fetched, consider the words of feminist poet Judy Grahn: "Plugging up of the anus, subcision, circumcision, cutting off the fingers in sacrifice, the slash in Christ's side and his blood-dripping crown of briars, the bloody bandage on the traditional hero—all are versions of male imitative 'menstrual' magic, and all have a similar underlying formula: The ability to shed blood equals the control of life powers."[4]

Two factors are necessary to understanding the great significance of this menstrual magic. One concerns very ancient beliefs about blood; the other, equally ancient beliefs about women. Worldwide, from the very earliest times of which we have record, until the eighteenth century in Europe, menstrual blood was thought to be the mysterious substance which held the key to creation. For example, Aristotle asserted that the male's contribution in the process of generation consisted in some obscure impulse to movement and that "the contribution which the female makes to generation is the *matter* used therein . . . found in the substance constituting the menstrual fluid. . . ."[5] The Roman naturalist Pliny, basing his notions on Aristotle's earlier formulation, wrote that menstrual blood is "the material for human generation, as the semen from the males acting like rennet collects this substance within it, which thereby immediately is inspired with life and endowed with body."[6] Various permutations of this idea, which is thought to have originated in ancient Hindu beliefs that the Great Mother creates the cosmos through her menstrual blood, have influenced the thinking of peoples around the world.

A crucial factor about this "menstrual magic" is the equally ancient cross-cultural belief that men wanting to attain such magical knowledge could do so by "becoming women," that is, through various forms of ritual transvestism. Transvestism was found in many ancient priesthoods. Tacitus says, for example, that the priests of Germanic tribes were *muliebri ornatu,* men who either wore some woman's emblem or dressed up as women.[7] Similarly, certain ancient Norse priests known as *Haddingnar,* who followed the cult of the Norse gods known as the Vanir were required to wear the dress and hairstyles of women.[8] And at the ancient Argive "Feast of Wantonness" men became women by wearing women's dresses and veils, temporarily assuming feminine powers.[9] Likewise, certain Cretan priests always wore female dress, as did Roman priests of the Great Mother.[10] Siberian shamans often wore women's clothes, some even living as homosexual "wives." Likewise, Amerindian *berdaches*—homosexual men—were gifted medicine men, who were originally told in dreams that henceforth they must live as women. These *berdaches* would don women's clothes and take husbands. Such men-turned-women were believed to have even greater powers of healing and spirituality than ordinary male shamans.

In contemporary Western cultures, such cross-dressing and transsexuality are seldom found in a sacred context. Instead, they typically appear on big city streets or nightclub stages.Such is the case with this overt surrogate male pregnancy and birth described by an eyewitness of a professional female impersonator:

> . . . the audience hears a loud POP. (This is done by sticking a pin in the "pregnant" stomach which, in reality, is a large balloon.) The "girl's" face freezes in stylized horror as "she" looks between "her" legs. "She" looks down at her feet, then stoops to pick up the "baby," a foot-long Norwegian troll with wild hair and a blank expression. "She" holds the "baby" at arm's length for a second, gazing at its face with dismay, then sadly and with resignation, "she" gathers it in her arms and shoves it up against one sagging "breast." This routine, relying entirely on the originality of the idea and the mimic genius of the performer, aided by sight gags, was always a huge success with the heterosexual audience for whom it had been created."[11]

A similar expression of male desire for motherhood occurs in John Rechy's *City of Night*. Here a nameless drag queen is being addressed by a "waitress" in a hustling bar.

> Hi, hon, . . . why aint [sic] I seen you in such a long time?—but then of course I've been in the hospital myself for about a week. I had this operation. . . . "An abortion?" an eavesdropping white queen asks. "Shut your nelly mouth, Mary," said the Negro queen—"or I'll have you eight-sixed out of this bar so fast you wont [sic] even be able to hold on to your makeup!"
> "Honey," said the other queen. "I wasn't trying to dish you, sweetheart. . . . Why dearest, *I'd* like to get pregnant myself!"[12]

In both examples humor supposedly hides the expressed male desire to carry and give birth to a child.

In some instances the motif of the male mother expands so that he-she is both "mother" and child. The 325-pound transvestite entertainer who goes by the name of Divine is a case in point. In January of 1984 "he" was reported to have landed a dual role in a musical called *Beverly Hills,* in which he plays both mother and son.[13]

In the 1970s some men did actually turn themselves into "women" through surgical alteration, although after about a decade, such procedures were largely halted. But trying to steal the mystery of giving birth by literalizing the desire for women's attributes does not necessarily gain a man the very deepest understanding of the way of the mother. First of all, he still cannot become pregnant, give birth, or (unless he is given massive doses of hormones) lactate. Furthermore, given the norms of patriarchal culture which overtly denigrate women's capabilities while secretly working to appropriate them, such behaviors are not socially desirable anyway. With rare exceptions, only those on the fringes of patriarchy—gay men, transvestites, and transsexuals—openly dare play out this patriarchal fantasy of appropriation of women's mysteries.

Far more desirable for most men is to command the external power granted to men-as-a-class and simultaneously enjoy the mysteries of women without appearing to do so. To actually *become* a woman is necessarily to lose the status of being a man. Far better to combine the power of the one with the mysteries of the other without openly seeming to do so.

This process whereby powerful males attempt to steal the mysteries of women without attempting, on the one hand, to become women, or, on the other, to pretend a fox-and-grapes attitude of disdain for them, dates back to the very beginnings of patriarchy. As noted in chapter 2, this long-standing desire of men to appropriate women's natural capacity for giving birth is nowhere more evident than in stories telling of the creation of humanity. From traditions as various as those of the Sumerians and the ancient Hebrews, Egyptians, Greeks, and Teutons come tales of male gods "giving birth" to the world.

In legend this same urge on the part of man to usurp woman's natural power of creating life out of our own bodies occurs most prominently in the Jewish Kabbalistic tradition. According to Jewish legend, the Rabbi Loew of Prague (1513-1609) received advice from Heaven telling him how to make a golem, a man-made creature which comes to life. The Rabbi was given this advice because the Jews needed help to battle the Jew-baiters who continuously accused them of murdering Christian children for ritual purposes. To make this quasi-human "man," Rabbi Loew enlisted help. Together with his son-in-law and a student, he used the three elements of fire, water, and air to create life out of the fourth, earth. When the three male creators recited from Genesis 2:7: "And he breathed into his nostrils the breath of life; and man became a living soul," the golem sprang to life. This popular tale renders the male theft of woman's deepest mystery in particularly vivid fashion.

Still another variant of this motif of man creating life informs Mary Shelley's classic, *Frankenstein,* published in 1818. In it Dr. Frankenstein learns the secret of creating life by vitalizing an inanimate body. In his words: "To examine the causes of life, we must first have recourse to death. . . . A new species would bless me as its creator and source; many happy and excellent natures would owe their being to me. No father could claim the gratitude of his child so completely as I should deserve theirs."[14]

Yet another variant of this motif occurs in Act II, scene ii of Goethe's *Faust,* when Faust's kindred spirit Wagner, working in his laboratory, manages to create life:

Of the old, senseless mode we're now well ridden.
. . . .
. . . Man must learn, with his great gifts, to win
Henceforth a purer, loftier origin.[15]

These legends celebrating the male theft of women's mysteries have their counterpart in ritual activities. Although it is actually Wagner and not Faust who creates life in the form of a homunculus, it is Faust, in his restless questing after more and more of the secrets of the universe, who has come to stand in Western culture for what we now call "Faustian man," exactly the sort of male who is not content with the natural order represented by the Goddess but must impose his own instead, following the patriarchal biblical injunction to assume dominion over the earth.

Some of the magical practices of such early magi figures as Faust fall into the realm of alchemy, in which the male desire to steal women's mysteries is a prominent theme. Alchemy is often described as a pseudo-science, although its physical practices eventuated in the science of chemistry. The physical purpose of alchemy was to learn the secret of transmuting base metals into gold, but it was also concerned with mystically perfecting the human soul, hence in learning the secret of rebirth. Exactly when alchemy started is unknown, for extant writings which date from the 3rd century C.E. reveal an already developed practice.

It was the twentieth-century psychiatrist Carl Gustav Jung who pointed out the psychological components of alchemy. These components made alchemy function, relative to its time, much the way psychoanalysis does in our own day. According to Jung, the philosopher's stone which alchemists sought so hard to create was an image of self. All the birth imagery so characteristic of alchemical treatises thus remains metaphoric for Jung, the repeated references to "new life" meaning new life in the sense that an analysand may feel new life after months or years of developing insights into the unconscious. By this interpretation, male desire to appropriate women's gifts for creating life is not operative in alchemy.

While much of what Jung says about this topic undeniably persuades, it is nonetheless the case that the language of alchemy strongly implies more literal birth as well. The alchemists sought their *prima materia* in: "excrement, one of the arcane substances from which it was hoped that the mystic figure of the *filius philosophorus* would emerge. . . ."[16] The *filius philosophorus* was both a longed-for savior and the philosopher's stone, capable of changing dross into gold. The excrement mentioned here, like the dirt or clay common to many creation myths including the golem legend, is the substance many children spontaneously believe responsible for making babies. The underlying logic inherent in this common belief readily connects expulsion of fecal material through the anus with production of a baby through the "stomach"—the exact opening usually being unclear to young children.

The formal discipline of alchemy, which so overtly reveals the desires of its practitioners, has long since given way to chemistry in its physical form and to psychoanalysis in its mystical-philosophic manifestations. In alchemy's varied offspring, chemistry, biology, and physics, man's desire for control of reproduction continues unabated. This desire has become increasingly apparent as the twentieth century becomes more and more technologically sophisticated. In the physical field of cybernetics, for instance, as Norbert Wiener points out in his book *God and Golem, Inc.: A Comment on Certain Points Where Cybernetics Impinges on Religion* (1964), the machine is the golem of the Rabbi of Prague.[17] Not only do we now have machines in profusion, such as washers and dryers, which function as household servants once did, we also have machines in the form of computers which may be said to "learn," even to "reproduce" themselves, if the terms are used loosely. And for those who want their golems to *look* human there are even androids, automatons in human form. With such figures, males are able to reproduce a technological analogue of humanity—not quite the real thing, but dangerously close enough to be frightening.

More directly threatening, however, to women's traditionally unique capacity to bear young alive are developments in the biological sphere, specifically molecular biology. In an article in the December 1983 issue of *Science,* called "The Shape of Things to Come," writer Paul Preuss says, "By mastering the special geometry of life's molecules, biochemists hope to splice several nerves, create synthetic vaccines, even sort gold from the sea."[18] How very like the dreams of the old alchemists. While the work of these "protein engineers" does not yet *directly* impinge on women's traditional role, consider what happens when this work is combined with computer technology: "The biocomputer represents the ultimate expression of the biotechnical age. By successfully engineering living material into an organic computer that can think, reproduce itself, and transform other living material into economic utilities, humanity becomes the architect of life itself in the coming age."[19]

Still more immediately threatening to women's traditional role as bearer of young at this point in history, however, are: cloning, fertility sperm banks, egg donors, test-tube impregnation, surrogate mothers, artificial wombs, artificial insemination, and in-vitro fertilization. While these scientific "advances" are undeniably very exciting, they also deserve to be viewed with caution by women for several reasons. First is the fact that these procedures are becoming more and more possible at just this moment in Western history. For the first time since the Industrial Revolution, great numbers of Western women have left their traditional roles as full-time mothers. And as they continue to do so, some are espousing the view of feminist thinker Shulamith Firestone who asserts that biological motherhood causes women's inferior status to men. In Firestone's vision, the ideal future encompasses "the freeing of women from the tyranny of their biology by any means available, and the diffusion of the childbearing and childrearing role to the society as a whole, to men and other children as well as women."[20] By this logic, what the Mother Goddess has to offer is not a gift, not an awe-inspiring mystery, but a tyranny from which women should be only too glad to escape.

For women who accept this position, the idea that babies may cease to be born from women's wombs is no threat whatsoever, but a highly desirable possibility. In this view women will now be free at last. But, one must ask, free to be . . . what? Human beings? Well, but "ain't I a human now?" to paraphrase Sojourner Truth. Free to be pseudo-men? Free never to become mothers? Just what is the nature of the freedom involved here? I ask this question because I perceive these new reproductive possibilities from just the opposite perspective. What if women are totally deluded in this regard? Did we not learn long ago to believe androcentric constructions of "reality" which assert that women's mothering is inferior to the "real" work of the world—that conducted not at home, but in the public sphere still largely dominated by men? Though some radical feminists claim this belief as authentically woman-centered, in fact, it is just the opposite. In believing it, women are rushing toward an illusionary concept of freedom we have devised out of a delusionary patriarchal context. In that context men are perceived as free (or at least freer) and women as confined.

But what if all the evidence pointing toward male envy of women's seeming capacity to create life is correct? Then, it seems to me, women, in defining the traditionally male world of work as "freedom," and then rushing to enter that world, may find ourselves duped. Remember when Tom Sawyer lured all his friends into whitewashing the fence by pretending to love painting it? I can foresee a possible reversal of the current Western social order, whereby women by the thousands will rush out every morning, briefcases in hand, coats almost on, coffee still being swallowed. "Bye, dear," they will shout as they start up the station wagon and wave to pregnant hubby, standing hand in hand with little Terry or Jane.

What if, just what if, standing off to the side in their self-created public sphere, men have all this while been patiently persuading us that those grapes of motherhood that we possess and that men can't yet quite reach are really sour, hence not worth our effort to retain them. Meanwhile, they have just been waiting for the time when they could finally reach them, having learned to control reproduction absolutely. Who knows, they might even want to implant those fertilized embryos directly into themselves as well as into sterile test tubes and infertile women. A ludicrous fantasy? Perhaps.

But whether or not most men actually want the physical experience of bearing children themselves, men as a group could well decide that vast numbers of women are expendable. We all know the horror of the Nazi extermination of Jews. Most women know of the huge number of witches (mostly women) liquidated in sixteenth- and seventeenth-century Europe by Inquisitors and other Church authorities. It could happen again. Women certainly are not essential for satisfying men's sexual needs. For those men who do not care for sex with other men, science can undoubtedly devise a surrogate more pleasing and less "uppity" than flesh-and-blood women. And if we no longer are needed as bearers of the young, why that makes us almost totally expendable, give or take a few thousand women worldwide to keep supplying eggs until that item of reproduction can also be synthesized. If such a world were to come to pass, the theft of women's greatest mystery would be complete.

But that negative drama need not occur. Women can stop to ponder the significance in our lives of the Mother image and of the mysteries and boons we can attain by following Her way. We can step back before it is too late, and see what enormous meaning motherhood and its boons have always had, and even now continue to have, not just for us, but for both sexes. And in that recognition lies a key. If men really do envy women this capacity, then it just may be that women have to learn how to *share* it—not to give it away unheedingly, not to allow it to be taken from us, not to disvalue it ourselves, nor to hoard it, but to pay attention to the urgency with which the condition and symbolization of motherhood cry out to both sexes. In a religious context that means that, above all, we must heed what the constellation of meaning generally known as the Mother Goddess actually signifies. In a mythic setting it means attending to the counterpart of the quest of the hero, the way of the mother.

Recall: Once upon a time the Mother in her deified form was worshipped everywhere. Then She was equalled by her own son; finally, She was eclipsed by the domineering patriarchal Father god. Now once again She is being reclaimed by numbers of feminists. Is there a way in which She and what She stands for can be more broadly shared?

If not, She is likely to be destroyed, so totally cut out of human awareness through patriarchal "advances" in artificial birth that She will disappear forever. And if She and what She stands for are destroyed, what about human beings? Who or what will we become instead when we are no longer of woman born? It might be well to remember that in many traditional societies a mother's curse is the most dreaded of all maledictions. In ancient Greek thought a mother's imprecation was so strong a pollutant that it would inevitably wreak destruction on the accursed and his descendants. The word for that kind of pollution is miasma. In speaking of this potent curse responsible for miasma, the ancient Aryan Laws of Manu sound this warning:

> Women must be honored and adored by their fathers, brothers, husbands, and brothers-in-law, who desire (their own) welfare.
> Where women are honoured, there the gods are pleased; but where they are not honoured, no sacred rite yields rewards.
> Where the female relations live in grief, the family soon wholly perishes; but that family where they are not unhappy ever prospers.
> The houses on which female relations, not being duly honoured, pronounce a curse, perish completely, as if destroyed by magic.[21]

This same curse, the *mutspell,* or *mudspell,* occurs also in the *Prose Edda* of the Icelandic scholar Snorri Sturluson (c. 1220) who decided to write down the old myths before they were totally lost. According to Snorri, in the beginning there were two regions, a world of snow and ice in the north called Niflheim, and one of brightness and fire in the South called Muspell. Between the two, connected by the great world tree Yggdrasill, lay a vast realm of emptiness known as Ginnungagap. In the ancient myths of these regions, recounted by Snorri, the final destruction of the world is foretold in the poem known as the *Voluspa,* alternatively, the *Ragnarok,* as it is called in Icelandic, or the *Götterdammerung,* in German. This twilight of the gods results from warlike behavior by the patriarchal Aesir, who torture Gullveig, a goddess of the opposing, pre-patriarchal Vanir.

On the fateful day, the sons of Muspelheim will follow their leader Surtur, riding out of Muspelhiem over the rainbow bridge Bifrost, which breaks under their hooves. On the battlefield all the gods, giants, and monsters do battle. The scene climaxes when Surt shoots flames all over the world, burning it up completely. Thus from "The Land of the Mother's Curse" comes the destruction of the world. I, for one, would prefer to maintain Her way instead.

NOTES

Introduction

1. Carol Gilligan, *In a Different Voice: Psychological Theory and Women's Development* (Cambridge and London: Harvard University Press, 1982).

2. Joseph Campbell, *The Hero with a Thousand Faces* (Cleveland and New York: World Publishing Company, 1968), p. 120.

3. Campbell, *Hero*, p. 3.

1. Mother Goddesses

1. Norman O. Brown, *Love's Body* (New York: Random House/Vintage, 1966), p. 133.

2. Much of the information on the Goddess appears in "Family," by Kathryn Allen Rabuzzi, *The Encyclopedia of Religion* (New York: Macmillan, 1986).

2. Father Gods

1. Much of the information on father gods appears in slightly different form in Rabuzzi, "Family" in *The Encyclopedia of Religion* (New York: Macmillan, 1986).

2. Cornelius Loew, *Myth, Sacred History, and Philosophy; The Pre-Christian Religious Heritage of the West* (New York: Harcourt, Brace & World, 1967), p. 25.

3. *The Ancient Near East, Vol. I, An Anthology of Texts and Pictures*, ed. James B. Pritchard (Princeton: Princeton University Press, 1958), p. 3.

3. Hero Sons

1. Much of the information in this chapter appears in slightly altered form in Rabuzzi, "Family," in *The Encyclopedia of Religion* (New York: Macmillan, 1986).

2. One source for this idea is *The Woman's Encyclopedia of Myths and Secrets*, ed. Barbara G. Walker (San Francisco: Harper & Row, 1983), pp. 392-93.

3. *The New York Times*, 7 May 1982, p. 10.

4. Carol Gilligan, *In a Different Voice: Psychological Theory and Women's Development* (Cambridge and London: Harvard University Press, 1982), passim.

4. Heroself

1. Joseph Campbell, *The Hero with a Thousand Faces* (Cleveland and New York: World Publishing Company, 1968), p. 109.

2. The following quote is representative: "'A woman's body is filthy, it is not a Dharma-receptacle. How can you attain unexcelled Bodhi?'. . . At that time, the assembled multitude all saw the dragon girl in the space of an instant turn into a man, perfect bodhisattva-conduct, straightway go Southward to the world-sphere

Spotless, sit on a jeweled lotus blossom, and achieve undifferentiating right, enlightened intuition, with thirty-two marks and eighty beautiful features setting forth the fine Dharma for all living beings in all ten directions." *The Scripture of the Lotus Blossom of the Fine Dharma,* tr. Leon Hurvitz (New York: Columbia University Press, 1976), pp. 200-201.

3. Campbell, *Hero,* p. 120.

5. Polytheistic Selves

1. Charlene Spretnak, *Lost Goddesses of Early Greece: A Collection of Pre-Hellenic Myths* (Boston: Beacon Press, 1981), p. 22.

6. Motherself

1. "Teddy," like all the names of people I have interviewed or talked with informally, is made up, but the child whose story is quoted here is known to me personally.

2. Victor Turner, *The Forest of Symbols: Aspects of Ndembu Ritual* (Ithaca and London: Cornell University Press, 1967), pp. 93-110.

3. Joseph Campbell, *The Masks of God: Primitive Mythology* (New York: Viking Press, 1970), p. 99.

4. This quote is transcribed from a conversation with a friend who wishes to remain anonymous.

5. Gail Godwin, *A Mother and Two Daughters* (New York: Viking Press, 1982), p. 284.

6. Merri Rosenberg, "The Hardest Choice of All," *Ladies' Home Journal,* Sept. 1985, p. 44.

7. Anne Tyler, *Celestial Navigation* (New York: Alfred A. Knopf, 1974), p. 58.

8. Comment from a personal friend.

9. This situation happened to an acquaintance of mine.

10. A friend of mine experienced this protectiveness from her children.

11. Godwin, *A Mother and Two Daughters,* p. 318.

12. "Marie" is a friend who prefers anonymity.

13. Idea given to me by another friend.

7. A Mother's Story

1. This mother's story is entirely of my own invention.

2. The Brothers Grimm, "The Water of Life," in Grimm's *Fairy Tales,* tr. Mrs. E. V. Lucas, Lucy Crane, and Marian Edwardes (New York: Grosset & Dunlap, 1945), p. 181.

3. Grimm, "Water of Life," p. 182.

4. Grimm, "Water of Life," p. 187.

5. "Serena" is based on the experience of a friend, although I have slightly altered her circumstances to preserve her anonymity.

8. Being a Mother: A Body Mystery

1. I am indebted to Robert Orsi, Associate Professor of Religious Studies, Fordham University, for this information.

2. John Rechy, *This Day's Death* (New York: Grove Press, 1969), p. 232.

3. Norman O. Brown, *Love's Body* (New York: Random House/Vintage, 1966), p. 52.

9. The Mother's Call

1. An exception is male gay literature. Interestingly, in this literature, sex is frequently portrayed as a "hunt"; thus sex and quest become synonymous for many gay men. See, for example, Dennis Altman, *The Homosexualization of America* (Boston: Beacon Press, 1982), p. 175, and the novels of John Rechy.

2. Lisa Alther, *Kinflicks* (New York: Signet/New American, 1975), p. 121.

3. Marina Warner, *Alone of All Her Sex: The Myth and the Cult of the Virgin Mary* (New York: Pocket Books, 1976), p. 72.

4. Stephen Crane, "Maggie, A Girl of the Streets," in *American Literature: Tradition and Innovation,* ed. Harrison T. Messerole et al. (Lexington, Mass.: D. C. Heath and Company, 1969), p. 2741.

5. Crane, p. 2770.

6. Crane, p. 2771.

7. "Alice" is a woman I once knew.

8. T. S. Eliot, "The Waste Land," in *Collected Poems 1909-1962* (New York: Harcourt, Brace & World, 1970), p. 62, line 252.

10. The Threshold

1. The Brothers Grimm, "Sleeping Beauty," in *Grimm's Fairy Tales,* tr. Mrs. E. V. Lucas, Lucy Crane, and Marian Edwardes (New York: Grosset & Dunlap, 1945), p. 104.

2. Johann Wolfgang von Goethe, *Faust; A Tragedy,* tr.Bayard Taylor (New York: The Modern Library, 1950), Part II, Act I, sc. v, p. 52.

3. Grimm, "The Twelve Dancing Princesses," in *Fairy Tales,* p. 3.

11. The Other Side of the Threshold

1. Joseph Campbell, *The Hero with a Thousand Faces,* (Cleveland and New York: World Publishing Company, 1968), p. 97.

2. Campbell, *Hero,* p. 90.

3. This story appears in Joseph Campbell, *The Masks of God: Primitive Mythology* (New York: Viking Press, 1969), pp. 74-75.

4. See, for example, John Rechy, *City of Night* (New York: Grove Press, 1963), pp. 40, 54; *Bodies and Souls* (New York: Carroll & Graf, 1983), p. 236; and J. M. Carrier, "Homosexual Behavior in Cross-Cultural Perspective," in *Homosexual Behavior: A Modern Reappraisal,* ed. Judd Marmor (New York: Basic Books, 1980), pp. 110-11, 117.

12. Supernatural Help

1. Hesiod, "To Demeter," in Hesiod, *The Homeric Hymns and Homerica,* tr. Hugh G. Evelyn-White, M.A. (Cambridge: Harvard University Press, 1914; reprinted 1974), lines 272ff., p. 309.

2. Joseph Campbell, *The Hero with a Thousand Faces* (Cleveland and New York: World Publishing Company, 1968), p. 77.

13. Pregnancy

1. Ann Oakley, *Women Confined: Towards a Sociology of Childbirth* (New York: Schocken Books, 1980), p. 291.

2. Marilyn French, *The Women's Room* (New York: Jove/Harcourt Brace Jovanovich, 1978), p. 69.

3. Shih Ming, "Fragment from a Lost Diary," in *Fragment from a Lost Diary and Other Stories: Women of Asia, Africa, and Latin America,*, ed. Naomi Katz and Nancy Milton (Boston: Beacon Press, 1973), p. 216.

4. Evelyn Scott, *Escapade* (New York: Thomas Seltzer, 1923), p. 5.

5. Anne Tyler, *Celestial Navigation* (New York: Alfred A. Knopf, 1974), p. 69.

6. "One Night in Paradise," in *Italian Folktales*, ed. Italo Calvino, tr. George Martin (New York and London: Harcourt Brace Jovanovich, 1980), pp. 119-21.

7. Anne Tyler, *Morgan's Passing* (New York: Alfred A. Knopf, 1980), p. 236.

8. Anne Tyler, *Earthly Possessions* (New York: Berkley Books, 1983), pp. 250, 251, 253.

9. "Delia" is a composite of several young women.

10. "Judy," like "Delia," reflects the stories of several young women.

11. Joan Didion, *Play It as It Lays* (New York: Washington Square Press/ Pocket Books, 1970), p. 140.

12. Gail Godwin, *A Mother and Two Daughters* (New York: Viking Press, 1982), p. 401.

13. Godwin, pp. 403-404.

14. Nadine Brozan, "The Grief of a Failed Pregnancy," *New York Times,* 7 Feb. 1983, p. B-5.

15. Gail Godwin, "Dream Children," in *Dream Children* (New York: Alfred A. Knopf, 1976), pp. 15-16.

14. Womansins

1. Valerie Saiving, "The Human Situation: A Feminist View," in *Womanspirit Rising: A Feminist Reader in Religion,* ed. Carol P. Christ and Judith Plaskow (New York: Harper & Row, 1979), p. 37.

2. Saiving, "Human Situation," p. 37.

3. Judith Plaskow, *Sex, Sin, and Grace: Women's Experience and the Theologies of Reinhold Niebuhr and Paul Tillich* (Washington: University Press of America, 1980).

4. Quoted in Kathryn Allen Rabuzzi, *The Sacred and the Feminine: Toward a Theology of Housework* (New York: Seabury Press, 1982), p. 193. The original is taken from Martin Buber, "The Query of Queries," from *Tales of the Hasidim—The Early Masters,* reprinted in *The Norton Reader: An Anthology of Expository Prose,* 4th ed. (New York: W. W. Norton, 1965), p. 1136.

5. "Amy" wishes to remain anonymous.

6. From discussion with a woman who wishes to remain anonymous.

7. From an oral interview with Agnes Massza, CUNY Oral History Project, May 1975, quoted in Elizabeth Ewen, "City Lights: Immigrant Women and the Rise of the Movies," in *Women and the American City,* ed. Catherine R. Stimpson et al.(Chicago and London: University of Chicago Press, 1981), pp. 53-54.

8. "Mrs. X" requested anonymity.

9. "Alice" wished to remain anonymous.

15. Temptation

1. Joseph Campbell, *The Hero with a Thousand Faces* (Cleveland and New York: World Publishing Company, 1968), p. 122.

2. Campbell, *Hero,* p. 122.

3. Quoted in Rozsika Parker and Griselda Pollock, *Old Mistresses: Women, Art and Ideology* (New York: Pantheon Books, 1981), p. 8. The original is from Octave Uzanne, *The Modern Parisienne: Parisiennes de ce Temps, en leurs divers*

milieus, états et conditions; études pour servir à l'histoire des femmes, de las société, de la galanterier francaise, des moeurs contemporaines et de l'egoisme masculin . . . , 2d ed. (Paris: Mercure de France, 1910).

4. Ellen Moers, *Literary Women* (Garden City, New York: Anchor Press/ Doubleday, 1977), p. 12.

5. Moers, p. 12.

16. Atonement with the Fathers

1. Joseph Campbell, *The Hero with a Thousand Faces* (Cleveland and New York: World Publishing Company, 1968), p. 147.

2. "Iris" told me her story in strict confidence.

17. Estrangement from the Fathers

1. *The Book of Common Prayer; and Administration of the Sacraments and Other Rites and Ceremonies of the Church* (New York: Edwin S. Gorham, Inc., 1929), p. 71.

2. *Book of Common Prayer,* p. 19.

3. Caroline A. was my paternal aunt.

4. This letter is in my possession.

5. From the nature of her story it should be evident why "Joan" wishes to remain anonymous.

6. "Clea" is an acquaintance.

7. "Jane" is a woman I knew for a brief time.

8. I have known "Rachel" for nearly twenty years.

18. Apotheosis: Decreation of Patriarchy

1. Joseph Campbell, *The Hero with a Thousand Faces* (Cleveland and New York: World Publishing Co., 1968), p. 151.

2. For more information on this topic, see Connie Brown and Jane Seitz, "Historical Perspectives," in *Sisterhood Is Powerful: An Anthology of Writings from the Women's Liberation Movement,* ed. Robin Morgan (New York: Vintage/Random House, 1970).

3. J. J. Bachofen, *Myth, Religion and Mother Right: Selected Writings of J. J. Bachofen,* tr. Ralph Manheim (Princeton: Princeton University Press, 1967), pp. 70-71.

4. *The Woman's Encyclopedia of Myths and Secrets,* ed. Barbara G. Walker (San Francisco: Harper & Row, 1983), p. 197.

5. Susan Griffin, *Woman and Nature: The Roaring inside Her* (San Francisco: Harper & Row, 1978), pp. 171, 173.

6. Monique Wittig, *The Lesbian Body,* tr. David Le Vay (New York: Bard/ Avon, 1976), p. x.

7. Wittig, p. 32.

8. Both my husband and my son accompanied me to this exhibit at MOMA; neither of them could bear to look at it. Both left and met me in the museum's permanent collection.

9. Quoted in Rozsika Parker and Griselda Pollock, *Old Mistresses: Women, Art and Ideology* (New York: Pantheon Books, 1981), p. 163.

10. Miriam Schapiro, "How Did I Happen to Make the Painting Anatomy of a Kimono?" in *Miriam Schapiro: A Retrospective 1953-1980,* ed. Thalia Gouma-Peterson (Wooster, Ohio: The College of Wooster, 1980), pp. 28, 30.

11. This information was given me by a close Roman Catholic friend who requested anonymity because of her own participation in such celebrations.

12. Information on this conference and this ritual was given to me in May 1984 by active Roman Catholic laywoman Nancy Murray of Syracuse, New York.

13. Cynthia Ozick, "Notes toward Finding the Right Question," *Lilith,* no.6, 1979, pp. 19-29.

14. E. M. Broner, "Honor and Ceremony in Women's Rituals," in *The Politics of Women's Spirituality; Essays on the Rise of Spiritual Power within the Feminist Movement,* ed. Charlene Spretnak (Garden City, New York; Anchor Press/Double-day, 1982), pp. 237-38.

15. Broner, "Honor," pp. 241-42.

16. Z. Budapest, "Self-Blessing Ritual," in *Womanspirit Rising: A Feminist Reader in Religion,* ed. Carol P. Christ and Judith Plaskow (New York: Harper & Row, 1979), pp. 269-72.

17. Kay Turner, "Contemporary Feminist Rituals," in *Politics of Women's Spirituality,* ed. Spretnak, p. 223.

18. Broner, "Honor," p. 242.

19. Nelle Morton, "The Dilemma of Celebration," in *Womanspirit Rising,* ed. Christ and Plaskow, pp. 162-63.

20. Judy Grahn, "From Sacred Blood to the Curse and Beyond," in *Politics of Women's Spirituality,* ed. Spretnak, p. 278.

19. The Meeting with the Goddess

1. Joseph Campbell, *The Hero with a Thousand Faces* (Cleveland and New York: World Publishing Company, 1968), p. 109.

2. C. S. Lewis, *Till We Have Faces: A Myth Retold* (New York and London: Harvest/Harcourt Brace Jovanovich, 1956).

3. Kim Chernin, *The Obsession: Reflections on the Tyranny of Slenderness* (New York: Colophon/Harper & Row, 1982), pp. 17-18.

4. Chernin, *Obsession,* p. 18.

5. Chernin, *Obsession,,* pp. 92-95.

6. Story revealed in private conversation with a medical student approximately twenty years ago.

7. Dorothy Dinnerstein, *The Mermaid and the Minotaur: Sexual Arrangements and Human Malaise* (New York: Colophon/Harper & Row, 1977).

8. Quoted in Philip Roth, "A Conversation with Edna O'Brien: 'The Body Contains the Life Story,'" *New York Times Book Review,* 18 November 1984, p. 40.

9. Anne Tyler, *Earthly Possessions* (New York: Berkley Books, 1983), p. 9.

10. Tyler, *Earthly Possessions,* pp. 179-82.

11. Chernin, *Obsession,* p. 71.

12. Sigmund Freud, *Beyond the Pleasure Principle,* tr. James Strachey (New York, Toronto, London: Bantam Books, 1928; 1959 ed.), p. 70.

13. Freud, *Beyond the Pleasure Principle,* p. 72.

20. The Mystical Marriage

1. Joseph Campbell, *The Hero with a Thousand Faces* (Cleveland and New York: World Publishing Company, 1968), p. 109.

2. Carroll Smith-Rosenberg, "The Female World of Love and Ritual: Relations Between Women in Nineteenth-Century America," in *A Heritage of Her Own: Toward a New Social History of American Women,* ed. Nancy F. Cott and Elizabeth H. Pleck (New York: Simon and Schuster/Touchstone, 1979).

3. From the Sarah Foulke [Emlen] Diary, 29 December 1808, quoted in Smith-Rosenberg, "Female World," p. 328.

4. Smith-Rosenberg, "Female World," p. 321.

5. John D'Emilio, *Sexual Politics, Sexual Communities: The Making of a Homosexual Minority in the United States 1940-1970* (Chicago and London: University of Chicago Press, 1983), pp. 10-11.

6. Sasha Gregory Lewis, *Sunday's Women: A Report on Lesbian Life Today* (Boston: Beacon Press, 1979), p. 40.

7. Shere Hite, *The Hite Report; A Nationwide Study on Female Sexuality* (New York: Macmillan, 1976), p. 294.

8. Hans Christian Andersen, "The Girl Who Trod on a Loaf," in *Andersen's Fairy Tales,* tr. Mrs. E. V. Lucas and Mrs. H. B. Paull (New York: Grosset & Dunlap, 1945), p. 85.

9. Dante Alighieri, *Inferno,* Canto VI, lines 10-13.

10. Dante, Canto VII, lines 127-30.

11. Sasha Gregory Lewis, *Sunday's Women,* p. 43.

12. Monique Wittig, *The Lesbian Body,* tr. David Le Vay (New York: Bard/Avon, 1976), p. 26.

21. The Mysteries of the Goddess

1. For an excellent source on this material, see Marija Gimbutas, *The Goddesses and Gods of Old Europe, 6500-3500 B.C.: Myths and Cult Images* (Berkeley and Los Angeles: University of California Press, 1982).

2. Similar mysteries are known to have attended the Goddess in various other of Her forms such as Isis and Cybele.

3. William Wharton, *Dad* (New York: Alfred A. Knopf, 1981), p. 307.

4. M. Esther Harding, *Woman's Mysteries, Ancient and Modern: A Psychological Interpretation of the Feminine Principle as Portrayed in Myth, Story and Dreams* (New York: Harper & Row, 1976).

5. Gwenda Blair, "Reviewing 'The Birth Project': Judy Chicago's Judgment Day," *Village Voice,* vol. 28, no. 44, December 1983, p. 92.

6. Susan Griffin, *Woman and Nature: The Roaring inside Her* (San Francisco: Harper & Row, Publishers, 1978), p. 198.

7. Marilyn French, *The Women's Room* (New York: Jove/Harcourt Brace Jovanovich, 1978), p. 73.

8. Ann Cornelison, *Women of the Shadows* (New York: Vintage Books/Random House, 1977), p. 132.

9. Anaïs Nin, "Birth," in *Under a Glass Bell and other Stories* (Chicago: Swallow Press, 1973), pp. 113-14.

10. John Layard, *Stone Men of Malekula, Vao* (London: Chatto & Windus, 1942), p. 652.

11. Gimbutas, *Goddesses,* p. 93.

12. Gimbutas, *Goddesses,* p. 125.

13. Virgil, "Aeneid," in *Virgil's Works: The Aeneid, Eclogues, Georgics,* tr. J. W. Mackail (New York: Modern Library, 1950), p. 104.

14. Layard, *Stone Men,* pp. 652-53.

15. Leo Nikolaevich Tolstoy, "The Death of Ivan Ilych," tr. Aylmer Maude, in *Short Novels of the Masters,* ed. Charles Neider (New York: Rinehart & Co., 1955), pp. 291-92.

16. Tolstoy, "Ivan Ilych," pp. 299-300.

17. Alfred Lord Tennyson, "Ulysses," in *Victorian Poetry and Poetics,* 2d ed., ed. Walter E. Houghton and G. Robert Stange (Boston: Houghton Mifflin Co., 1968), lines 30-33, p. 32.

18. T. S. Eliot, "Four Quartets," in *Collected Poems 1909-1962* (New York: Harcourt, Brace & World, 1970), p. 209.

22. Perils: Dead Babies, Infanticide, and Postpartum Depression

1. Gail Godwin, "Dream Children," in *Dream Children* (New York: Alfred A. Knopf, 1976), p. 17.

2. Alfred Lord Tennyson, "The Lotos-Eaters," VIII, lines 153-55, in *Victorian Poetry and Poetics,* 2d ed., ed. Walter E. Houghton and G. Robert Stange (Boston: Houghton Mifflin Co., 1968), p. 26.

3. Charlotte Perkins Gilman, "The Yellow Wallpaper," in *The Oven Birds: American Women on Womanhood 1820-1920,* ed. Gail Parker (Garden City, New York: Doubleday/Anchor, 1972), pp. 334-35.

23. Repudiation

1. Anne Tyler, *Celestial Navigation* (New York: Alfred A. Knopf, 1974), p. 160.

Conclusion: Theft of Women's Mysteries and Boons

1. The Brothers Grimm, "The Water of Life," in *Grimm's Fairy Tales,* tr. Mrs. E. V. Lucas, Lucy Crane, and Marian Edwardes (New York: Grosset & Dunlap, 1945), p. 185.

2. Gail Godwin, *A Mother and Two Daughters* (New York: Viking Press, 1982), p. 262.

3. Ashley Montagu, *The Natural Superiority of Women* (New York: Macmillan, 1953), pp. 35ff.

4. Judy Grahn, "From Sacred Blood to the Curse and Beyond," in *The Politics of Women's Spirituality: Essays on the Rise of Spiritual Power within the Feminist Movement,* ed. Charlene Spretnak (Garden City, New York: Anchor Press/Doubleday 1982), p. 274.

5. Aristotle, *Generation of Animals,* I:xix, tr. A. L. Peck, M.A., Ph.D. (London: William Heinemann Ltd. and Cambridge: Harvard University Press, 1943), p. 101.

6. Pliny, *Natural History, II, Libri III-VII,* in the Loeb Classical Library, ed. E. H. Warmington, M.A. (London: William Heinemann Ltd. and Cambridge: Harvard University Press, 1969), p. 549.

7. Tacitus, *Complete Works* (New York: Modern Library, 1942), p. 730.

8. E. O. G. Turville-Petre, *Myth and Religion of the North: The Religion of Ancient Scandinavia* (New York: Holt, Rinehart & Winston, 1964), p. 219.

9. Wolfgang Lederer, *The Fear of Women* (New York: Harcourt Brace Jovanovich, 1968), p. 145.

10. Theodore Gaster, *Myth, Legend and Custom in the Old Testament: A Comparative Study with Chapters from Sir James G. Frazer's "Folklore in the Old Testament"* (New York: Harper & Row, 1969), p. 316.

11. Esther Newton, *Mother Camp: Female Impersonators in America* (Chicago and London: University of Chicago Press, 1979), p. 54.

12. John Rechy, *City of Night* (New York: Grove Press, 1963), p. 173.

13. Susan Mulcahy, "Eavesdropping," in the *Syracuse Herald-Journal,* 9 January 1984, p. B-3.

14. Mary Shelley, *Frankenstein* (New York: Magnum/Lancer Books, 1968), pp. 77, 81.

15. Goethe, *Faust,* p. 76, Act II, sc. ii.

16. Carl Gustav Jung, *Symbols of Transformation: An Analysis of the Prelude to a Case of Schizophrenia,* 2d ed., tr. R. F. C. Hull (Princeton: Princeton University Press, 1956), p. 189.

17. Norbert Wiener, *God and Golem Inc.; A Comment on Certain Points Where Cybernetics Impinges on Religion* (Cambridge: M.I.T. Press, 1964).

18. Paul Preuss, "The Shape of Things to Come," *Science 83,* vol. 4, no. 10, December 1983, p. 81.

19. Jeremy Rifkin in collaboration with Nicanor Perlas, *Algeny* (New York: Viking Press, 1983), p. 22.

20. Shulamith Firestone, *The Dialectic of Sex: The Case for Feminist Revolution* (Toronto, New York, and London: Bantam Books, revised ed., 1971), p. 238.

21. Manu, *Laws of Manu,* III:55-58, in *The Sacred Books of the East,* ed. Max Muller (Oxford: Clarendon Press, 1886), p. 85.

INDEX

Theology, 6–7, 54, 68, 122–23, 177
"There and then," 137–38
Thesmophoria, 197–98
This Day's Death (Rechy), 72
Threshold motif, 11, 16, 88–91, 92–98
Tiamat, 30
Tillich, Paul: on sin, 122–23
Till We Have Faces (Lewis), 179
Titans, 32
Title: use of husband's, 145
Token women, 161, 163, 179
Tolstoy, Leo, 206–207
Toothed vagina *(vagina dentata)*, 94–95, 97
Transsexuality: among men, 224, 226
Transvestism. *See* Cross-dressing
Trials. *See* Ordeals
Tribal cultures, 50–51, 52, 81, 201, 223
Tunnel image, 205
Turner, Victor, 50
"Twelve Brothers, The" (Grimm), 34
"Twelve Dancing Princesses, The" (Grimm), 89–90
Tyler, Anne, 114, 183–84; *Celestial Navigation*, 57–58, 110, 218

Ugliness, 179, 181, 184–85
"Ulysses" (Tennyson): quote from, 209
Ulysses, story of, 101
Uma, 184
Unconscious, 38
Underworld, 100, 102
Unfulfillment, 128
Ungit, 179
Unitary selfhood: manhood as, 220
Unitary self-image: of women, 48, 57–58
Unity, 43–44

Vagina, 94–95, 97
Vagina dentata (toothed vagina), 94–95, 97
Venus of Willendorf, 22, 66
Virgin birth: belief in, 27
Virginity, 4, 25, 82–86
Virgin-Mother-Crone triads, 24
Virgin/mother/whore triad, 112
Virilocal cultures, 81

Walker, Barbara G., 164
Waste Land (Eliot), 84–85
"Water of Life, The" (Grimm), 66–67, 222
Way of the mother, 12–18, 21, 45, 63–106, 141;

call to, 79, 86–87; construed metaphorically, 12; decreation of patriarchy, 157–71; estrangement from the fathers, 151; experience of childbirth, 71–72, 73, 75–77; inclusion of mate, 28; Klein bottle as image, 40–41; meeting with the Mother, 175; need to follow, 230, 231; threshold motif as challenge to, 88, 89–91, 92; as quest tale, 10, 11, 34; and selfhood of mother, 54–58; supernatural help, 99–106; temptation for woman following, 134–39, 143, 144–50; theft of boons and mysteries connected with, 223–31. *See also* Motherselfhood
Weaning, 220
Weston, Jessie, 218
White-male, pseudo: pseudo-man as, 136
Wholeness: virginity as, 82–83
Wiener, Norbert, 228
Willing: as different from the call, 80
Witchcraft, 34, 35, 170, 183, 230
Wittig, Monique, 165, 196
Woman, 11, 21–22, 134, 175; man's attempts to become, 224–26; relationship to death and sex, 100–101; relationship of pseudo-man to, 136
Woman and Nature: The Roaring inside Her (Griffin), 165
Womanhood, 11–12, 23, 36, 41, 121–22, 191; rejection of, 134–36, 139
Womanhouse (feminist environment), 167
Woman of color: as a pseudo-man, 136
Woman's Encyclopedia of Myths and Secrets, The (Walker, ed.), 164
Womansins, 16, 121–33, 137–38. *See also* Sin
Womb, 73, 75, 93, 102–103
Womb envy, 17, 223–30
Women and Work (exhibition), 166
Women-Church Speaks (conference), 168–69
Women's history (herstory), 160–64
Women's Liberation Movement, 158
Women's Room, The (French), 109, 202–203
Women's Studies: as scholarly field, 159

Yahweh, 29
"Yellow Wallpaper, The" (Gilman), 216
Ymir, 30

Zelig (film), 162–63
Zeus, 29